# QUAND McKINSEY ARRIVE EN VILLE

L'influence cachée du cabinet de conseil le plus puissant du monde

WALTERS and JOHN

*[L'influence cache]*

# Quand McKinsey Arrive en Ville

**WALTERS and JOHN**

*[L'influence cache]*

# QUAND MCKINSEY ARRIVE EN VILLE

*L'influence cachée du cabinet de conseil
le plus puissant du monde*

### WALTERS and JOHN

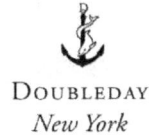

DOUBLEDAY
*New York*

# [L'influence cache]

## Contents

**Presentation**
    At the point when McKinsey Comes to Town

### Section 1
    Abundance without Responsibility
    McKinsey's Qualities

### Section 2
    Champs and Failures
    The Disparity Machine

### Section 3
    Playing The two Sides
    Assisting Government With aiding McKinsey

### Section 4
    McKinsey at ICE
    "We Do Execution, Not Arrangement"

### Section 5
    Become friends with China's Administration

### Section 6
    Watching the Entryways of Gehenna
    Tobacco and Vaping

### Section 7
    Turbo charging Narcotic Deals

### Section 8
    "Transforming a Coal Mineshaft into a Precious stone"

### Section 9
    Poisonous Obligation
    McKinsey on Money Road

### Section 10
    ALL state's Mystery Slides
    "Winning Will Be a lose Situation"

### Section 11
    "The Enron Astros"

*[L'influence cache]*

Section 12
>   "Clubbing Seals"
>
>   The South Africa Catastrophe

Section 13
>   Serving the Saudi State

Section 14
>   Chumocracy
>
>   50 years at England's NHS

**Epilog**

**A Note on Sources**

**Affirmations**

# [L'influence cache]

## Presentation

### At the point when McKinsey Comes to Town

In Gary, Indiana, simply past the rusting spans, stripping paint, and railroad exchanging station sits a green very much tended plot of land that appears to be strangely awkward. It is a lush meadow of shrubs and trees eclipsed by the boring, lumbering remaining parts of a plant run by what was once the world's greatest, most beneficial organization, the U.S. Steel Organization.

To one side, a transcending heater and smokestacks rise high against the northeastern sky. Fundamental steel is made there, produced in heat so serious the metal looks like white-hot magma moving from a well of lava. Nothing is dElicate or pardoning, just concrete, fire, and metal. To one side, lines of structures with gabled rooftops stretch toward the western skyline. This is where steel is blessed to receive make it less fragile prior to folding it into huge curls for shipment to places all over.

Possessing seven miles of lakefront, the steel plant has 200 miles of railroad tracks, its own medical clinic, local group of fire-fighters, and police force. In years past, the organization carried out its metro responsibility by sending laborers with great voices and formal hats to sing holiday songs at grade schools across the city.

Inside the green desert spring is a rock remembrance with a book depicting how 513 Individuals passed on from mishaps inside the steel plant. This book of the dead, shrouded in thick plastic and residue, recounts laborers squashed by railroad vehicles, trucks, and steel. Others tumbled to their demise, were destroyed by blasts, suffocated, consumed, covered alive, and, surprisingly, suffocated. 41 passed on by electric shock. The work correspondent Joseph S. Pete composed that steelworker burial services are many times shut coffin issues. The book of the dead makes sense of why.[*]

Gary once held the commitment of 20th century modern America, a blend of racial and ethnic gatherings in quest for a superior life, cash for school, paid excursions, and benefits. From this arose a strong working class, two Nobel Prize champs, and the Jackson Five, as well as contamination that befouled the air and streams.

In the last quarter of the 20th hundred years, the organization's fortunes fell pointedly in light of modest unfamiliar steel, old gear, and suspect administration. The labor force dipped under 8,000. Divisions were shut or pared down.

The rot spread to Gary, the city U.S. Steel established over 100 years back as "a victory of logical preparation." Before the century's over, Gary had slid into a scene of deserted places of business, stores, and chapels. Instead of burn through cash it didn't need to destroy them, Gary leased the areas to teams recording dystopian and blood and gore flicks, remembering A Bad dream for Elm Road and Transformers. Indeed, even a scene from the miniseries Chernobyl was recorded there.

## [L'influence cache]

Wrongdoing spiked, and Gary's populace dropped to 69,000 from a high of 177,000 out of 1960. Bulletins along the steel plant's southern boundary mirror a populace that had lost its moorings. "Shackled by Desire? Jesus liberates You," understands one, trailed by promotions for a strip club, a physical issue lawyer, and a gambling club.

The year 2014, notwithstanding, brought Gary's steelworkers a hint of something better over the horizon. The organization's new CEO, Mario longhi, recruited a tip top counseling firm, McKinsey and Company, to infuse novel thoughts into the maturing producer. For a really long time McKinsey sold clients on standing as a firm conveyed logical answers for complex issues. Blue-chip organizations and state run administrations all over the planet employed its advisors, as did the CIA, the FBI, and the Pentagon, among others, accepting McKinsey had the insight and fortitude that their chiefs needed.

McKinsey came to U.S. Steel fully intent on reestablishing the steelmaker to notorious status as an organization constructed the country's scaffolds, structures, and weapons that crushed America's foes. With McKinsey's assistance, U.S. Steel vowed to recover that soul through "a tenacious spotlight on monetary benefit, our clients, cost construction, and development" — all without forfeiting wellbeing or hurting the climate. Gary's workforce had little thought of what's in store from these generously compensated experts, a few alumni of Elite level business colleges.

Yet, steelworkers would advance soon enough, as did others before them, what can happen when McKinsey comes to town.

Development on U.S. Steel's Gary plant had started in 1906 under the course of the organization's executive, Elbert Gary, a previous appointed authority who maintained that the city should bear his name, however he would have rather not live there himself. Called "a morose moralist" by one history specialist, Judge Gary thought often less about the government assistance of inhabitants than about the productivity and benefit of his steel plant.

Judge Gary searched out European eminence and gathered Renaissance workmanship, while steelworkers were stuck living in "the fix," a crude, sickness contaminated locale that had 200 cantinas with names like Can of Blood. They worked twelve-hour days, seven days per week. A congregation bunch considered this 84 hour long week of work a "shame to civilization," and a legislative panel named it "a merciless arrangement of modern servitude." Judge Gary couldn't have cared less. He went against associations, thought about work pioneers his Social inferiors, and accepted his representatives liked to fill in whatever number hours as could reasonably be expected.

The pioneer behind McKinsey and Company, James O. McKinsey, a bookkeeper from the Ozarks, likewise had faith in productivity and benefits. His young organization started prompting U.S. Steel in the Economic crisis of the early 20s. The organization immediately turned into the company's greatest client; in excess of forty advisors were appointed to the record. At a certain point, U.S. Steel produced around 50% of the billings in McKinsey's New York office. At the point when the Wagner Demonstration of 1935 expected organizations to haggle with

## [L'influence cache]

laborers looking for better compensation and more secure working circumstances, McKinsey set up an extraordinary unit to encourage corporate leaders on the most proficient method to manage their requests. However, McKinsey in the end lost its greatest ally at the steel organization, and during the 1950s the two organizations moved separated. After sixty years, the notorious steelmaker was fumbling, and U.S. Steel's new CEO, Mario longhi, chose to reestablish their cozy relationship.

The Brazilian-conceived longhi became Chief of U.S. Steel in 2013. He acquired an organization burdened with old, wasteful assembling strategies. More modest organizations with fresher innovation had been gouging out enormous pieces of business from stumbling U.S. Steel, which had not turned a yearly benefit in years.

Like Adjudicator Gary, longhi inclined toward a mustache and lavishness. He purchased a house in Florida with ten showers, a guesthouse, a different exercise center, media room, and pool. longhi sold the complex for $9.8 million. He additionally possessed property on Fisher Island, one of the country's most affluent areas, open off the Miami coast exclusively by ships, helicopter, or personal ships.

Longhi had no involvement in a major, completely coordinated steel organization — the greater part of his past work experience was at Alcoa — yet he knew Individuals who could direct him, and that was his "long time confided in consultant," McKinsey and Company.

At longhi's heading, McKinsey carried out a "groundbreaking" strategy called "The Carnegie Way," to pay tribute to U.S. Steel's prime supporter Andrew Carnegie. The arrangement meant quite a bit to U.S. Steel's future that the maker referred to the Carnegie Way multiple times in its 2014 yearly report. Among the arrangement's most significant objectives was tracking down a more reasonable, cost-effective method for keeping up with the organization's maturing gear and foundation. There appeared to be no more excellent firm to oversee upkeep costs than McKinsey, broadly perceived as the world's head effectiveness specialists.

The next January, longhi told an exchange distribution that U.S. Steel's change was a "remarkable" achievement. As verification, he referred to his specialists "who have seen what we are doing" and have finished up "there could be no more profound, more extensive change exertion occurring in the country." longhi tried anybody to say his organization had not considered each choice to further develop productivity. "We are doing all that is required — and pretty actually, incidentally."

With another CEO and a circle back plan, U.S. Steel stock started rising, and in 2014 it posted its first yearly benefit in quite a while. Yet, the advancement was more deception than reality. The maker posted a $75 million misfortune in the primary quarter of 2015. The slump affected laborers as well as financial backers. 9,000 representatives at organization plants, including Gary Works, got notification of potential cutbacks. Upkeep laborers were hit hard: Many them were laid off. 200 others were downgraded to meandering work groups at a critical decrease of pay and shipped off work in new pieces of the plant.

# [L'influence cache]

Patrons came to accept that the Carnegie Way was basically a main story for the organization's arrangement to reduce expenses — an arrangement that laborers said imperiled their wellbeing. Mike Millsap, Region 7 head of the steelworkers' association, said McKinsey had no experience running a steel plant or "the stuff to safeguard the workers from hurt."

The admonition demonstrated prophetic. In June, laborers in Gary found Charles Kremke oblivious with severe singeing on his head. A U.S. Steel representative said the worker couldn't be resuscitated. The coroner decided that Kremke had been shocked, however months would pass without the organization's unveiling the reason for his demise.

In light of the casualty, the Territory of Indiana referred to U.S. Steel for four wellbeing infringement, all considered serious: neglecting to "de-empower" the live association preceding upkeep; neglecting to sufficiently prepare representatives to recognize a live association; neglecting to test hardware to guarantee live associations were de-stimulated before support; and neglecting to give defensive stuff to those functioning around live associations in a bound region.

The cutbacks and security concerns didn't deter U.S. Steel from going ahead with its arrangement to give 21.7 million new portions of stock. This unique stock contribution, which raised $482 million, happened in August, that very month the association blamed the organization for destroying its upkeep office. Irate over security issues, the association on August 26 drove a dissent Walk to U.S. Steel's principal door in Gary. Ordinarily association fights happen just during contract dealings. laborers recited, "McKinsey sucks! McKinsey sucks!" Patrons conveyed signs that drove home their opinion:

"Hi Mario! McKinsey should go."

"McKinsey took."

"McKinsey = contract infringement."

"Association indeed, McKinsey no."

"McKinsey takes."

"Give McKinsey the (image of a boot)."

In the days after Kremke's passing, Jonathan Arrizola, a thirty-year-old naval force veteran and father of two small kids, stressed that his support work was turning out to be excessively hazardous, so he started searching for other work. Arrizola told his better Half, Whitney, that he had as of late gotten an electric al shock at work. "He was continually grumbling about the McKinsey bunch scaling back specialists," she told The Hours of Northwest Indiana. "There was in every case some sort of near calamity with somebody he worked with."

Then, at that point, toward the finish of September 2016, Arrizola was on a four-man group investigating an electric al issue on a crane when he came into contact with 480 volts and was shocked.

## [L'influence cache]

"ALL they care about is cash," his significant other said subsequent to learning of her better Half's passing. "I have no spouse. My kids have no dad. I have no clue about how I will pay for my home, or my vehicle, any of my bills. I was a housewife. I have no encounters. Jon was everything to me." Companions and well-wishers raised $14,000 for her benefit through a GoFundMe crusade.

Billy McCall, leader of Joined Steelworkers Nearby 1066 during the Carnegie Way, said Arrizola was popular. "U.S. Steel took this large number of actions through McKinsey plans, and at last he was moved from one region where he was very capable into another area where he was not as capable," McCall said. "That potentially was the immediate explanation he passed on."

For the electric shock passing's of Kremke and Arrizola, the public authority fined U.S. Steel a terrific complete of $42,000, however that sum was diminished to $14,500 through discussions with the organization. The steelmaker consented to make ten restorative activities to forestall comparable mishaps later on. Adam Finkel, the previous boss administrative authority for laborer security under President Clinton, said fines start low and afterward get "thumped endlessly down." He added, "The fine is greater for hassling a wild jackass on a public touching area than for killing a specialist."

Association objections about security were reverberated by U.S. Steel financial backers who recorded a legal claim, charging that U.S. Steel deluded them on the organization's monetary wellbeing. Dependent generally upon secret meetings with eleven current or previous U.S. Steel representatives, a large number of them chiefs or managers, the financial backers considered the Carnegie Way a "farce," a cover for outrageous expense slicing through "gigantic cutbacks and conceding frantically required support and fixes." They said these strategies left the organization "with a skeleton group of unpracticed plant workers who didn't have the foggiest idea how to keep up with or fix gear, were expected to work extended periods of time of as long as 90 hours out of each week, and which brought about serious spontaneous blackouts."

The organization embraced a strategy of "don't buy, squeeze by," by which supervisors purchased things just when totally important, as per a previous U.S. Steel buying expert whose essential occupation was to arrange machine parts for the organization's American plants. Instead of make required fixes, the authority said, support groups were asked to "jury-rig" bombing machines to keep them working.

Orders for certain parts required endorsement of a "control tower," comprising of McKinsey and the plant director. "The execution of the control tower brought about a huge decrease of order endorsements," the financial backer claim expressed. A previous overseer of support at another U.S. Steel office said that McKinsey would have rather not caught wind of "basic" primary support due to the expense and that the specialists assumed a part in cutting the maintenance and upkeep spending plan. (McKinsey and U.S. Steel said specialists had no endorsement authority over the acquisition of parts.)

Billy McCall, the previous association official, said he comprehended that McKinsey got a level of what U.S. Steel purportedly saved. As a matter of fact,

## [L'influence cache]

McKinsey's remuneration was tied Halfway to the steelmaker's monetary presentation, bringing up issues about the company's rationale in suggesting cuts in costs.

After Donald J. Trump won the November 2016 official political race, to some degree by promising to reestablish common positions, longhi and his second-in-order, David Burritt, concluded everything looked good to trade out. The two sold a joined $25 million in stock more than eight exchanging days. longhi let CNBC know that he expected to reestablish 10,000 positions, referring to a better administrative climate and lower charges.

Longhi's confidence persisted to mid 2017, when he consoled financial backers that the most obviously terrible was finished. Days after President Trump got to work, he named longhi as one of 28 business pioneers to serve on his Blue collar positions Drive.

ALso, that is where things remained until 90 days after the fact, when U.S. Steel announced first-quarter profit for 2017. Investigators had anticipated a sound benefit. ALL things considered, the organization stunned Money Road by posting a $180 million overal deficit, setting off a 27 percent drop in the stock value, the organization's biggest day to day drop in excess of a fourth of a really long period.

Gordon Johnson of Maxim Capital Administration called the misfortune all the really disturbing "considering that it happened in a market where U.S. steel costs are high versus earlier years." He further noticed that the business had "delighted in critical security from imports from both the Obama and Trump organization." That's what Johnson reasoned on the off chance that the organization played out this ineffectively in great times, the remainder of the year "looks set to look like a 'Bad dream on Elm Road,' " an accidental gesture to Gary's job in that film.

In somewhere around fourteen days of that profit report, longhi left U.S. Steel with a $4.54 million reward. longhi wasn't the main loss. His vaunted Carnegie Way vanished like impressions on lake Michigan's sandy shore. Though the Carnegie Way justified in excess of forty references in U.S. Steel's 2016 yearly report, it got not a solitary notice in the 2017 yearly report. History had been deleted, Soviet-style.

U.S. Steel refocused and in 2018 made another arrangement and another motto.

"Fundamental our endeavors," the organization expressed, "is our conviction that we should work as a principled organization focused on a set of rules that is established in our Gary Standards and our basic beliefs." Those basic beliefs are "verbalized in our S.T.E.E.L. standards... : Wellbeing First, Trust and Regard, Harmless to the ecosystem Exercises, Moral Way of behaving, and legal Business Direct."

S.T.E.E.L. — with a hint of Ayn Rand. As a Christmas present, the organization's new CEO, David Burritt, gave the previous association official Billy McCall an unexpected present — the book Map book Shrugged. "This is the way of thinking at present," McCall said in a meeting. "This is corporate way of thinking, for the love of all that is pure and holy."

## [L'influence cache]

With longhi and the Carnegie Way having passed their termination dates, McKinsey actually stayed fastened to the steelmaker, taking in somewhere around $13 million in expenses from 2018 through 2020, as per McKinsey records.

Three McKinsey experts even composed an article that made sense of, with zero trace of incongruity, "why upkeep staffing matters." The writers recognized that support staffing is not difficult to misunderstand. "Cut excessively profound and excessively quick and unwavering quality endures. Furthermore, botches are precarious to fix."

Particularly, they could have added, when Individuals kick the bucket.

There is no book of the dead at Disneyland, not at a spot sold as the "Most joyful Put on The planet." Walters Disney planned the recreation area to be unadulterated dream. "I don't believe that people in general should see the world they live in," Disney said. "I believe that they should feel they are in a different universe." Disneyland offered a blend of past and future, experience, boat rides, animation characters posturing for pictures, and topic based thrill rides. A few rides planned to frighten, yet not imperil. Under Walters Disney, who kicked the bucket in 1966, the recreation area had an excellent wellbeing record, procuring a standing as the business chief for security.

Quite a long while after it opened, the recreation area had proactively turned into a Social peculiarity. At the level of the Virus War, the Soviet head, Nikita Khrushchev, attempted to visit the "Enchantment Realm" yet was denied section. "I inquired: Why not?" Khrushchev said. "What do they have, rocket-take off platforms there?"

Floated by the outcome of Disneyland, the organization's impression developed. Other Disney parks opened, including the greatest of all, Disney World Hotel in Orlando. The organization moved forcefully into filmmaking, distributing, TV, and Broadway plays. Then, at that point, in 1994, a previous toy leader, Paul S. Pressler, turned into Disneyland's top chief.

Depicted as attractive, magnetic, and a number one of Disney's CEO, Michael Eisner, Pressler set off to influence the organization by recruiting McKinsey to assess the recreation area's activity completely.

After over a time of study, on May 13, 1997, McKinsey gave Pressler its discoveries in a secret report named "Changing Support: Characterizing the Disney Standard."

McKinsey purported to have figured out how to make Disneyland more productive and increment benefits without forfeiting quality, yet that required reevaluating how upkeep ought to be performed. "Instinct or science?" McKinsey wrote in its examination for Pressler. The right response, the firm clarified, was science, as McKinsey characterized it.

Support choices ought to be put together not with respect to the judgment of veteran representatives, McKinsey expressed, however on an examination of

## [L'influence cache]

upkeep narratives, breakdowns, and cost. Called dependability focused support, the cycle started in the flying business, where security is central.

At Disneyland, however, the interaction developed principally into an order to cut costs. Utilizing terms like "cost aversion," McKinsey suggested scaling back park support, taking out positions, paying certain Individuals less, and employing outside workers for hire. In an extensively disagreeable move, most upkeep laborers were moved to the short-term, or burial ground, shift. To manage the shock of such an unexpected move, McKinsey prescribed getting guides to resolve issues of rest, nourishment, and connections. Each short-term laborer would likewise get a one-year membership to the Pulling all nighters pamphlet.

Just a little group, the Upkeep Reaction Group, would deal with mechanical breakdowns during the day. And, surprisingly, that gathering, McKinsey said, could ultimately be trimmed somewhere near 30%.

Specialists unquestionably realized the gamble in rearranging an amusement park, currently the jealousy of the diversion world . Yet, the compensation for carrying out the changes, they contended, would be "Elite support," at last saving the organization a huge number of dollars.

McKinsey let no self-question hose its energy for the changes. "The size of the open door provides a single opportunity to stop and think," the firm told Pressler. "Change of this greatness isn't overseen — it is driven." To address this difficulty, "pioneers should rouse and foster a seat of genuine change champions."

Finding those "genuine change champions" may be troublesome on the grounds that McKinsey held a low assessment of many park directors, saying they needed "basic abilities," requiring the evacuation or rectifying of 50% of the recreation area's initiative. In the wake of concentrating on one workspace, the experts stated, "Gatherings, administrator and security utilizing an excess of time." McKinsey likewise suggested cost reserve funds through "execution estimates in light of above rate and dollars. Consider shop directors responsible for area above."

"Nothing bad can be said about setting aside cash," Mike Goodwin, a previous upkeep boss, told the los Angeles Times. "Yet, not to the detriment of your superb goal, which is to keep the spot running securely." McKinsey asked another upkeep manager, Weave Klostreich, why lap bars on an exciting ride were examined day to day when records showed they won't ever fall flat.

Klostreich, a twenty-year Disney representative, became enraged. "The explanation they don't fizzle is on the grounds that we really take a look at them consistently," he said. Goodwin said Disney saw not checking lap bars as an adequate gamble. "It resembles a pilot saying, 'Hello, we haven't crashed in some time, we should skirt the preflight.' "

Five months after McKinsey suggested reducing upkeep expenses, Klostreich cautioned Disney that wellbeing worries at the recreation area were developing. "As you probably are aware," he stated, "I have communicated to you and others on a few events my profound worries over what I feel has been a serious decrease

## [L'influence cache]

in administration's preparation, eagerness and capacity to appropriately and securely keep up with the rapid attractions doled out to the thrill ride group. Our staffing and work circulation has been and is conflicting with powerful day to day preventive administration."

Klostreich said he got no reaction.

The next year, on Christmas Eve, Disneyland encountered a lethal mishap that shook the business. 1uan Dawson, a 34 year-old software engineer at Microsoft, and his better Half, a drug specialist, were standing by to board a dated riverboat, Columbia, which had quite Recently gone full circle through the recreation area. Mooring the weighty boat required ability obtained exclusively through preparing and experience. However, on this day, a manager filled in for a missing representative despite the fact that she had never prepared on that boat and had never attempted to moor it.

With the boat actually moving, excessively quick as it ended up, the boss tied a substitute nylon rope to a metal fitting on the boat. The power of the moving boat tore free the metal projection, obviously connected to decaying wood, driving it like shrapnel from a bomb, killing Dawson and seriously distorting his significant other before their child, as indicated by court records documented by a Dawson family lawyer, Christopher Aitken. The manager was hospitalized with wounds too.

Aitken said a more secure rope that breaks under extreme strain had been utilized before, yet wasn't utilized on this day.

The casualty provoked a public reevaluation of security at the country's carnivals and driven straightforwardly to another state regulation in California requiring a free examination of serious mishaps there. Already, park authorities explored themselves. The Dawson family arrived at a classified settlement with Disney answered to be $25 million.

Aitken said McKinsey's expense saving measures straightforwardly added to the Columbia mishap, among others. At McKinsey's idea, Disney had dispensed with the more generously compensated master supervisors on each ride — called ride leads — remembering for the Columbia. They were answerable for guaranteeing that the rides worked securely. Upkeep likewise endured. At the point when workers called mechanics to fix issues, they didn't quickly answer, so they quit calling, Aitken said. It didn't help, he added, that laborers with the most institutional information on rides were "getting constrained into a super late shifts."

In February 1999 — two months after the Columbia casualty — Klostreich disdain his prior advance notice to Disney authority. "I'm worried that the attractions are crumbling significantly more so presently than at the time I composed the joined reminder," he composed.

Sometime thereafter Klostreich was ended — a move he said was reprisal for being an informant. Disney said he would not work the super late shift for

## [L'influence cache]

wellbeing reasons and no employment opportunities were accessible during the day. Klostreich documented suit, yet it was excused.

In July 2000, security issues turned out to be more articulated. A wheel gathering tumbled off a ride in Space Mountain, harming nine Individuals. Unfortunate upkeep was referred to as a reason.

After two months, a four-year-old kid, Brandon Zucker, dropped out of the Roger Hare ride and was squashed under another vehicle, where he stayed for ten minutes. Before his salvage, he went into heart Failure, bringing about long-lasting cerebrum harm. He at absolutely no point ever strolled or talked in the future. Representatives had put him in a seat that was less protected given his size and neglected to completely bring down the lap bar. Brandon kicked the bucket at age thirteen. State authorities requested Disney to ro11 out critical improvements to work on the ride's security.

David Koenig, who has expounded widely on Disneyland in books and articles, said the organization needed a firm like McKinsey in light of the fact that administration felt park tasks had become excessively costly. "They urged the Disneyland the board to lessen staffing, diminish preparing, decrease upkeep, diminish, lessen, decrease — lessen everything to the place where it became hazardous," Koenig said. He was unable to say whether the issue rested with McKinsey's suggestions or Disney's execution of them. "I simply realize they kicked the ball off, and we as a whole know where it wound up."

John J. Lawler, who showed in the College of Illinois' School of Business and Work Relations, accepts the executive's advisors predominantly legitimize the objectives of their clients. "Clients like to be informed they are making the best choice," Lawler said, adding that administration procedures saw as best practices "are frequently engendered by counseling firms and hence these strategies become to a great extent standardized in the business world."

The mishaps addressed a significant disaster for Disneyland's standing, yet they didn't slow the corporate progression of the expense shaper in boss, Paul Pressler. As detailed by the Los Angeles Times, Pressler "partook in a fleeting ascent, jumping over different chiefs, remembering supervisors of the a lot bigger Disney World for Florida." He joined the internal circle of Disney's President, Michael Eisner.

ALL things considered, it was a list of references set apart by mishaps. What's more, it wouldn't be some time before new inquiries emerged over the insight of Pressler's support arrangements and McKinsey's job in suggesting them.

In the pre-fall of 2003, Disney representatives started hearing weird commotions coming from an exciting ride, worked to seem to be a train, as it zoomed through large Thunder Mountain. Mechanics supplanted an aide haggle the ride once more into administration. Yet again after "a similar uncommon clicking sound" happened once more, support supplanted a wheel. A yellow tag was put on the train, named I. M. Fearless, demonstrating it ought not be utilized, however it was.

# [L'influence cache]

On September 5, 2003, as the temperature rose toward its high of 87 degrees, Marcelo Torres, 22, and three companions ready to board the large Thunder Mountain train not long after 11:00 a.m. Prior in the day, Disney representatives had kept on hearing strange commotions yet didn't Eliminate the thrill ride for examination. The yellow label cautioning remained.

Torres and his companions didn't realize they had Recently boarded a ride with a background marked by mechanical issues. The earlier month, riders must be cleared after the train separated. Of more prompt concern, two holding bolts had quite Recently separated from the pivot on the past ride, causing the wheel manual for fall inconspicuous onto the track.

At 11:17 a.m., the injured train left with 24 travelers on its thirteenth run of the day, a three-minute roller coaster with exciting bends in the road arriving at velocities of 41 feet each second.

At the point when the surprising sounds proceeded, the choice was made to Eliminate the train for investigation at the finish of the thirteenth ride. That demonstrated past the point of no return. As the train left a banked bend, the development broke a hub bar. The shaky pivot in the long run wedged itself between the track tie and the train, driving the train up and ease off the main vehicle, pounding Torres inside. He passed on and ten others were harmed. A short time later, state reviewers found pieces of the ride dispersed up and down the track.

The state revealed critical support and preparing deficiencies. Representatives neglected to fix two screws holding the wheel gathering set up and neglected to introduce a security wire as a component of the "wheel gathering connection." Ride administrators were not prepared on the most proficient method to answer uncommon sounds on exciting rides and didn't comprehend the labEling framework used to keep dangerous rides sidelined until they were fixed. The upkeep "dependability group" didn't follow appropriate system including the utilization of labels on different rides. ALso, mechanics were permitted to finish paperwork for work finished by different engineers.

California expected Disney to retrain all external engineers at Enormous Thunder Mountain as well as those relegated to the meandering "dependability" group, including their directors. The state ordered that all workers get clear guidelines on what to do when a surprising clamor is distinguished. Engineers were likewise illegal to finish paperwork for work they didn't perform.

Christopher Aitken's law office documented suit for the benefit of the Torres family, faulting Disney for taking on McKinsey's suggestions. "Disney knew, or ought to have known, that making broad reductions in their wellbeing and upkeep projects would eventually devastatingly affect the security of people in general." The claim referred to pressure the organization put on representatives to keep rides in help, organization motivating force designs that compensated cash saved, and a "race to disappointment" reasoning.

Disney arrived at a classified settlement with the family, while McKinsey said its work "was not connected with the shocking episodes at Disneyland."

## [L'influence cache]

Pressler, the Disney leader who requested and carried out McKinsey's recommendation, wasn't around to manage the repercussions of the casualty on Huge Thunder Mountain. He left the prior year to become CEO of Hole, the apparel store chain. His order: cut costs. He endured four years prior to being pushed out.

McKinsey was not considered responsible for what occurred at U.S. Steel and Disneyland. Nobody sued the firm. No administration organization blamed it for bad behavior. Advisors were just doing what they were paid to do: offer guidance, not orders.

Thus, on the off chance that something awful occurred, the spotlight didn't radiate on them. They assumed no praise openly when their clients got along admirably, and for a really long time they acknowledged no fault when their suggestions sent organizations off the street into the trench.

U.S. Steel and Disneyland could never have been more unique — one a remnant of a once incredible regular organization, the other a radiant dream fueled by the most recent innovation. They were not McKinsey's most worthwhile clients or generally questionable. However they exemplified the virus cost-cutting counsel that transformed the firm into the guardian of the executives counseling.

This center counsel isn't recorded in the company's loved articulation of values, yet consistently that is what McKinsey discreetly prescribed to chiefs — as laborers and networks all through the world would come to realize when McKinsey came to town.

## *[L'influence cache]*

### Section 1

**Abundance Without Responsibility**

**McKinsey's Qualities**

For the savviest, most refined undergrads, a task at McKinsey and Company can appear to be a way to riches and notoriety as well as a potential chance to show off their abilities by tackling the business world's hardest issues.

As an administration consultancy, McKinsey has no friend, and behaves like it. At the point when it selects every year, the firm could draw in 200,000 candidates, recruiting just 1 to 2 percent. A spell at McKinsey, in any event, for a brief time frame, is a deep rooted visa to industry and government, because of the company's immense graduated class network stretching all over the planet.

Other top organizations hang commitments of wealth and the status that accompanies them. That's what McKinsey offers, yet in addition something else — the chance for youthful enlisted people to involve their gifts for a higher reason, to make the world a superior spot. "Change that is important," McKinsey tells work competitors, an attempt to close the deal of abundance without culpability. "We are a qualities driven association," McKinsey demands.

By depicting itself as an organization with a heart, in addition to a desire for benefits, McKinsey requests to more youthful, hopeful understudies worried about issues like an Earth-wide temperature boost, imbalance, and racial equity. It is an intense attempt to sell something and a solid message to the future wolves of Money Road that they need not have any significant bearing. Yet, the firm additionally offers something comparably inebriating: impact.

For as far back as century, McKinsey has deliberately constructed its marquee consultancy by offering its way of thinking of logical administration to the world's most popular blue-chip organizations. At some time most Fortune 500 organizations have paid McKinsey for exhortation. So have in excess of 100 government organizations all over the planet.

Since the firm will not distinguish clients or unveil the exhortation it gives, Americans and, progressively, Individuals the world over are to a great extent ignorant about the significant impact McKinsey applies over their lives, from the expense and nature of their clinical consideration to the positions that compensation for their kids' schooling.

A pursuit of records, including interior organization reports, found that the firm has exhorted practically every significant drug organization — and their administration controllers — alongside wellbeing guarantors, carriers, colleges, exhibition halls, weapons producers, confidential value firms, gambling clubs, bookmakers, Elite athletics groups, and media organizations, including The New York Times. large numbers of its specialists were similarly as open to exhorting Trump authorities as they were Obama's.

## [L'influence cache]

Working in beyond what 65 nations, they can murmur in the ears of tyrants and chosen pioneers the same. In fifteen of those nations, the firm has prompted the military, police and safeguard, and equity services. Its specialists have said something regarding the upkeep and backing of "shielded faculty transporters; minesweepers, destroyers and submarines." Countries employ McKinsey to exhort sovereign abundance subsidizes worth more than $1 trillion. McKinsey's own powerful profit make it feasible for the firm to run a confidential mutual funds for senior accomplices, with enormous pieces of its generally $31.5 billion in resources under administration disguised behind a knot of Shell organizations on an Island expense safe house in the English Channel.

McKinsey's standing is improved by the progress of its previous advisors, including Tom Cotton, the moderate U.S. congressperson from Arkansas; Pete Buttigieg, U.S. secretary of transportation; Bobby Jindal, previous legislative head of Louisiana; Sheryl Sandberg of Facebook; Lou Gerstner of IBM and American Express; and James P. Gorman of Morgan Stanley and Merrill lynch. Outside the US, McKinsey's graduated class have additionally arrived at magnified positions, including Kirill Dmitriev, top of Russia's sovereign abundance store; William Hague, England's previous unfamiliar secretary; and the previous Credit Suisse Chief Tidjane Thiam.

ALbeit the firm is named after its pioneer, James O. McKinsey, its profound chief was Marvin Grove, who joined the consultancy in 1933, introducing a time of amazing skill designed after the lofty Cleveland law office where he once worked. Splendid yet solid, he characterized how experts ought to function and dress. He demanded that McKinsey call itself a firm, not an organization; that it run a training, not a business; and that client work be a commitment, not a task. As indicated by the company's true history, "The very word business, when spoken about anybody at McKinsey, is likened to foulness," one specialist said. As a result of Grove's standards — the most significant being "client first" — the consultancy flourished.

An alum of Harvard Regulation and Harvard Business college, Grove accepted experts are best enrolled youthful and prepared in-house since "it is simpler and more powerful to prepare remarkable Individuals in their early stages." He didn't need specialists offering exhortation separated through their earlier business experience or, more terrible yet, their instinct.

Grove likewise fostered the association's important connections to Harvard Business college by forcefully enlisting its lofty Cook researchers, who acquired scholarly distinctions and positioned in the main 5% of their graduating class. Duff McDonald, who has composed profoundly announced books about McKinsey and the Harvard Business college, found that starting around 2010 approximately 500 Harvard Business college graduates were working for McKinsey, more than its fundamental selecting rivals, Goldman Sachs, Google, and Microsoft.

The business college's standing developed as McKinsey recruited a greater amount of its alumni and McKinsey acquired openness through the Harvard Business Survey. Beginning around 1959, the Audit has given out the "McKinsey Grants"

## [L'influence cache]

for something good "down to earth and pivotal administration thinking" distributed in the magazine during the year.

Assuming there was an honor for extracting the most from clients, McKinsey may be the #1 to win it. A senior accomplice let youthful volunteers know that when he began at the firm, a McKinsey chief aided him by offering tips on building client connections. "Wedge yourself in and spread like a single adaptable cell," he said. "Once in, you ought to spread yourself in the association and do everything." as such, he said, behave like "a diversion."

Albeit situated in New York City, McKinsey works through semiautonomous workplaces in urban communities all over the planet. Assuming New York is the city that never rests, so it is for McKinsey, its specialized staff prepared at any hour to help advisors in various time regions set up their discoveries in the association's standard configuration: PowerPoint slides.

McKinsey's attempt to close the deal engaged Rogé Karma, a Notre lady graduate. He picked the firm since it stressed the chance to work on Individuals' lives. "That is not Goldman Sachs' pitch. That is not the ExxonMobil pitch," he said. Karma, presently a staff supervisor for the Ezra Klein digital recording at The New York Times, took the long view. "By coming to McKinsey, you will get familiar with a tool compartment — an approach to working that will assist you with being a change creator when you go out into the world. Regardless of what you need to do, regardless of what influence you need to have, you will have this tool stash."

One college alumni worked at Goldman prior to joining McKinsey, and he said the distinction couldn't be all the more obvious. At Goldman, "there was never at any point, ever an endeavor to be something besides what they were — 'We are the sharks and that is the reason we are awesome and everybody needs to work here since we are the sharks' — and that is invigorating. Nobody was deceiving themselves around evening time."

McKinsey held itself out to appear as something else. "It is more clear than any time in recent memory that we really want to work with our clients to think about the full effect of our work together, on their exhibition, however on society in general," the company's previous overseeing accomplice Kevin Sneader wrote in 2018. Toward that end, McKinsey supports projects to elevate ladies, hindered youth, and ethnic minorities, as well as other philanthropic work.

Erik Edstrom joined McKinsey to battle an unnatural weather change. Caitlin Rosenthal, a Rice graduate, joined McKinsey's Houston office not knowing what's in store, but rather was enjoyably shocked by her merciful partners. "On my most memorable day," she reviewed, "I said, 'I would rather not work for any oil organizations.' "Karma said he would have rather not worked for a drug organization. McKinsey respected the two solicitations. "My most memorable undertaking was working for a neighborhood gallery," said Rosenthal, presently a set of experiences teacher at the College of California, Berkeley.

Different organizations discuss doing great by accomplishing something beneficial. Google once had a straightforward witticism: "Don't be detestable."

## [L'influence cache]

That proverb vanished from the prelude to its set of principles in 2018 during the residency of its CEO, a previous McKinsey specialist, Sundar Pichai.

Not many organizations advance "values" as a selecting instrument with the intensity of McKinsey.

The attempt to Seal the deal frequently starts when applicants are approached in meetings to tackle business issues, for example, how to further develop immunization dispersion in Africa, an issue McKinsey really managed in Nigeria. "It was particularly made to seem like the sort of work I would get to do routinely in the event that I joined," Karma said.

One Harvard undergrad said he had never known about McKinsey however applied on the grounds that his companions did. "Nobody grows up and fantasies about being a McKinsey specialist," he said. However, one night after class, while drinking wine from a Performance cup, he chose to finish up an application. After two rounds of meetings, he got a deal. "They do all that to inspire you to join on the spot." And when you do, he said, your McKinsey controllers bust opens a container of champagne.

In their most memorable year at McKinsey, business college graduates can make as much as $195,000, reward notwithstanding, however are frequently expected to work long into the evening, with a requesting itinerary. "I left following one year," Louis Hyman, an academic administrator of financial history at Cornell College's School of Modern and Work Relations, said. "One of the criticisms I got after a commitment was I was excessively scholarly. We don't require scholastics. We want competitors. It's tied in with persevering through torment, but at the same time it's tied in with being centered around the group, zeroed in on the triumph."

After a short direction, fresh recruits are relegated to projects run by commitment directors, who are thusly managed by the company's accomplices. If the beginners have any desire to propel, they should foster associations with accomplices who can organize work for prominent, beneficial clients, the sort that senior accomplices notice. Without a support, workers are "on the ocean front," significance unavailable for general use, either sitting tight for a task or attempting to foster their own ventures.

"At the point when I was a first-year partner, I encountered a great deal of tension when I was on the ocean front while others were staffed on examinations," one McKinsey accomplice reviewed. "I would absolutely giggle at myself [now] for having loathed ocean side time accomplishing client advancement work." Without finding new clients, the firm would wilt away.

McKinsey utilizes around 34 thousand Individuals, a large number of whom withdraw or, in McKinsey-talk, are "directed to leave" after not exactly heavenly assessments. The Individuals who remain have exhibited their counseling ability as well as their capacity to join themselves to notable Individuals in the firm, opening the way for headway. A little rate are ultimately chosen accomplices or senior accomplices, with a pay in the large numbers of dollars.

## [L'influence cache]

Leaving McKinsey isn't a shame. It is more similar to school graduation, with the endowment of significant level associations for future positions. McKinsey realizes that by cultivating the business world with previous workers, it stands to receive new clients consequently.

McKinsey's height permits it to draw in, for the most part without analysis, in rehearses that others could see as abnormal or unseemly. It all the while counsels for organizations contending in a similar market, so one bunch of specialists may be advising Organization a how to beat Organization B while one more set is advising Organization B how to beat Organization A. McKinsey additionally counsels for government organizations that control McKinsey clients. As well as exhorting the U.S. Food and Medication Organization, McKinsey has counseled for no less than nineteen drug clients — all dependent upon FDA guideline.

McKinsey shields these counsels in light of the fact that adequate protections exist to guarantee classified data isn't improperly shared.

McKinsey's qualities are in excess of a promoting device; they are the company's divine messengers, as per McKinsey's non circulating official history. "Whenever the firm has committed errors or has permitted its desires to rush extravagantly, its qualities have gotten control it over," McKinsey says. "An arrangement of values fills in as a fundamental underpinning of long haul institutional achievement."

To commute home the point, McKinsey representatives are approached to take part in a "Values Day" coordinated by workplaces all over the planet. Senior accomplices can involve the amazing chance to explain applying McKinsey's qualities in everyday work. In 2019, the Australia overseeing accomplice, John lydon, talked about how, at the very least, McKinsey shouldn't work with clients who mischief or kill Individuals or cheat their clients.

Not long before his passing in 1968, the association's administrator, Gilbert Clee, pondered the significance of those qualities. He expressed, "No matter what a singular's field of interest or how he needs to manage his life, I trust the firm offers two other extraordinary fulfillments: the capacity to look yourself in the mirror each day and to say, There's nothing I should be embarrassed about."

Those are the expressions of a pleased McKinsey pioneer from another period. In any case, there are others, numerous truth be told, who looked and could have done without what they saw. As of late, the decisive moves' frequently appeared to deceive its vaunted esteem framework. Starting in 2018, as one media report followed another, McKinsey chiefs mixed to counter what had turned into the gravest danger to the company's standing in its long and pleased history. Crisis gatherings were held, statements of regret gave, a new overseeing chief dominated, and risk the executives strategies were fortified.

As the firm looked for the purposes for these issues, one clarification sat up front, so clear it was barely noticeable. Also, it incidentally turned out to be the very Establishment whereupon Marvin Arbor had constructed the firm.

Up to this point, McKinsey's site recorded fifteen explicit qualities that "illuminate both our drawn out methodology as a firm and the manner in which we serve our clients consistently." A significant number of those values are standard and self-evident, for example, "construct getting through connections in light of trust" and "get developments the executives practice to all clients."

Some are coordinated toward establishing a friendly climate for experts to flourish, for example, "support a mindful meritocracy." One empowers freethinking: "Maintain the commitment to disagree."

After some time, these qualities have been refreshed in little ways, however the most importantly esteem — number one on the rundown — has never truly changed: "Put client interests in front of the company's." McKinsey had once embraced a more broad proclamation where clients started things out, the firm second, cash third, and individual premium fourth. In time, the cash reference vanished, maybe on the grounds that in a spot fixated on impressive skill that word seemed improper.

Clients felt alright with McKinsey's qualities. What's more, according to their point of view, that is as it ought to be, since McKinsey charges a premium for its administrations. At the point when a telecom required help quite a long while back, the firm charged the organization more than $120 million out of two years. For that sort of cash, clients ought to get what they need.

Rosenthal, the advisor who began in McKinsey's Houston office, said the proclamation to focus on client intrigues sounds caring yet ought not be mixed up as open help. "The language around client administration causes it to seem like serving a client, all by itself, is significant without respect for what that organization is doing," Rosenthal said. "I found it bumping that client administration is so high at the top with no capabilities."

Karma, the webcast proofreader, sees a contrast between working for an assembling organization and working for McKinsey. At an organization, he said, "you are likewise going to have a loyalty to the item, and a faithfulness to Individuals. You have a different upsides of some kind." At McKinsey, "your whole occupation is to get investors more cash-flow."

This brings into play McKinsey's subsequent worth, the basic to "notice high moral guidelines." Does that recommend that specialists, in addition to other things, shouldn't work for clients who participate in unsafe way of behaving or who overemphasize benefits to the hindrance of their representatives? This is no little issue for a consultancy that has frequently said its principal resource beside its kin is its standing.

What occurs on the off chance that a client sells habit-forming items known to cause passing, or denies settle rs sympathetic treatment, or supports bad and undemocratic states? These are not speculative inquiries. For each situation, McKinsey had a decision and favored the clients. "If you have any desire to accomplish moral work, on the off chance that that is fundamentally important, you must turn down beneficial open doors. It was never obvious to me that McKinsey was truly able to do that," Rosenthal said.

## [L'influence cache]

Seth Green, who joined McKinsey out of Yale Graduate school, shares her anxiety. "In the event that we don't bring an ethical reason into these organizations, then the reason unavoidably turns into the client and anything that the client is attempting to accomplish," Green, presently a dignitary at the College of Chicago, said. In an exposition distributed in Fortune, Green inquired, "Could daring to tell a failing to meet expectations tobacco organization to seek after more aggressive showcasing strategies be an illustration of our qualities in real life? Assuming this is the case, are these any qualities whatsoever?"

Post Beautiful joined McKinsey to a limited extent to track down ways of diminishing savagery in penitentiaries. "I came to my occupation as a McKinsey specialist expecting to influence the world from within, assuming the most effective way to gain ground is through impacting the people who control the switches of force," Wonderful wrote in a 2019 exposition. "Rather than being a power for good, I found myself involved with the most harming powers influencing the world: the resurgence of tyranny and the proceeded with creep of business sectors into all pieces of life."

In a long time past, the firm had to a great extent got away from public examination — the most remarkable special case being McKinsey's job in the Enron calamity — to some degree in view of the imperatives of one more of the company's fifteen qualities: "Safeguard client confidences." people in general and their administration delegates are not in that frame of mind to pass judgment on the off chance that they don't have any idea what McKinsey does or what it expresses and to whom.

Not until 2018, when the media, drove by The New York Times and ProPublica, started doing profound jumps into the company's undertakings, did a significant number of McKinsey's young experts initially discover that they and their manager had an alternate understanding of values. The Times expressed, "when majority rules systems and their fundamental qualities are progressively enduring an onslaught, the notable American organization has helped raise the height of dictator and degenerate state run administrations across the globe, in some cases in manners that counter American interests."

McKinsey's clients remembered degenerate states for Russia, South Africa, and Malaysia. There were the Russian organizations put under UN authorizations to rebuff President Putin for holding onto Crimea. Furthermore, state-possessed Chinese organizations that gives the financial and military help for its strong ruler, Xi Jinping, who most certainly doesn't keep McKinsey's "commitment to contradict."

Different debates followed, including a revolt that ejected inside McKinsey's Washington, D.C., office over the company's work for President Trump's unforgiving migration strategies and a worldwide dissent by in excess of eleven hundred specialists against the company's broad work with the world 's greatest supporters of rising ozone depleting substances.

## [L'influence cache]

The most stunning disclosure, be that as it may, was McKinsey's choice to assist organizations with selling more narcotics when the maltreatment of those medications had killed great many Americans. Two senior accomplices examined perhaps cleansing records, clearly to conceal their association. McKinsey consented to pay more than $600 million to settle examinations by many state lawyers general into the association's job in fanning the narcotic pandemic. The firm likewise put out an uncommon conciliatory sentiment, and terminated the two workers, yet said it did nothing unlawful.

"This is the cliché of wickedness, M.B.A. version," said Anand Giridharadas, a previous McKinsey specialist and creator of Victors Take ALL: The Tip top Act of Impacting the World. "They realized what was happening. Furthermore, they figured out how to look past it, through it, around it, to address the main inquiries they thought often about: how to make the client cash and, when the walls shut in, how to safeguard themselves."

One previous senior accomplice accused the narcotic disaster on the insufficiency of the company's administration structure, saying the firm became too large to be represented as an organization, which he said is generally founded on trust. "It was an extraordinary firm, and I say 'it was' on the grounds that I can't ensure what it is today."

McKinsey's inconveniences in the end turned into an issue in the 2020 Vote based official primaries. With the previous South Twist city chairman Pete Buttigieg ascending in the surveys, new Titles about the firm provoked inquiries regarding a subject he seldom referenced — his work as a McKinsey specialist. He at first declined to respond to those inquiries, referring to a nondisclosure understanding he endorsed with the firm. In any case, as his quietness took steps to overpower his mission subjects, Buttigieg looked for authorization from McKinsey to examine his time there.

The firm, awkward with the new examination it was getting, made the uncommon stride of permitting Buttigieg to depict his work, which ended up being genuinely commonplace. He told The New Yorker he was glad for his work at McKinsey on issues like staple estimating and sustainable power. "It was a sensational learning a potential open door," he said.

However, reports of McKinsey's inappropriate lead — about aiding the narcotic business and despotic countries — left him irate. "It stuns the still, small voice whenever that a lethal despot can depend on the authenticity of a Western counseling organization, particularly the most esteemed organization out there, to additional their objectives." In a meeting with the Times, Buttigieg likewise talked powerfully against McKinsey's distraction with investor esteem. "That is not sufficient when we are perceiving the way that the economy keeps on turning out to be increasingly inconsistent, and we are seeing the manners by which a ton of corporate way of behaving that is in fact lawful is likewise not OK."

A more close to home reaction came from quite possibly of McKinsey's most popular previous specialist — and successive pundit — Tom Peters, co-writer of one of the top rated business books ever, looking for Greatness. "It's sickening,"

## [L'influence cache]

he expressed, alluding to McKinsey's work for the narcotic business. "I'm stunned. I'm horrified and am irritated."

Peters expressed that until he heard that McKinsey had suggested "turbocharging" narcotic deals, he was still "enigmatically pleased" to list the firm on his CV. "That's it. How would you do that and afterward imagine you are a qualities driven organization? How would you have a Qualities Day and do that poop? It's unfathomable."

A significantly more concerning issue, Peters said, may be the "disinvestment in Individuals" for greater benefits. "I truly think the investor esteem augmentation thing has caused more damage than any single thing perhaps in the country. It is the dad of imbalance, and disparity is the dad of Trump."

A few previous experts said they struggled with understanding how a firm with such kind and caring Individuals could take on such unsavory clients. Green, the college dignitary, gauges that the vast majority of his partners wouldn't work for a tobacco organization or an undemocratic government, yet they would serve them under the name McKinsey.

McKinsey permits specialists to decline tasks that contention with their ethics. Tobacco and Coal-mining organizations frequently top that rundown. Be that as it may, a few veterans of the firm said this main foisted the moral and moral decisions on low-level partners, as opposed to the company's initiative. What's more, turning down work can prompt unfortunate surveys and being guided to leave the firm.

"There was an ethical evaluation that I saw at the top, meaning the manner in which we discussed extraordinary accomplices — the quantity of clients they got — and I saw them commended for cases that were, best case scenario, problematic," Green said, adding that in the event that you take on these polluted clients you have a superior possibility progressing. "There's complete responsibility to the client; there is no responsibility to society."

Karma, the digital broadcast supervisor, said his extraordinary second happened when he was doled out to assist a client with terminating fifteen hundred of its workers overall — "not on the grounds that it was battling, but since they needed to get more cash-flow," Karma said. "Get them out of the entryway as fast and proficiently as conceivable with next to no prosecution." As far as he might be concerned, that undeniable the end. "I was unable to come into work consistently knowing all that I had worked as long as I can remember for — every last bit of it was being utilized to aggravate others' lives."

At the point when McKinsey experts hear again and again that they are splendid and the most ideally suited to take care of an organization's most complicated issues, it can cause them to feel like they couldn't possibly step out of line. Accounting sheets — the soul of calculating McKinsey experts — can additionally protect them from Individuals who may be hurt by their choices.

McKinsey isn't anxious to promote its standing as the counseling business' most productive work slasher. A direction booklet for newcomers secretly examines this

## [L'influence cache]

part of the business while focusing on that it was "composed and secretly printed for readership by just the faculty of McKinsey and Co." The writer, Manish Chopra, presently a senior accomplice, recounts the narrative of how not long after beginning at McKinsey he was relegated to a car parts maker whose new CEO needed a lower head count — a choice Chopra saw as upsetting. Chopra said he had asked why the firm was not hoping to develop income, as opposed to cut finance. "I found it unscrupulous to track down approaches to lay off Individuals, and it was discouraging to stro11 into the client HQ with the workers knowing why we were there."

So Chopra concentrated on ways of supporting the client's income through more reasonable valuing. This, nonetheless, prompted "endless" contentions with his boss. "He was outraged, feEling that I was not conveying what I was approached to do." Chopra thought his McKinsey profession was ill-fated, yet amazingly it wasn't. "The lovely thing about our firm qualities is that you are committed, not simply permitted to disagree. On the off chance that you fee1 something is off-base, it's anything but a choice to remain silent about it."

That might be in this way, yet Carl Pechman, overseer of the Public Administrative Exploration Establishment, said other McKinsey specialists are not by any stretch hesitant to suggest terminating representatives. Pechman recounts this account of his McKinsey experience:

I will always remember when a youthful troublemaker from McKinsey came into my office at the New York Public Help Commission and excitedly made sense of how they were rightsizing one of the state's utilities that was in monetary difficulty. I said, "You mean laypeople off?" He answered that they were not laying Individuals off, but rather rightsizing. I let him know I want to believe that he had the delight of being right sized. Primary concern — these imbeciles right sized linemen with institutional memory — like where the lines truly were — and the utility needed to employ them back as specialists.

In February 2018, McKinsey revealed that 560 senior accomplices had chosen Kevin Sneader, a Glasgow local, as McKinsey's world wide overseeing accomplice. Sneader turned out to be only the twe1fth accomplice to lead the firm since its establishing.

McKinsey involved Sneader's declaration as a valuable chance to proclaim its new achievements, like multiplying the quantity of accomplices over the course of the past ten years to multiple thousand and fortifying its work in "computerized change, progressed examination, plan, and execution." It additionally procured twelve organizations as well as establishing a not-for-profit association to address youth joblessness.

"REliably named the world's most esteemed counseling firm, McKinsey keeps on conveying the top administration exhortation [that] pioneers have trusted for almost 100 years," McKinsey crowed. As of now not zeroed in principally on delivering guidance, the firm said it likewise works "next to each other with clients, at each level of their associations, filling in as an 'influence accomplice' to assist them with building their abilities and execute their methodologies."

## [L'influence cache]

Sneader realized he'd need to revamp the company's South African office, destroyed by its connections to a significant political embarrassment — one that cut down the nation's leader. McKinsey took in more than 1,000,000 bucks in expenses, however under tension later consented to reimburse the cash. Past that, however, any issues seemed reasonable. "We stay focused on McKinsey's essential qualities," Sneader pronounced. "The firm you see today is still traditionally McKinsey, however how we can help our clients, and the effect we have, keeps on reclassifying the calling of the executives counseling."

Sneader additionally understood the firm needed to reevaluate how it worked. So on May 11, 2019, McKinsey embraced another code of expert lead, a lot of which tended to client choice and client conduct. "Every one of us has a commitment to keep up with the most elevated proficient guidelines in our client administration; establish a climate wherein our kin are regarded, enlivened and persuaded; think about the more extensive ramifications of our activities on society; and maintain the company's standing" (italics added).

Sometime thereafter, at an official Q&A event in the company's Washington, D.C., office, Nora Gardner, a senior accomplice who sits on an interior panel entrusted with screening new clients, gave the gathering an advancement report. Specialists, she said, were currently more mindful of the need to all the more thoroughly vet clients, with 30% more cases submitted for institutional surveys. "Generally 50% of those commitment, approximately 50% of them, we banter, talk about, and say, 'looks alright, continue.' 35% or so get guardrails. 'Kindly shape it in an unexpected way.' Avoid this piece of the work and whatnot. Furthermore, around 15% have been off limits, we won't accomplish the work."

McKinsey didn't name the clients it dismissed.

Old propensities, nonetheless, can be difficult to break, as McKinsey found in January 2021.

In a proclamation, "satisfying our obligation to society," McKinsey had underlined the significance of common freedoms. "Our obligation to basic freedoms illuminates whom we serve and on what points, and we won't take care of business that backings or empowers common liberties infringement."

However, when fights were arranged in Moscow over the treatment of the Kremlin pundit and harming casualty Alexei Navalny, McKinsey suddenly restricted its representatives from supporting the fights. "In accordance with strategy, McKinsey representatives should not help any political movement either freely or secretly," the firm expressed in a message to workers, as per the web-based news website The Moscow Times.

The request upset Individuals from McKinsey's Moscow office who spilled it to Individuals outside the firm. Under open tension, McKinsey backtracked and said it lamented sending the message. "Our Moscow office's correspondence generally distorted our strategies and values," a representative for the firm said. "McKinsey representatives are free, in their own ability, to practice their opportunity of articulation remembering partaking for municipal and political exercises."

## [L'influence cache]

As far as numbers, McKinsey's struggles haven't harmed enlistment, as per Brian Rolfes, the accomplice accountable for worldwide enrolling. On February 3, 2021, he shared some uplifting news in a proclamation posted on the company's site: "We are meaning to employ more new partners this year than any earlier year throughout the entire existence of the firm."

These newbie's, be that as it may, will proceed without Kevin Sneader as the overseeing accomplice who squeezed for every one of the changes. In February 2021, without precedent for 45 years, the company's senior accomplices removed an overseeing accomplice after only one three-year term.

After seven months, Sneader joined Goldman Sachs.

# [L'influence cache]

## Section 2

**Champs and Failures**

**The Disparity Machine**

As the final part of the 20th century started, Americans longed for one thing more than some other — soundness. Having survived the Economic crisis of the early 20s, a universal conflict, and fierce showdowns among work and the executives, they needed no more shocks. There were homes to fabricate, kids to raise, and success that appeared at long last reachable.

The overall climate of this time was reflected in an earth shattering work understanding arrived at between the Unified Car laborers and General Engines, the world's biggest automaker. Known as "The Settlement of Detroit," it gave laborers interestingly their pass to the working class — medical coverage, cost for many everyday items changes, and a benefits. In return, laborers made a deal to avoid striking, permitting General Engines to bank consistent benefits without disturbance. The two sides got what they trusted was an anticipated future. Seeing this, Passage and Chrysler immediately endorsed on.

While not evident at that point, the year 1950 would become significant for America's laborers for different reasons. Sam Walton moved to Bentonville, Arkansas, to open a five-and-ten store, the harbinger of what became Walmart, the country's biggest confidential manager and a layout for building a corporate realm on modest work. Marvin Nook turned into McKinsey's overseeing accomplice, transforming the firm into the consigliere of America's most impressive partnerships. ALso, General Engines leaders, seeing what work had achieved, started to ponder themselves: Would they say they were being adequately paid?

General Engines responded to that inquiry by posing to McKinsey to concentrate on leader remuneration at 37 distinct organizations and report back. What McKinsey found was startling: laborer compensation were rising quicker than leader remuneration.

Nobody might have anticipated how critical that study would become, for it helped generate quite possibly of the most politically charged, destructive issue in America today: pay and abundance disparity. In 1950, the CEO of an ordinary enormous organization made multiple times a creation laborer's pay. By 2020, Chiefs made something like 351 fold the amount. What's more, that didn't represent laborers who lost positions from reevaluating and corporate rebuilding — business choices frequently suggested by McKinsey's steady of very much associated specialists.

The McKinsey study, distributed by the Harvard Business Survey and Fortune, hit the business local area with such power that it resounded long into the future. Interestingly, leaders had a vibe for the market worth of their positions. "The compensation of the singular chief was one of an organization's most carefully hidden mysteries," Curve Patton, the McKinsey expert who coordinated the

## [L'influence cache]

review, composed. Presently chiefs could figure out how they estimated facing the opposition.

Juan Trippe, organizer and CEO of Skillet American World Aviation routes, requested that Patton work on his organization's investment opportunities. Different organizations immediately followed with comparative solicitations. "Individuals just originated from all over to get some of Mr. Patton's enchantment and furthermore get more extravagant," said Macintosh Stewart, a previous individual from the company's administration council.

Chiefs at rail lines, public utilities, and banks were alarmed to learn they were paid not exactly those in the car, material, and steel ventures. One organization president in a lower-paid industry kept in touch with Patton, saying he "put our industry in a difficult spot five years," since it suggested their leaders were worth short of what others. Another chief needed more pay essentially for gloating privileges. No one needed to be close to the base, and the rush to the top had started, gradually right away, just to advance quickly as each new ten years showed up.

Patton made it more straightforward for corporate chiefs to endorse higher remuneration by connecting significant salary to greater organization benefits. Enterprises that paid rewards, he said, delivered two times the benefits of organizations that didn't. He additionally examined improving compensation bundles through benefit sharing, stock honors, including choices, and different advantages. A few advantages were Particularly significant in light of the fact that they helped offset what Patton called "the crippling impact of the graduated personal duty." He referred to limited investment opportunities as the most ideal way for leaders to fabricate a bequest while expanding organization benefits.

Patton's examinations were not intended to help assembly line laborers or administration representatives. McKinsey was, all things considered, an administration specialist, not a work expert. Two years after the Wagner Demonstration of 1935 gave most specialists the option to join associations and to altogether deal with their bosses, McKinsey began a modern relations practice that, as per the company's inside history, "was no question an endeavor to exploit the general progress of worker's organizations in coordinating the shop floors."

The association's indifference with regards to laborers made news when its pioneer, James O. McKinsey, assessed Marshall Field's, an enormous retail chain and a venerated Chicago foundation. To guarantee his proposals were carried out, McKinsey took over as the store's top leader. Then, at that point, things got revolting. In what became known as "McKinsey's Cleanse," almost twelve hundred positions were wiped out. The aftermath from that cleanse is depicted unsparingly in McKinsey's own authentic documents: "The generally paternalistic Marshall Field had become, in the public eye, simply one more wanton Gloom period enterprise that safeguarded its investors by terminating representatives with scarcely any severance and little to no benefits. Faulting McKinsey for all that and more was simple."

## [L'influence cache]

Patton was substantially more thoughtful to organization supervisors. He refreshed his remuneration concentrates on many years in high-profile distributions. At the point when McKinsey specialists should stay behind the scenes, he was one whom organizations requested by name. "His productive state of the art works regarding the matter pulled in popularity for him and fortune to the firm," as per McKinsey's inward history. Patton ultimately represented right around 10% of the association's billings. Patton likewise wedged the entryway open for other McKinsey experts to sneak in and exhort organizations on other business matters, producing much more pay for the firm. "Then, at that point, I would do the review and figure out what their different issues were and acquire their certainty, and afterward we would feel free to do increasingly a one and another," one accomplice reviewed.

Patton's work wasn't generally appreciated in the firm. Peter Walker, who joined McKinsey in 1972 from the actuarial firm Pinnacles Perrin, scrutinized Patton's decisions, hinting that he controlled the numbers "with the overall target of attempting to demonstrate that the Chief was come up short on — which I didn't view as an especially honoring process."

Patton's work made partners anxious for another explanation. They thought it represented an irreconcilable circumstance. How is it that consultants could impartially assess the value of leaders who recruit and pay them? Yet, uneasiness is a certain something, benefits are another, and Patton's leader remuneration practice went on for a long time before it was closed down. By then, remuneration advisors had become huge business, Following the Model set by McKinsey, irreconcilable situations what not. Furthermore, the remuneration pattern proceeded — more cash for leaders and a developing hole among them and their workers.

Walker never got to demonstrate his worth to the firm after he addressed why he was approached to investigate country-club enrollments for organization leaders. "What I was approached to do is absolutely superfluous," he said. Walker's exhibition survey procured him a zero, and a talk that caught in a couple of sentences McKinsey's expanded perspective on itself, as well just like own advantage in greater paydays. "You must comprehend," his manager said. "You don't have a MBA, you were a 2.7 number related major from Association School. We could not have possibly even evaluated you, if not for your experience at Pinnacles Perrin in leader pay. So to do any more remuneration studies, then, at that point, you won't remain at McKinsey." Walker quickly exchanged over to counseling on protection issues and partook in a long and prosperous vocation at the firm.

As enterprises advanced, their needs different, including their disposition toward representatives. During the 1950s and the vast majority of the 1960s — the time of goliath aggregates — Chiefs were risk disinclined, content to take the long view in working for what's to come. As John Kenneth Galbraith wrote in his 1967 book, The New Modern Express, these organizations inclined toward dependability, not benefit expansion, permitting time to foster items that superior Individuals' lives. Inside limits, they tried to keep their workers content, if not well

## [L'influence cache]

off. While not every person got what they needed, most by and large found that their lives appeared to be more unsurprising and secure.

The previous McKinsey advisor Louis Hyman, a financial student of history, portrayed the advantages of this methodology: "Paper pushers of the working class could depend on their positions as their families developed. Regular workers realized the plant would be open the Following year and that their modern association would get them a raise, however not an upset."

Soundness as an excellence in American life didn't stand the test of time, giving way to the fights of the 1960s, as society tended to rotting Social issues. What's more, it wasn't long after Galbraith's book that the American partnership started its transformation from a steady mainstay of American culture into a substance that served the impulses of Money Road, first and foremost, frequently to the impediment of workers and their encompassing networks. More streamlined, not greater, turned into the objective. ALso, McKinsey was available to dress its clients in the design existing apart from everything e1se.

This change outgrew what Hyman called "a new, rigorously monetary perspective on companies, a way of thinking that inclined toward stock and bond costs over creation, of transient increases over long haul speculation." Experts, he said, excitedly supported this change, controlling enterprises toward compensating the couple of over the many, and financial backers over society. "The partnership under the specialists' rudder was as of now not a getting through adventure; it turned into a flashing collection whose worth was not in the upcoming advancement but rather in the present stock cost."

To keep in sync with the times, McKinsey soaks itself in the most recent administration hypotheses, satisfying accomplices anxious to move past basic statistical surveying into business technique, hierarchical plan, and troublesome scientific issues. This recalibration disappointed the McKinsey specialist Tom Peters, who accepted that administrators had failed to remember the rudiments, for example, client support and perceiving the worth of workers.

In a segment for The Money Road Diary, Peters dumped on the firm where he actually worked. "As a rule, they have been enticed by the accessibility of MBAs, furnished with the 'most recent' in essential arranging procedures." Peters recognized that McKinsey didn't see the value in his remarks, with one accomplice in any event, proposing he be terminated. That didn't occur; Peters quit before looking for Greatness was distributed and he proceeded to compose another smash hit.

Chiefs and their advisors had genuine purposes behind needing to reconsider the American partnership. Modest, excellent Japanese items were testing U.S. makers, particularly in the car business, provoking General Engines back to look for help from McKinsey. Yet, rather than zeroing in on quality-control issues, a significant justification behind Japan's prosperity, GM and McKinsey left on a gigantic corporate rearrangement, eminent generally for the amount it cost and how little it achieved. Eventually, the specialists addressed the stiffest cost for this error through employment misfortunes.

# [L'influence cache]

The 1980s brought greater precariousness, starting a winded series of tales about unexpected wealth, corporate strikes, utilized buyouts, and the blurring allure of once stable organizations. "Billions could be made by purchasing up American organizations and stacking them with piles of obligation," said les leopold, head of New York's Work Foundation and creator of Out of control Imbalance. As these pillagers got rich off what leopold called "the deindustrialization of America," their defenders commended them for making organizations more effective. A few organizations had to be sure become careless, however marauders frequently purchased organizations to split them up and auction the pieces, leaving huge number of representatives without occupations. "This isn't the undetectable hand of the market," leopold said. "This is the monetary extraction process."

The Business Roundtable, with a participation of the country's most impressive corporate managers, didn't completely accept that that organizations ought to have cultural interests past their own prosperity. The business bunch had a basic way of thinking: a company ought to "create financial re-visitations of its proprietors." all in all, investors. End of story.

The fealty of enterprises to Money Road implied professional stability turned out to be less significant. "It was the corporate scaling back of the last part of the 1980s that previously broke the conventional contract that exchanged professional stability for devotion," three McKinsey experts wrote in their book, The Battle for Ability. "Inside a couple of brief years, the old restrictions against work jumping had dissipated and it had turned into a praiseworthy symbol to have various organizations on one's list of references." The book included graphs with explanations like this one: "The old reality: Representatives are steadfast. The new reality: Individuals are portable and their responsibility is present moment."

McKinsey's disposition toward professional stability is reflected in its own, up-or-out training, where every individual is routinely reexamined and the people who disappoint are, in McKinsey's speech, advised to leave. By far most leave, generally on the grounds that the firm pushes them out, or they detested the work, or they saw McKinsey as an entrée to dealing with their own organization. Yet, leaving McKinsey is boundlessly unique in relation to common laborers losing their positions. A list of qualifications that incorporates a spell at McKinsey nearly ensures another lucrative work. Common laborers, then again, occupy a grimmer world with less choice.

In an article, "How McKinsey Obliterated the Working Class," distributed in The Atlantic, the Yale regulation teacher Daniel Markovits expounded on this deficiency of faithfulness. "While the board counseling untethered leaders from specific ventures or firms and tied them rather to the executives as a rule, it likewise drove them to embrace the one thing normal to all enterprises: bringing in cash for investors." As per McKinsey, unobtrusive benefits were as of now not OK. "Exceptional organizations really do win the option to get by, yet not the capacity to acquire better than expected and, surprisingly, normal investor returns over the long haul," McKinsey advisors composed.

To make an "remarkable company," administrators needed to keep their stock value high, and reducing expenses through cutbacks was normally more

*[L'influence cache]*

straightforward and faster than helping income. CEOs profited from higher stock costs to some degree in light of the fact that their pay was progressively attached to the worth of that stock. Cutbacks were many times framed as important to further develop proficiency, and no organization could match McKinsey's long record of running up an organization's body count. Call it scaling back or rebuilding, the outcome was something very similar: sending laborers home without a task. Duff McDonald, who composed a background marked by McKinsey, put this piece of the company's business in setting. "There is an unmistakable chance," he expressed, "that McKinsey might be the single most prominent legitimizer of mass cutbacks than anybody, anyplace, whenever in current history."

Trade guilds, with their declining impact, gave little insurance. In 1954, in excess of 34% of hourly and salaried workers were endorsers. By the 1980s, just 20%. In 2020, only 10 percent.

With no dependability to laborers, organizations started re-appropriating great, working class positions to southern states where wages were lower. These employment misfortunes were only the start. Before long the quest for modest work ventured into different nations as new innovation made it simpler to work a business large number of miles away. Called offshoring, it had no greater team promoter than McKinsey, which had come to consider itself to be a greater amount of a global firm than an American one. "We have unrivaled involvement with prompting associations on how, where and with whom to accomplice for an extensive variety of worldwide rethinking and offshoring open doors," McKinsey gloated.

Steven Nursery, the regarded previous New York Times work essayist, wrote in 2008 that offshoring, more than some other financial power since the Downturn, incited dread among American laborers since it impacted authentic and middle class laborers the same. "Globalization used to hurt simply the Bud swarm, yet presently it is likewise raising a ruckus around town swarm."

McKinsey at first centered around India, where it forcefully advanced that nation's informed, English-talking populace as an arrival spot for U.S. partnerships looking for modest work. With McKinsey's assistance, India turned into the world 's top offshoring area, procuring the epithet "Seaward istan." As per Anita Raghavan, who has expounded on the rising impact of the Indian first class, McKinsey's progress in India was expected generally to two senior forerunners in the firm, Rajat Gupta, the company's overseeing accomplice from 1994 to 2003, and Anil Kumar, who had fostered the company's web practice in Silicon Valley. Kumar, bombastic and rough, was not well known in the firm, however he had a strong partner in Gupta, who shared his longing to prod financial improvement in India.

McKinsey worked intimately with two of India's greatest re-appropriating organizations: the exchange bunch NASSCOM; and Infosys, which has some expertise in data innovation and business counseling. McKinsey kept on exhorting Infosys as of late as 2020. Off shoring hurt American laborers, however it was awesome for India's economy. "Our worker investment opportunities program

## [L'influence cache]

made a portion of India's most memorable salaried moguls," Infosys flaunted on its site.

McKinsey, as an issue of strategy, doesn't distinguish clients, however an off shoring facilitator said the five U.S. organizations re-appropriating the most positions to India were five McKinsey clients — Passage Engine Organization, American Express, Microsoft, General Electric , and Cisco.

To find the best off shoring areas, the firm assessed 28 low-wage nations for framework, ability, cost, and business climate. McKinsey commended offshoring in open proclamations and in a 2006 book, Offshoring: Understanding the Arising Worldwide Work Market. Among the advantages, the firm said, were financial development, advancement, and the capacity of purchasers to purchase items at lower costs.

"Organizations move their business benefits seaward since they can get more cash-flow — and that implies that abundance is made for the US as well concerning the nation getting the positions," McKinsey said. The advantage, the firm said, was a "greater cake" for everybody to share. McKinsey highlighted how the aircrafts set aside cash through offshoring: "By utilizing modest work, carriers are presently ready to pursue delinquent records receivables that they would prior be compelled to overlook."

Indeed, even organizations with seaward activities were urged to accomplish more. "Organizations aren't capitalizing on their offshoring programs," McKinsey finished up, Particularly in finance. However, McKinsey commended a few General Electric units for effectively offshoring as much as 35 to 40 percent of their money tasks, including creditor liabilities, administrative readiness, charge consistence, and money the executives.

McKinsey proclaimed its perspectives on offshoring through its research organization, the McKinsey Worldwide Establishment, which the firm depicted as free and profoundly respected. How "autonomous" the foundation truly was is begging to be proven wrong. In a 2003 report on offshoring, McKinsey said the organization's "basic role" was to all the more likely grasp the world wide economy "to help McKinsey clients and experts."

Josh Bivens, a financial expert and an exploration chief at the liberal-inclining Monetary Strategy Establishment, sees the McKinsey Worldwide Foundation with incredulity. The gathering needs to depict itself as "nonpartisan public intelligent people, simply taking a gander at the proof, and isn't it astounding?" Bivens said. At the point when as a matter of fact, he added, the gathering was attempting "to give a scholarly gleam" on a benefit making try. "They love to zero in on the triumphant side while overlooking or imagining there isn't so much as a terrible side," Bivens said.

Worried about the deficiency of American positions, Congress held hearings on rethinking, remembering one for June 14, 2007, where Marcus Courtney, addressing tech laborers, assessed that somewhere in the range of 3.3 and 14 million help industry occupations were defenseless against offshoring. Courtney referred to one distributed report that said currently more than 1.1 million

## [L'influence cache]

positions in programming, semiconductors, and telecoms had left the country in the past five years.

McKinsey recognized that a few American laborers might experience temporarily, however said that shouldn't eclipse the advantages. "Zeroing in the offshoring banter on employment misfortunes misses the main point: offshoring makes an incentive for the US economy by making an incentive for US organizations," McKinsey composed. It additionally delivers new income and localizes profit that in a roundabout way assist with making position for uprooted laborers. A few dislodged laborers can move to "other, high worth added exercises," McKinsey said.

Regardless, McKinsey said, "employment misfortunes should be viewed as a feature of a continuous course of financial rebuilding, with which the U.S. economy is all around familiar" — limited consolation for abandoned laborers attempting to take care of their families.

The Nobel Prize-winning business analyst Joseph E. Stiglitz said McKinsey's perspectives on deregulation and Globalization are imperfect. "Indeed, even in the best of conditions," he wrote in The New York Times, "the old deregulation hypothesis said just that the victors could remunerate the Failures, not that they would. ALso, they haven't — a remarkable inverse." Yet international alliances held help due to what he calls "counterfeit, exposed monetary hypothesis, which has stayed available for use generally on the grounds that it serves the interests of the most well off."

With assembling and work area occupations vanishing, McKinsey in any case kept on supporting paying leaders more cash, referring to elevated contest for administrative ability. ALbeit the firm had shut its leader pay practice, that didn't mean it couldn't advocate openly for higher President pay. "Gifted directors hope to rake in boatloads of cash," McKinsey experts composed.

So what comprised ability? That was the very thing the three McKinsey specialists attempted to reply in their book The Battle for Ability. "Ability is an enchanting word, one which Individuals appear to see certainly. Furthermore, they wonder about their relationship to it. Am I 'ability'? How would I increment my ability?" An inquiry, no question, for the expert who composed that sentence. And afterward there was this fortune-treat exhortation: "Information give unquestionable proof that better ability the board brings about better execution." Pity the chiefs who required McKinsey information to let them know that.

Since McKinsey will not talk about chief pay at explicit organizations, its reasoning regarding this situation can be gathered to some degree by inspecting the compensation structure at Enron, the bombed energy organization. Over and over, the firm held out Enron as a Model of the cutting edge, effective company. It was controlled by a previous McKinsey accomplice, with assistance from McKinsey specialists, one of whom even participated in executive gatherings. As per Forbes, Enron's best five chiefs took in almost $300 million out of a solitary year and more than $500 million north of a five-year length finishing in 2000, the majority of it from changing out investment opportunities. Enron in the end fell

## [L'influence cache]

in the midst of claims of misrepresentation, bringing about the deficiency of thousands of occupations. (McKinsey was not accused of any bad behavior.)

Much obliged to some degree to remuneration specialists, the posterity of Curve Patton's training, chief pay has ascended to beforehand incomprehensible levels, provoking a board of the U.S. Place of Delegates to explore. At a legislative hearing in December 2007, the board revealed that close to Half of the country's 250 greatest public organizations had utilized remuneration experts with irreconcilable situations. Those with the greatest struggles, the board of trustees' exploration found, would in general compensation their Presidents more. "Chiefs don't simply get pay rates any longer," said Delegate Henry Waxman. "They get investment opportunities, limited stock units, conceded remuneration, chief benefits plans, worthwhile severance bundles and a huge range of advantages from corporate planes to burden and monetary arranging administrations and nation club enrollments." Around 80% of a President's pay is stock related, one review found.

The consistently supportive McKinsey distributed a report in 2002 contribution a tip for leaders on the best way to keep their stock cost raised. Chiefs ought to invest energy, the report expressed, getting to know their biggest financial backers so that after knowing about a significant new corporate choice, the financial backers don't frenzy and dump their portions, sending the stock cost lower. Yet, understanding the opinions of financial backers without uncovering nonpublic data is precarious. Thus, McKinsey encouraged chiefs to peddle their financial backers in a manner that can't be understood "as passing insider data." A high stock cost, obviously, benefits the organization and the President, whose pay is progressively connected to the stock cost.

As the working class proceeded to endure, and the situation of America's laborers became more enthusiastically to overlook, even McKinsey started to understand that a company's nearsighted obsession with investor benefits probably won't be really great for society. "While investor free enterprise has catalyzed huge advancement, it additionally has battled to resolve profoundly vexing issues, for example, environmental change and pay disparity," McKinsey recognized in 2020.

The firm even reevaluated its inadequate commendation of offshoring. As per a Bloomberg report, Richard Dobbs, a McKinsey senior accomplice and an individual from the McKinsey World wide Organization in London, depicted his company's perspective on Globalization as a development. McKinsey actually upholds Globalization, he said, yet added, "There's a be that as it may, and we should be more mindful of the in any case."

What happens when Walmart plants its banner locally is certainly not a new story. less expensive items and market power force nearby retailers to bring down their costs or close their entryways while by and large discouraging wages locally. However, for 1.5 million Americans, Walmart extends to something they need — an employment opportunity and the self confidence that accompanies it. What it doesn't offer is simple entry to the working class or the assurance of remaining there.

## [L'influence cache]

By 2005, the normal yearly compensation at Walmart, a McKinsey client, was generally $17,500, while the middle family pay in the US was nearly $50,000. Almost around 50% of the offspring of Walmart representatives, called partners, were on Medicaid or uninsured. Without an association to address them — the organization is violently hostile to association — the main influence workers had for better treatment was public openness, and the tension that could present as a powerful influence for the executives.

Notoriety was a significant Walmart worry in 2005 as the organization enrolled McKinsey to take a gander at how it could slow the development of worker costs, Particularly medical services. "Walmart's medical services benefit is one of the most squeezing notoriety issues we face," Susan Chambers, a Walmart leader, wrote in a private reminder — ready with the assistance of McKinsey — to the organization's governing body. She accused "very much financed, efficient pundits, as well as state government authorities," who were cautiously investigating Walmart's advantages.

Chambers recognized a few reactions were substantial, remarkably that the inclusion was costly for low-pay families and that "a huge rate" of partners and their kids were on open help. Hence, a more modest level of workers signed up for the organization's protection plan contrasted and most public bosses. Another issue, Chambers finished up, was discernment. "We have not really conveyed the liberality of our medical care advantages to the overall population."

To resolve these issues, Walmart requested that McKinsey assist with driving a fifteen-man group entrusted with making proposals.

One prickly issue uncovered by the team was that laborer residency at Walmart had developed, genuinely influencing the organization's funds. In light of longer residency, more partners equipped for advantages and more took care of time. "A significantly more significant variable is compensation, which expansion in lock-step with residency and straightforwardly drive the expense of many advantages."

Though different organizations could celebrate workers for their dependability and experience, clearly Walmart was not one of them. "Given the effect of residency on wages and advantages, the expense of a partner with seven years of residency is just about 55% more than the expense of a partner with one year of residency, yet there is no distinction in their efficiency," the team found. "Besides, on the grounds that we pay a partner more in compensation and advantages, as their residency builds, we are evaluating that partner out of the work market, improving the probability that the person in question will remain with Wal-Shop." More than anything, this showed how perspectives toward work had changed since the Settlement of Detroit once held out the commitment of a safer future for laborers, one in which their youngsters could have a preferable life over their folks.

Walmart relates normally spent almost two times the public normal on medical care for them as well as their families. Walmart's protection didn't cover routine kid vaccination. "State run administrations are progressively worried about medical services costs, and many view Walmart as a feature of the issue," as per the team report. Walmart dreaded states could begin expecting organizations to report the

## [L'influence cache]

number of their workers required Medicaid inclusion. As a matter of fact, when Minnesota lawmakers attempted to do precisely that, Walmart campaigned hard against it, delivering a letter expressing that the bill was just a "misinformed, disastrous attack on a business attempting to make 100,000 new positions this year."

The team, with the assistance of McKinsey, suggested that the organization increment the level of seasonal laborers, however that would bring down the organization's medical care enlistment, perhaps affecting the organization's "public standing." The gathering likewise said administration ought to consider lessening its general interest in benefit sharing and 401(k) programs, bring down its organization paid life coverage inclusion, and move workers to "buyer driven" wellbeing plans. At long last, to fight off analysis that an excessive number of workers required Medicaid, the team recommended reevaluating the discussion by proposing that Medicaid "is everybody's concern, in addition to Walmart's."

However unique as Walmart seems to be from other enormous organizations, it imparts one business practice to them. At the point when items or supplies can be bought all the more efficiently in low-wage nations, Walmart will do that. In 2005, a long-term Walmart provider of sprinklers laid off practically the entirety of its laborers. The organization president faulted Walmart for demanding that his organization produce the sprinklers all the more efficiently in China, as per Charles Fishman's book The Wal-Shop Impact.

Fishman visited representatives who lost their positions following quite a while of working for the sprinkler organization. He tracked down a combination of sharpness, trouble, and stress.

Rose Dunbar: I returned home and sobbed for seven days. I was overpowered. I didn't have the foggiest idea what to do. I began at Nelson at $4.50. I left at $10.85 an hour fifteen years after the fact... . I'm sixty years of age. I'm too youthful to even think about resigning. Yet, I'm not alluring. I'm separated, my girl lives with me — she doesn't make a lot — and my two granddaughters.

Terri Graham: Recently, they had... Individuals strolling around the plant and recording us working. That was awful, horrible. Squarely in front of us.

Sally Stone: Nelson is sending a portion of Individuals over to China, similar to the group chiefs, the groundskeepers, they are going to China to prepare Individuals there and set up the hardware for them.

Those meetings don't completely catch the degree of Walmart's dependence on modest unfamiliar work. In the primary long stretches of the new thousand years, Walmart imported a bewildering $30 billion in products from China alone. Peter Walker, who conflicted with Patton 50 years prior and has accomplished broad work in China, told a Fox News have, "In the event that my McKinsey mates were here today, I figure they would agree, as I have, that deregulation was so the predominant mantra of the time that whatever might be finished to cultivate that and make anything anyplace was essentially unchallenged."

## [L'influence cache]

Fishman reminded perusers that Walmart had done other disagreeable things. It once secured representatives in certain stores for the time being; constrained a few representatives to finish off and continue to work; and utilized undocumented outsiders to clean a few stores for the time being. (McKinsey played no part in these episodes.) considering this, Fishman finished up,

Wal-Store just can't embrace a fundamental reality: the organization has the very notoriety it merits. No, we don't give the organization sufficient credit at low costs. In any case, the wrecked pledge Sam Walton had with how to treat workers; the tireless tension that hollows out organizations and weakens the nature of their items; the harassing of providers and networks; the destructive mystery... none of these is fanciful or trifling.

Since Fishman's book, Walmart has changed a portion of its more questionable practices by expanding medical care, accomplishing other things to safeguard the climate, and acting in an all the more socially mindful way. Following a mass shooting in one of its stores, Walmart prohibited the offer of handguns and ammo for military-style weapons. In any case, representatives will in any case battle to cover their bills. In 2020, Walmart started testing an arrangement in 500 stores that raised the lowest pay permitted by law from $11 to $12 an hour for specific representatives.

McKinsey has kept on exhorting Walmart. In one late two-year time frame, the retailer paid the firm more than $5 million in expenses, alongside $3.2 million to a McKinsey drive pointed toward assisting youthful specialists with securing positions.

In late November 2017, the CEO of AT&T, Randall Stephenson, came to the Monetary Club of New York on the 50th floor of the Domain State Working to commend President Trump's tax reduction proposition and to make a guarantee to his representatives. Reclining in his seat in front of an audience, that's what stephenson said assuming Trump's $1.5 trillion tax break became regulation, he would recruit 7,000 additional laborers, put somewhere around $1 billion in capital upgrades, and pay $1,000 rewards to 200,000 representatives. The positions wouldn't be section level, he said. "These are 7,000 positions of Individuals placing fiber in the ground, hard cap occupations that make $70,000 to $80,000."

AT&T made sense of that the rewards would go to patrons, non management representatives, and forefront supervisors.

AT&T could stand to be charitable. Under Trump's proposition — which leftists said helped for the most part enormous enterprises that didn't require help — AT&T would save an underlying $21 billion in charges. "In the event that the President signs the bill before Christmas, representatives will get the reward over special times of year," AT&T said.

Three days before Christmas, Trump marked the bill into regulation and tweeted his gratitude to organizations like AT&T. "Our large and extremely famous Tax reduction and Change Bill has taken on a startling new wellspring of 'Affection' — that is enormous organizations and partnerships giving their laborers rewards." A representative for AT&T said the rewards were paid as guaranteed.

## [L'influence cache]

In the three years after the tax break, AT&T paid McKinsey more than $35 million. It didn't take long for AT&T's vows to unwind. Rather than adding position, AT&T disposed of almost eleven thousand positions in the initial a Half year after Trump's tax reduction became regulation, as per the Correspondences laborers of America. ALso, occupations continued to vanish. By June 2020, a bigger number of than 40,000 positions were disposed of, the association said. One previous McKinsey specialist said the firm brought in its cash revamping portions of the organization.

Stephen Smith had worked for over twenty years at a call place in Connecticut when, with no advance notice, he took in the organization was shutting three region call focuses, including his. At age 46, Smith needed to look for a new position. As revealed by The Watchman, Smith said around ninety representatives were offered severance bundles or the choice of migrating to Georgia or Tennessee — not a suitable choice for workers with companions who worked, or who had youngsters in school. Cindy liddick had worked at the AT&T call focus in Harrisburg, Pennsylvania, for a considerable length of time before it shut in 2018. "My significant other is exceptionally sick, I'm going to lose my medical coverage and beginning once again in the gig market at my age will be extreme," liddick said.

Joe Snyder, leader of a CWA neighborhood in Akron, said, "It seems as though AT&T is pushing the work to low-paid project workers who don't have a similar preparation, experience, and responsibility as CWA Individuals. The cash they are saving goes into the pockets of well off investors searching for momentary benefits." Exhorting AT&T has been remarkably worthwhile for McKinsey. In only one five-year time frame in the mid 1990s, the organization paid McKinsey $96 million.

Another telecom organization, Verizon Correspondences, paid McKinsey a stupendous complete of something like $120 million of every 2018 and 2019. Almost 200 McKinsey experts — 200 — dealt with the Verizon account, a previous McKinsey worker said in a meeting. "We were running fifteen to twenty separate groups," the previous representative said, adding that there were comparative numbers from other counseling firms. "We were continuously running into cohorts in the break room. It was a running joke."

Now and again, there were however many experts as Verizon representatives, the previous McKinsey worker said. Verizon could have spent in some measure part of the $120 million to enlist extremely durable representatives or overhaul their own staff. Expressed another way, Verizon — and AT&T — re-appropriated their responsibilities to advisors who might travel every which way, with practically no steadfastness to the organizations they exhorted, past satisfying the supervisors who employed them, guaranteeing that the Following flood of specialists would be pretty much as welcome as they were.

By late 2018, in excess of 10,000 Verizon representatives had taken a willful buyout. McKinsey said finance decreases were "not a focal point of our work." ALL things considered, Nell Geiser, research facilitator for the Correspondences laborers of America, said the work slices were made to meet Money Road's

## [L'influence cache]

assumptions. "The quickest method for arriving is through staff decrease," Geiser said.

Anand Giridharadas, a previous McKinsey specialist, trusts the country's inability to address pay imbalance has turned Individuals against government and against one another. "A huge number of Americans, on the left and right, feel one thing in like manner: that the game is manipulated against Individuals like them," he wrote in Victors Take ALL. "Maybe to this end we hear steady judgment of 'the framework.' "

A concentrate by the Central bank Board in Washington, D.C., reported that throughout the course of recent many years the rising business sector force of organizations added to a portion of society's most obstinate issues: wage development deteriorated as efficiency developed; before-charge benefit of U.S. companies rose forcefully as pay disparity deteriorated; and family obligation rose as monetary insecurity expanded. Indeed, even the Business Roundtable in August 2019 reconsidered its place that enterprises ought to serve just investor interests — a reflection, McKinsey said, "of strains that have been bubbling over."

With offshoring undesirable with numerous Washington strategy creators, the McKinsey Worldwide Establishment guarded its help of Globalization, saying reevaluating and more fragile worker's organizations had been wrongly referred to as driving reasons for money imbalance. The almost certain guilty parties, McKinsey said, were the "win and fail cycles in the economy" and mechanical advances. "While a significant part of the public discussion on this issue has been about positions lost and positions uprooted, the more significant story is one about change," McKinsey said.

Giridharadas said McKinsey's concern includes something other than whom it prompts. "Indeed, even at its ideal, a large part of the work is tied in with expanding financial backers' portion of the benefits by diminishing work's portion."

Apparently consistently, McKinsey peppers the web with considerations and ideas on how organizations can adapt to the effect of pay imbalance. They are a genuine inventory of McKinseyisms. "What is your organization's center justification behind being?" the firm inquires. "What's required is generally clear : it's profound reflection on your corporate character — what you truly depend on." While the inquiry might be clear, McKinsey said, the responses are not. "How would you pull this off? What are the mechanics of making it happen and making it genuine?"

McKinsey offered some New Age shrewdness: "As you endeavor to interface the superpower of your business with its effect on society, you're probably going to distinguish a rich group of stars of potential reason drives." For Individuals uncertain of their convictions, McKinsey recommended an application through which they can "investigate their qualities and reason and make working environment associations with empower the quest for those points."

McKinsey seldom apologizes for previous slip-ups, yet it appears to be fitting to glance back at Curve Patton, who began the Walk toward higher leader pay.

## [L'influence cache]

Further down the road, he was asked by a journalist how he had an outlook on the effect of his work.

His single word answer: "Blameworthy."

## Section 3

**Playing The two Sides**

**Assisting Government With aiding McKinsey**

During the 1990s, a group of McKinsey experts plummeted on the Illinois capital of Springfield in quest for an idealistic dream: to break the pattern of neediness by weaning the poor off government assistance with the assistance of a redesigned state government. The experts were brought there by a previous accomplice, Gary MacDougal, who years sooner had passed on the firm to maintain a fruitful business, then went to legislative issues, dealing with the 1988 official mission of George H. W. Shrub.

During a disrupted time in his life, including a separation, MacDougal had set off on a trip across the Himalayas to contemplate what came straightaway. He got back with a thought: perhaps he could utilize his authority abilities and political contacts to reconsider how government could more readily go after destitution. In the same way as other conservative partners, MacDougal accepted government assistance time after time sustained neediness, so he promised to assist beneficiaries with becoming independent.

MacDougal convinced Illinois' lead representative, Jim Edgar, an individual conservative, to approve a team, with him in control, to concentrate on destitution programs, put forth objectives, and measure progress. The lead representative proposed collaborating with his wellbeing counsel, FElicia Norwood, an amazing youthful alumni of Yale Graduate school who felt comfortable around state government. Norwood turned into a confided in comrade.

Given the intricacy of his errand, MacDougal turned for help to Individuals he knew and regarded — his previous associates at McKinsey. They addressed his call with energy, dispatching a group of seven specialists, including senior accomplices, who assumed control over an enormous office close to the Illinois State legislative hall. The specialists dealt with and off for a really long time, investigating documents on 365 families that got help through eighteen projects controlled by state organizations and confidential foundations. They talked with government assistance beneficiaries and government authorities and visited unfortunate areas. By and by, MacDougal said, the specialists understood the authoritative deficiencies of public help better compared to anybody.

The best part is that McKinsey did everything free, an in-kind commitment with an expected worth in the large numbers of dollars in light of current costs. "The way that the firm was chipping in their time and had no yearnings to get the territory of Illinois as a paying client improved their validity," MacDougal said, taking note of that the firm avoided the chance to impossible work for the public authority, accepting that genuine change there was.

In any case, genuine change happened in 1997 when another regulation redesigned wellbeing administrations in the state. MacDougal said the government assistance caseload dropped 22% in the main year under the redesign. Furthermore, it happened on account of MacDougal and his partners. "This was the greatest

## [L'influence cache]

redesign of state government beginning around 1900," said MacDougal, who proceeded to seat the Illinois Conservative Alliance and to exhort different states on destitution issues.

Later it gave the idea that the company's free work might have filled a need less honorable than MacDougal accepted. By learning the functional subtleties of Free State clients, McKinsey established the groundwork for getting work later — this time for benefit.

That system delivered huge prizes in Illinois. The state was privatizing Medicaid administrations through oversaw care, a framework intended to control expenses and quality part of the way by guiding patients to specific specialists and emergency clinics. In mid 2017, state authorities needed to extend the program by enlisting 650,000 extra Individuals yet concluded it wasn't possible without assistance. Enter McKinsey. It knew the state, having worked there years sooner with Gary MacDougal.

The new lead representative, Bruce Rauner, a moderate, supportive of business conservative, selected a previous McKinsey official as his delegate lead representative. Furthermore, FElicia Norwood, presently the state's Medicaid chief, knew McKinsey from its past work revamping the state government. Norwood likewise worked numerous years for a McKinsey client, Aetna, in its overseen care division.

lead representative Rauner, who had vowed to cut spending and debilitate associations, immediately cruised his organization into the stones. The state had no spending plan for over two years as Rauner went head to head with Majority rule officials. To give a beware of the lead representative's monetary choices, electors chose Susana Mendoza as Illinois specialist.

little in height and loaded with battle, Mendoza visited hospices, nursing homes, and medical clinics to see firsthand the effect of the spending plan stalemate on the destitute. She tracked down broad concern and languishing. The state owed $800,000 to one organization that gave home consideration to seniors, compElling the organization to cut the quantity of clients from 900 to 300.

"They were shouting for help, in a real sense," Mendoza said. "I went to an aggressive behavior at home focus in Carbondale, the only one out of 200 miles. Assuming they shut, ladies planned to pass on." Andrea Durbin, who ran an affiliation that served families out of 1uck, said the hardest hit were "Individuals who are debilitated, who need the help from the state to be protected and solid and financially recover."

It was during this spending plan emergency that Mendoza made a surprising disclosure.

With lifesaving administrations starving for cash, Illinois authorities were discreetly scooping a huge number of dollars out the way to McKinsey experts. These choices were much of the time brought forth in obscurity, without regulative oversight or endorsement, as per Mendoza. Only three months into her new position, in Walk 2017, she froze $21.6 million the state had consented to pay

## [L'influence cache]

counseling firms for innovation exhortation — its vast majority reserved for McKinsey.

Mendoza needed to know why private experts "have all the earmarks of being focused on for installment in front of basic administrations like senior communities, hospice care offices and instructive foundations." She gave the lead representative five days to respond to explicit inquiries, however she said the cutoff time traveled every which way without replies.

Mendoza didn't yet understand the bigger story she was assisting with revealing — how government turned into a willing associate in McKinsey's work to fabricate a medical services domain around playing all sides of the game.

State officials had close to zero familiarity with the counseling installments, provoking a Chicago lawmaker, Greg Harris, to meet three hearings to realize the reason why the state decided to pay McKinsey more than $75 million with the state in monetary pain. Right off the bat he zeroed in on two sole-source contracts adding up to generally $24 million. The state granted both to McKinsey without as much as talking a solitary other organization.

At one hearing, Harris clarified his interests for Norwood, whose office had granted the agreements: "When you discuss a sole source contract, where there is no offering, no valuable chance to see who else is out there, who could have better insight, better costs, that... as you can envision brings up a great deal of issues."

Not a great explanation to stress, Norwood answered. She and her partners were exceptionally acquainted with McKinsey's work, so there was compelling reason need to ask somewhere else.

"Is there no inner ability to do any of this work without going out and burning through huge number of dollars more?" Harris inquired.

Norwood said no. "The work most certainly isn't possible by those representatives." Planning authoritative change was considered past their abilities.

lawmakers were in good company to have a problem with the McKinsey contracts. The state's central acquirement official voided one of them — worth $12 million — in light of the fact that Norwood mistakenly reasoned that contending offers were not needed. After one day Mendoza froze installments on a second McKinsey contract.

However it was McKinsey's connect to another consumption that raised the most concern. Norwood, with McKinsey's direction, organized to pay $63 billion — the biggest acquisition in state history — to seven oversaw care organizations to oversee and pay for clinical benefits through the extended Medicaid program. The use circumvent regulative oversight, a choice that Mendoza said was terribly off track. "That implies this proposition isn't managed the cost of a similar free oversight as, say, an agreement to buy paper cuts," she said.

## [L'influence cache]

McKinsey, as far as one might be concerned, was not especially keen on having anybody investigate its shoulder, in any event, for its administration work. At one hearing, Harris suggested the company's propensity for mystery with Norwood. He referred to an arrangement in McKinsey's agreement "that neither the state nor McKinsey can allude to one another or trait any data to the next party in an outer correspondence including news discharges relating to this agreement."

"Is this a standard arrangement in Illinois contracts?" Harris inquired.

Norwood said she thought it was, yet couldn't say without a doubt.

"That doesn't appear to be extremely helpful for straightforwardness," Harris closed.

Yet again Norwood said there was no reason to worry. She made sense of that the goliath oversaw care contracts, for instance, were put out for offers and would be assessed by Individuals without any irreconcilable situations. "While it is valid," she said, "that I have Recently worked for an overseen care plan, very nearly 19 years to be definite," neither she nor two partners with connections to the medical services industry would partake in the assessment.

Norwood's response was precise the end of the line, yet neglected to resolve other essential inquiries, for example, who composed agreement particulars, which can possibly lean toward one firm over another. Gotten some information about this, Norwood said McKinsey assisted state representatives with setting them up. Helping, she said, were Individuals from the lead representative's office, including another delegate lead representative, Three pointer Childress, who a year after the fact joined McKinsey's Chicago office. In other declaration, Norwood changed her record to say Childress didn't partake. Norwood didn't answer messages looking for a meeting.

Nobody at the consultation remembered to find out if McKinsey had any likely irreconcilable circumstances. The company's client list, a strictly confidential mystery, could not have possibly been accessible to state authorities. Yet, the writers of this book acquired restrictive admittance to that rundown, and it showed McKinsey's profound monetary connections to the oversaw care industry.

Lately, McKinsey charged organizations that give oversaw care more than $200 million, making it one of the association's most rewarding areas. Additionally, four of the seven organizations that won pieces of the $63 billion Medicaid contract were subsequently procured by McKinsey clients. What's more, a fifth, the parent organization of Blue Cross and Blue Safeguard of Illinois, was McKinsey's landowner in midtown Chicago. At the point when McKinsey rented three upper-level floors in a structure claimed by the safety net provider, Crain's Chicago Business called it a major success for the insurance agency, which had "a strong speculation to recover" in the structure.

McKinsey didn't openly unveil these ties. A McKinsey representative said experts who obtain private data from a client's rival are taboo from serving the contender "however long the data has huge serious worth (ordinarily two years)." The firm

## [L'influence cache]

added: "Clients work with us since they believe that we will protect their classified data."

Lawmakers needed to understand how McKinsey acquired month to month expenses of generally $1 million. Or on the other hand in the dialect of experts, what were the "expectations"? Harris, investigating reports at a consultation, saw something that grieved him. "Consistently they rehash similar expectations. So why would that be something very similar without variety?" Harris inquired. "I believe that is a consistent inquiry."

"It is," Norwood answered.

Harris said a few expectations seemed unclear, like aiding support and get ready initiative "for supplier commitment meetings at suitable rhythm to be characterized." As of now, certain Individuals started to snicker, he said.

"Do we have a rhythm characterized?" Harris asked with a hint of mockery.

"Is that your inquiry?"

"Definitely, I'm simply going through these, considering what we have gotten for the million bucks."

"We will return and get something to you that entirely frames all that we've paid and the expectations that we've gotten," Norwood guaranteed.

A Half year after the fact, Norwood left her state work for quite possibly of McKinsey's greatest client, Song of devotion, a huge oversaw care organization. McKinsey has charged Song of praise more than $90 million starting around 2018. A critical piece of those billings came while Norwood filled in as leader of Song of devotion's administration business division. Notwithstanding Song of devotion, McKinsey has counseled for undoubtedly nine other insurance agency clients.

In any case, before Norwood left state business, another lawmaker, Delegate William Davis, found out if she was sure that McKinsey had a spotless record doing this sort of work. He was asking, Davis made sense of, on the grounds that an organization could have an extraordinary standing, "then a modern day miracle, someone digs somewhat more profound and pulls back a layer of the onion" and finds issues.

"No issues with this organization that you know about?" Davis inquired.

"Supposedly, Delegate, there are no issues with this organization that we know about."

"Is it true that you are beyond a doubt certain? I need to be sure."

"I'm certain about that, Agent."

To pull back a layer of the onion, they could have thought about a little excursion across the Mississippi Waterway to St. Louis, and afterward one more 380 miles to little Shake. Had they done as such, they would have found that Missouri and

## [L'influence cache]

Arkansas had uncovering stories to tell about how McKinsey wins government contracts.

As Illinois demonstrated, McKinsey knew the fine subtleties of overseen care as well as how to contact Individuals in power — the chiefs — like the previous Missouri lead representative Eric Greitens.

In January 2017, only days after Greitens was confirmed, he made another position explicitly for Drew Erdmann, a previous McKinsey accomplice who had once been a chief with the Public safety Board zeroing in on Iraq and Iran. It wasn't some time before Missouri employed McKinsey — once more, at no charge — "to help us with understanding the vital initiative and Social components that we really want to fabricate a high-performing association."

After McKinsey's free work, the firm stood prepared to begin gathering cash. At the point when Erdmann communicated interest in upgrading Medicaid, the state soon thereafter welcomed McKinsey and four other counseling firms to offer on an agreement to quickly assess the Medicaid program and suggest changes, including ways of combatting waste, extortion, and misuse.

McKinsey's accommodation stuck out, most observably in light of the fact that it included many pages that were either shut down completely or generally passed out, disclosing any examination unimaginable. No other counseling firm did that.

A feature writer for the St. Louis Post-Dispatch, Tony Courier, became dubious. He expressed, "Since Erdmann was recruited, McKinsey has turned into a key part in Missouri state government. A critical element of their work has all the earmarks of being mystery." The state head legal officer said the redactions seemed inappropriate.

The enormous redactions foreshadowed what was to come.

The state at first said the triumphant bidder would be chosen in view of the accompanying measures: cost 40%, philosophy 40%, and experience 20%. However, promptly after giving those particulars, the state out of nowhere pulled out them and gave another rating framework that de-underscored cost. Presently, rather than the expense being 40%, it dropped to just 15%. The change permitted McKinsey to all the more serenely request more cash nevertheless accomplish a high score.

ALso, that occurred. McKinsey won the agreement for $2.7 million — multiple times higher than the most reduced bid or more than the consolidated all out of the three least offers. Missouri authorities seemed to have reordered indistinguishable assessments in numerous segments, granting each a 100% score. Contenders were made a decision about more cruelly, with explicit reactions.

There were different peculiarities. Subsequent to presenting its ideal and last bid, McKinsey mentioned a gathering with state authorities and got consent to modify its proposition — over a month after the documenting cutoff time. A contender, Navigant, dissented, saying state records lay out that McKinsey "was managed the cost of the valuable chance to modify and resubmit material that was used in

## [L'influence cache]

scoring." A previous solicitation by Navigant for additional opportunity to present its unique proposition was dismissed.

Navigant likewise protested McKinsey's broad redactions, saying it impeded contenders from checking on the arrangement "as to consistence or substance." Navigant added, "A bid interaction is expected to be open and straightforward once finished. This is everything except that." The state said it had no commitment to distribute a full offered proposition on the web, yet later Eliminated the redactions. State authorities dismissed Navigant's dissent, it were observed to say every single pertinent rule.

The Missouri House minority pioneer, Gail McCann Beatty, a leftist, blamed the Greitens organization for gear the determination interaction for McKinsey, a charge state authorities, including Erdmann, denied. Another house part, Peter Merideth, said the agreement didn't breeze through the smell assessment. "I have little to no faith in them briefly," he expressed, alluding to McKinsey. Merideth likewise considered it odd that McKinsey appeared to follow nearby officials via web-based entertainment. "One person in New York is normally quick to 'like' something I post via online entertainment. For what reason is it?"

A customer bunch, Missouri Medical care for ALL, likewise had inquiries regarding McKinsey. "We can't be aware assuming that McKinsey has any irreconcilable situations since we don't have the foggiest idea who all their ongoing clients are," the gathering composed.

That demonstrated insightful. The three organizations Missouri employed to oversee the new Medicaid program were either McKinsey clients or destined to-be McKinsey clients. One of them, the St. Louis-based Centene Organization, "had to deal with serious penalties of bungle coming about in something like $23.6 million in punishments in excess of twelve expresses," The Des Moines Register revealed in 2018. Those charges, which didn't blame McKinsey for bad behavior, included "deficiencies" in furnishing poor people and older with admittance to specialists, as per the paper. McKinsey charged Centene more than $50 million out of 2018 and 2019.

Shawn D'Abreu, the shopper gathering's strategy chief, said Missourians didn't get much for their $2.7 million. While McKinsey's report contained a few smart thoughts, the firm recognized that a significant number of its ideas were at that point known to state authorities.

"Anyone might have gone to the Division of Social Administrations, talked with several Individuals, and in the span of a day or so composed precisely the same report as far as the things that we recognize as great," D'Abreu said. A misrepresentation? Maybe. In any case, the McKinsey report brought up different issues also.

"Virtually the significant proposals for 'change' can be all tracked down in different reports on McKinsey's site," the customer bunch composed. "It's reasonable to address whether Missouri is getting custom fitted proposals for our state or cutout arrangements."

## [L'influence cache]

McKinsey's assessment tried not to offend Missouri's conservative administrators. "The report appears to put the state's financial plan misfortunes on the Medicaid program, disregarding the effect of rehashed tax reductions," the buyer bunch composed. Generally speaking, McKinsey seemed to lean toward oversaw care benefits over admittance to medical services benefits, the gathering said.

By 2019, Missouri's new vehicle for conveying Medicaid administrations started spilling oil. A sharp drop in the quantity of Medicaid enlistments — Particularly among kids — stressed Spice Kuhn, CEO of the Missouri Clinic Affiliation. "At the point when we see north of 50,000 kids fall off the Medicaid rolls, it brings up certain issues about whether the state is doing its checks suitably," he said. Merideth, the state delegate, put the number more like 100,000.

Either McKinsey didn't suggest an arrangement that would have forestalled this, or the state overlooked McKinsey's recommendation. A third chance is that Missouri's economy improved, however advocates for the poor limited that clarification. legitimate Administrations of Eastern Missouri put a greater amount of the fault on McKinsey's report, which prescribed ways of reducing Medicaid expenses. "In view of its emphasis on cost reserve funds, the report for the most part neglects to break down the expected effect of its proposals on wellbeing access and results," the lawful administrations bunch wrote in a report.

Merideth said oversaw care flopped in another space. "They sold us on setting aside cash," he said, yet Missouri has among the most noteworthy per-patient Medicaid costs in the country. How much obligation, if any, McKinsey bears for these significant expenses is an open inquiry.

Overseen care in the event that done right have some control over costs, work on clinical results, and convey preferable worth over the conventional charge for-administration framework, which rewards volume over quality and cost. However, when overseen care doesn't follow through on those commitments, the business has been known to put resources into lobbyists to push for better Medicaid rules, as per Dr. Joshua M. Sharfstein, a wellbeing strategy master at Johns Hopkins. "I'm in favor of overseen care plans in Medicaid, however their commitment is definitely not a mystical arrangement," he said. In the event that the plans are to fill in as planned, he added, states should give "vigorous oversight."

McKinsey's nearby connections to safety net providers were obvious in adjoining Arkansas, where Blue Cross Blue Safeguard made the strange stride of offering the express a $1.5 million award on the off chance that it would employ McKinsey to assess the Medicaid program. The state took the cash, added another $1.5 million, then, at that point, gave everything — $3 million — to McKinsey through an "crisis" sole-source contract.

A while in the wake of granting the agreement, Arkansas had another shock. Andy Allison, a wellbeing financial specialist, recounts talking with for the gig of Arkansas Medicaid chief and winding up in an office with a McKinsey senior accomplice, David Nuzum. "A McKinsey accomplice was sitting in my meeting," Allison reviewed. "They required exhortation to sort out whether or not I could do what I was being employed to do." Nuzum declined to be evaluated. Yet, as

## [L'influence cache]

per McKinsey, Nuzum "was welcomed in extemporaneous to talk with Mr. Allison for a couple of moments" and assumed no part in verifying him.

Allison landed the position. He came needing to involve Medicaid assets to purchase private health care coverage for low-pay people. However, it was McKinsey that benefited the most, figuring out how to parlay that $3 million introductory agreement into state business adding up to more than $100 million — while never presenting a bid. Very much a take for one of the country's most unfortunate states. Afterward, a regulative review presumed that the first, $1.5 million Blue Cross-facilitated agreement, granted before Allison showed up, was given out inappropriately and ought to have been put out for offers.

In a meeting for this book, Allison said McKinsey got sole-source contracts in light of the fact that no other firm had the important abilities to change Medicaid. "Development and installment change requires a lot of comprehension of the clinical market," he said. "No consultancy can pull that off other than McKinsey." Had he looked for cutthroat offers, Allison said, McKinsey would in any case have arisen as the best. "It would have been a similar response — just a whole lot more slow."

McKinsey probably loved what it saw in Allison, in light of the fact that the firm recruited him in 2015, somewhat more than a Half year after he left his state work, an improvement that regulative evaluators figured huge enough to remember for a profoundly basic report on the state's stewardship of Medicaid reserves.

McKinsey's progress in Illinois, Missouri, and Arkansas is more than karma and provincial information. The company's long reach expands well past the lines of those states and incorporates an impressive rundown of clients crossing the whole medical services production network, alongside their administration controllers. It additionally makes a practically unquantifiable potential for irreconcilable circumstances.

Perceiving that medical services could be a significant benefit place, McKinsey tunneled profound into state and bureaucratic organizations by selling that normal government laborers coming up short on preparing and experience to comprehend the subtleties of medical services financial matters. The firm advanced its exclusive examination, implanted with large number of informational indexes from clients all over the planet. At this point not the space of just generalists, McKinsey currently had specialists, scientists, and previous government controllers on staff.

McKinsey was gigantically effective, getting more than one billion bucks in state and government counseling contracts, frequently without serious offering. A significant number of those agreements included prompting government organizations that direct McKinsey's confidential clients in drugs, emergency clinics, and protection.

McKinsey's medical care group played a significant — and much-scrutinized — job in the discussion over President Obama's unmistakable homegrown accomplishment, the Reasonable Consideration Act, the main medical services regulation since Federal medical care and Medicaid 50 years sooner. The law

## [L'influence cache]

finished long periods of bombed Popularity based endeavors to help the uninsured. A large number of Americans would now approach reasonable protection since Medicaid extended to incorporate the poor as well as the close to poor. The Individuals who didn't qualify due to pay could utilize tax reductions to purchase protection through a public commercial center and couldn't be denied inclusion as a result of previous circumstances.

The law enraged conservative pioneers, who saw it as a stage toward an administration takeover of medical care. Wellbeing guarantors freely upheld the regulation yet secretly attempted to kill it by covertly diverting huge number of dollars through the U.S. Office of Business to campaign against the bill.

The protection business didn't overcome the Reasonable Consideration Act, however debilitated it by forcing lawmakers to Eliminate the "public choice," an arrangement that would have permitted the public authority to offer contending inclusion as a fence against unnecessary insurance agency benefits. President Obama dropped that arrangement to win the concluding vote of Representative Joe lieberman of Connecticut, home to a few significant insurance agency. legislative conservatives lost the fight however didn't quit attempting to sabotage the new regulation through court difficulties and different means.

In June 2011, conservatives got a surprising lift. McKinsey stunned Washington by delivering a review that extended close to 33% of managers "without a doubt or most likely" would quit offering wellbeing inclusion when the law produced full results in 2014. The review proposed the fix was more terrible than the sickness, taking steps to sabotage the law before it carried out.

McKinsey's discoveries conflicted with different examinations, including those by the Rand Company, the Metropolitan Foundation, and the neutral legislative Financial plan Office, inciting liberals to request that the specialists discharge their procedure.

For almost fourteen days McKinsey rejected, saying its examination was restrictive, further maddening legislative liberals. "The discoveries of this study are so Particularly clashing with different evaluations that it has brought up real issues about the item, including how and why it was made," liberals on the House Available resources Board of trustees wrote in a letter to McKinsey's overseeing accomplice, Dominic Barton. "The actual report expresses that McKinsey 'taught respondents' about the ramifications of the Reasonable Consideration Act, without really any sign of the substance of this 'training.' "Congressperson Max Baucus, executive of the Senate Money Board of trustees, composed a comparative letter to Barton.

"It isn't each day that the director of the Senate Money Board and three House councils all the while request that an organization hack up the internals of a review like this one," the Washington Post feature writer Greg Commander composed. "This comprises genuine tension, and highlights how high the stakes have become for liberals, since conservatives have been consistently refering to the concentrate as a weapon against the wellbeing regulation."

## [L'influence cache]

McKinsey at last bowed to political strain and recognized its review was not tantamount to other, more thorough examinations and that it was not intended to be "prescient." That didn't fulfill Representative Baucus, who said the report "is loaded up with filtered out realities and skewed questions." Nancy-Ann DeParle, vice president of staff to President Obama, likewise speared McKinsey's report, saying that almost 50% of the study's respondents knew scarcely anything about a business' liability under the law and almost a quarter were "not by any stretch natural" with it. DeParle declined to theorize concerning McKinsey's inspiration to compose such a report.

Had liberals realized how close McKinsey was to wellbeing guarantors, they could have said much more.

The McKinsey report streamed directly from its standard playbook, where the firm recognizes an issue hiding around the bend — an issue more serious than Individuals understand, requiring a speedy reaction in the event that damage is to be stayed away from and flourishing accomplished. Arrangements are accessible. What's more, McKinsey can help — for a charge.

To build its perceivability, McKinsey set up the Middle for U.S. Wellbeing Framework Change "to track and display the effect of administrative change on market and customer elements." The middle is unambiguous about its interest group. "We support financial backers — including key purchasers and confidential value — to comprehend potential open doors arising out of the most recent authoritative and administrative change patterns [and] distinguish appealing venture regions and resources across the medical care esteem chain."

"Throughout recent years," McKinsey wrote in April 2018, "our medical services practice has directed in excess of 2,500 commitment with medical services frameworks, confidential back up plans and government payers, expert emergency clinics, scholastic clinical focuses and subordinate specialist co-ops." That incorporates twenty of the greatest oversaw care firms, nine of the biggest U.S. emergency clinic frameworks, and seven of the best ten scholarly clinical focuses, "as well as numerous administration payers at the government and state level — including 12 states to change organization activity [and] upgrade their oversaw care draws near." furthermore, the firm serves "driving retail drug stores, auxiliary specialist co-ops, industry affiliations, confidential value firms and a significant number of the biggest U.S. businesses."

With tip top clients across the medical care scene and an elevated standing, it is not difficult to envision how McKinsey could maneuver government organizations into its circle.

*[L'influence cache]*

## Section 4

## McKinsey at ICE

### "We Do Execution, Not Arrangement"

The late-harvest time sun was going to set over Arlington Public Graveyard, noticeable from the housetop deck, as 200 McKinsey workers fit into a 10th floor meeting room in the company's Washington, D.C., office. McKinsey chiefs had assembled the conference on a Friday evening — generally a movement day for specialists heading home Following seven days out and about — to examine a pressing matter.

McKinsey was under attack.

For an organization familiar with continuously being in charge, late occasions had shocked and panicked many in its positions. 18 months sooner, articles started showing up in the media that scrutinized McKinsey's judgment and morals. There was its work for a bad power organization in South Africa, claimed irreconcilable situations in its liquidation practice, and a ruckus over the company's work with narcotic makers, despots, and kleptocrats.

McKinsey had trusted this unwanted examination would shrink and pass on in a climate where the media is more acclimated with adulating the organization than to scrutinizing it.

In any case, that hadn't occurred.

In June 2018, The New York Times incorporated a short notice of McKinsey's work with Migration and Customs Requirement — otherwise called ICE — in an extended insightful article about the company's work in South Africa.

It set off a downpour of analysis inside McKinsey and among its huge number of graduated class, fastened to the firm through customary email briefings. Experts the world over took steps to leave. "It caused a gigantic issue inside," one London-based specialist reviewed.

McKinsey safeguarded its agreement with ICE, saying that it principally involved "managerial and authoritative issues."

Kevin Sneader, then only days into his residency as the company's overseeing accomplice, guaranteed the McKinsey majority and its numerous graduated class that the firm represented more than earning anything. "We will not, for any reason, take part in work, anyplace on the planet, that advances or helps arrangements that are in conflict with our qualities," he composed. In addition, he added, McKinsey's work with ICE had finished.

Inside the firm, the discussion over ICE b1urred out of spotlight.

That changed on Tuesday, December 3, 2019.

## [L'influence cache]

That day, Republican, a philanthropic insightful newsroom, distributed a significant story in The New York Times reporting McKinsey's work with ICE — the government office liable for gathering together undocumented settle rs and expelling them.

For over a year, the country had watched reports of shouting youngsters effectively isolated from their folks at the boundary — sights and sounds difficult to neglect. Some were shunted into holding pens, locked inside steel walled in areas no better than confines. One columnist got a sound recording of young men and young ladies at a Texas confinement focus, wailing for their moms and fathers.

Presently specialists in the room needed to defy the truth that their firm could have assisted with empowering these approaches.

After Trump was chosen, there was an open inquiry regarding how McKinsey's scientific, exceptionally requested perspective on government would work with a president who doubted science, followed evaluations driven TV characters, and embraced paranoid ideas of all shapes and sizes. Trump's working way appeared to be absolutely incongruent with McKinsey's information driven way to deal with divining the most reasonable method for running government.

As it ended up, the main thing the Trump organization didn't do was set up McKinsey a party. It granted many counseling contracts across the scene of government organizations, creating a large number of dollars in income for the firm.

In any case, presently, toward the beginning of December 2019, with the president only days from being reprimanded, his cruel enemy of migration approaches were tearing through the firm.

The article uncovered a few awkward bits of insight about how far the firm would go in serving clients. As indicated by the article, McKinsey suggested that ICE save on food, clinical consideration, and management of prisoners — recommendations that frightened even some ICE authorities who addressed whether the reduces supported the human expense.

Regardless, ICE's initiative embraced the company's work, saying it brought "an eminent reduction in an opportunity to Eliminate outsiders with a last request of evacuation."

The article resounded external the firm also. Pete Buttigieg, then, at that point, an official competitor and a veteran of McKinsey's Washington office, referred to the decisive moves' as "revolting." Another previous McKinsey specialist, Andy Slavitt, a previous wellbeing official under Obama, took to Twitter, referring to the proposals as "savage."

Undeniably more significant for McKinsey was the means by which its ongoing workers were engrossing the information. Large numbers of the youthful, hopeful specialists in the room that evening had been influence d by McKinsey scouts,

## [L'influence cache]

who regularly stressed the company's Social-area work. McKinsey enlists said they tried to make the world a superior spot.

Presently they needed to deal with the hazier side of what they had pursued. Vocations were on the line. Stand up and confront the results? Or on the other hand keep quiet, controlled by the possibility of losing a liberal compensation and a high-glory work?

No less than two among them had burning individual encounters that stirred up their displeasure. One would stand up that evening. The second would follow, days after the fact, with an emotional mass email to Individuals from the firm. Others, Particularly senior experts, were more irresolute.

For some McKinsey representatives, the spirit looking through over the company's work with ICE had really started three years sooner during the tumultuous opening a long time of the Trump organization.

McKinsey had marked an agreement with ICE, worth more than $20 million, and started work on it during the last year of Obama's administration. By Trump's introduction on January 20, 2017, the group was at that point a ways into their task, implanted at the organization's base camp close to the Potomac Waterway, working in gatherings of four in austere workplaces intended for two Individuals.

However, Trump's proceeding with hot air over outsiders concerned a few more youthful Individuals from the firm.

McKinsey's work with ICE took on added significance since Trump required the organization to satisfy his center mission vow to get the country's southern boundary. His position reverberated with many white Americans who were responsive to his not so subtle bigoted castigations against migrants, a subject Trump explained when he pronounced his bid in the hall of Manhattan's Trump Pinnacle on June 16, 2015.

"At the point when Mexico sends its kin, they're not sending their best," Trump said, two minutes into his brief discourse. "They're bringing drugs, they're bringing wrongdoing, they're attackers, and some, I expect, are great Individuals. Yet, I address line watchmen, and they let us know what we're getting." He kept, telling the Trump Pinnacle crowd travelers were coming "from everywhere South and latin America" and, he proposed, "likely — presumably — from the Center East."

"Furthermore, it has must stop. Furthermore, it has must stop quick."

Once in power, Trump moved quick. Five days into his administration, he marked two chief orders. One approved the structure of a wall on the southern line, a commitment from that 2015 discourse. The other managed undocumented travelers currently inside the US, a significant number of whom, he said, "are crooks who have spent time in jail in our Government, State [sic] and nearby prisons." He needed them out and guided ICE to employ 10,000 new officials to get it going.

## [L'influence cache]

With no advance notice, Trump likewise restricted travel from a few Muslim countries, leaving numerous legitimate U.S. visa holders and, surprisingly, long-lasting occupants in an in-between state, unfit to enter the country.

McKinsey's Washington office unexpectedly wound up in the center of a politically unstable circumstance. A few Individuals from the group were probably not going to savor making life significantly more hard for Individuals escaping neediness and brutality. One expert aided Individuals who were visually impaired and driven a development for jail change — all while in secondary school. One more partook in the counter Trump ladies' Walk the day after the initiation.

Detecting there may be inconvenience fermenting below decks, the venture chief, Richard Senior, booked a 8:00 a.m. multi-city phone call with Individuals from the ICE group, including ranking directors. Senior permitted audience members to voice their interests. However, he likewise needed to convey a message: McKinsey wouldn't avoid this work.

"ICE is taking a different path," he reported. "ALso, McKinsey must change with it."

At the point when his remarks set off new inquiries, Senior offered a recognizable reaction, one that helpfully permitted McKinsey accomplices to evade extreme moral choices.

"We don't do strategy," he said. "We do execution."

Not every person purchased that clarification, including one youthful individual from the ICE group who made some noise. "With that rationale," he said pointedly, "you could legitimize working for any tyrant, even the Nazis." In poker, his remark was what might be compared to betting everything — win all that or lose everything. At that point, he understood McKinsey was not his future. The time had come to leave, and he in the long run did, without any second thoughts.

It wasn't whenever the company's Washington first work had caused disagreement among youthful McKinsey recruits. During the last part of the 1960s, a few experts who went against the Vietnam War would not work with Robert McNamara's Pentagon.

There would be undeniably more inner unrest over the ICE contract. In any case, in February 2017, all that was from now on. Senior had taken care of his business. He let the soldiers air their complaints. Presently the work proceeded.

McKinsey was hustling to give "expectations" for the Requirement and Expulsion Tasks division of ICE, liable for keeping unlawful migrants and expElling them. The venture, began in 2016, was named ERO 2.0, and, in the expressions of an ICE representative, the point was "to audit ERO's activities and mission execution, hierarchical Model, and ability and culture the board."

A short portrayal of the work on McKinsey's interior site slice through the language: "Change plan to increment captures. Lessen handling time for prisoners, and further develop association wellbeing."

## [L'influence cache]

As one previous senior ICE official depicted it, McKinsey's specialists went about as a facilitator for the ICE chiefs, proposing thoughts, talking with representatives in Washington as well as in field workplaces around the nation, ordering notes, and "running the numbers" on potential drives. Furthermore, obviously, their PowerPoint slides. Many slides. Fasteners loaded with them.

On February 13, 2017, under a month into the Trump organization, McKinsey conveyed a sixteen-page slide deck to ICE named "Ability The executives," a profoundly redacted rendition of which became public because of the Opportunity of Data Act claim welcomed on by ProPublica.

The show mirrored the new truth of ICE under Trump, beginning on slide 14: "The recruiting framework can work better and meet extra employing needs welcomed on by the leader Request."

Trump's leader request.

McKinsey's huge thought was "very one-quit employing." This idea was introduced to ICE authority the next month. The arrangement was to unite whatever number strides in the employing system as could be expected under the circumstances into one day, at one area. "We are intending to diminish time to employ by 30-Half (many days)," one slide read.

Employing 10,000 new ICE specialists would mean the organization would need to sign on four and a Half times a larger number of Individuals a year than it at any point had. Be that as it may, enrolling qualified specialists in a terrible economy was sufficiently hard. With America at close full work, a fast increase was inordinately difficult.

"With Trump, who will work there now?" the youthful McKinsey advisor pondered. The response: a many Individuals who concurred with Trump's perspectives on migration.

A portion of McKinsey's ideas on the most proficient method to accelerate recruiting were embraced by ICE, however financial plan requirements held the organization back from meeting Trump's objective.

McKinsey retaliated against the ProPublica report in the Times, saying the article "on a very basic level distorts McKinsey's work." The firm likewise paid Google to rank its reaction over the article on web look, as it had done when it answered past New York Times articles. McKinsey said that the "extension and objectives of our work were laid out during the earlier organization, and they changed in no material way after the progress in organizations."

However, McKinsey's own slides recounted an alternate story. The firm was assisting ICE with completing Trump's migration strategy Full stop.

McKinsey had accomplishment at ICE doing what it excels at — reducing expenses. Its experts guaranteed ICE could save $385 million per year, generally from reconsidering contracts for privately owned businesses like CoreCivic

## [L'influence cache]

(previously Redresses Organization of America) that worked large numbers of the multiple hundred detainment communities ICE utilized the nation over.

The experts found six regions where it could manage costs, and they doled out a number and a letter to every one of them. Region La was staffing; 1b was "clinical." Different things included supplies, capital consumptions, and charges. One that started truly furious obstruction inside ICE was lc — food.

McKinsey had established that ICE was spending over the "industry standard" on food at certain offices. The issue from Mckinsey's perspective: ICE's principles for food quality, which had been surveyed and supported beginning in 2011, were excessively high, and it upheld it with a slide.

Regardless of ICE's standing, key Individuals there really needed to work on the personal satisfaction for prisoners, and they battled against the McKinsey ideas. Where McKinsey saw a bookkeeping sheet and the capacity to satisfy a KPI (key execution pointer) for a client, they put a human face on what it would intend to cut food spending.

"ICE spends such a huge amount on confinement — shaving pennies from dinners isn't the right strategy," a previous senior ICE official, who had protested a significant number of McKinsey's ideas, said.

That got under the skin of Tony D'Emidio, the McKinsey accomplice who was accountable for the work. He grumbled to the manager of the senior ICE official, saying that individual was being "obstructionist." D'Emidio rejects that this occurred.

After the ProPublica article, McKinsey safeguarded itself, saying it was looking for cost reserve funds "without forfeiting quality, security and mission." That was not difficult to say. The truth was unique.

For instance, McKinsey took a gander at the "day to day bed rate" for various offices and observed that some were far less expensive than others. Why not move prisoners to the less expensive offices and fill those beds first? By all accounts, it checked out, however the truth was that those beds were less expensive on the grounds that many were in city and region prisons. Provincial regions desired ICE gets that paid them to house Individuals in any case empty cells, producing genuinely necessary income.

"They are less expensive on the grounds that they are crappy sheriff's correctional facilities, and they simply need the cash," one previous Division of Country Security official said, referring to them as "trash beds."

One of the offices McKinsey focused on was the ICE family confinement focus at Dilley, Texas — one of a handful of the spots endorsed to hold moms and their youngsters — somewhere between the Rio Grande and San Antonio. At a certain point in 2018 it housed sixteen youngsters under two years of age.

## [L'influence cache]

In August 2017, messages show that McKinsey specialists met with ICE "authority" at Potomac Center North — the ICE place of business in Washington. The McKinsey group had a PowerPoint show they needed to show.

ICE was paying CoreCivic $157 million per year for it to run Dilley, the greatest family detainment office in the ICE archipelago. McKinsey's slides showed the "ought to cost" was radically lower: $40 million, near a 75 percent cut. Everything being equal, McKinsey gathered, the organization could push for slices to the agreement of up to $90 million. Where could the fat have been? The subtleties are redacted, yet the cuts came in regions, for example, "staffing," "food and supplies," deterioration, and "other." An unredacted note on the lower part of the page made sense of that training and clinical "won't be a focal point of the dealings."

ICE authorities, helped by calls from CoreCivic, effectively scotched the McKinsey plan. The cuts didn't come full circle, yet they made a few onlookers can't help thinking about how much more terrible the compassionate emergency that was going to overpower Dilley and other confinement communities might have been had McKinsey's proposition won the day.

Dilley was where, in Walk 2018, a nineteen-month-old young lady, Mariee Juárez, had contracted pneumonia, kicking the bucket not long after being released. Her mom documented a $60 million unfair demise guarantee that itemized a reiteration of clinical deficiencies at Dilley. Just a single time during Mariee's visit was she, a her seen by a specialist Vicks VapoRub for clog.

Martin Garbus, a notable common liberties legal counselor, chipped in at Dilley in mid 2019 to assist ladies and their youngsters with traversing their "bElievable trepidation" interview so they might have a shot at getting shelter in America. Before their appearance, many had been handled through a hielera or "fridge," a holding cell run by line watch specialists. They talked about escaping the hopelessness of life in Focal America, depicting assaults, constrained prostitution, and ruthless pack viciousness. Many were profoundly damaged. "I never considered anybody to be powerless as these ladies with their children," Garbus said.

"I saw the South African police mistreat demonstrators, incorporating moms with youngsters. I saw Southerners in the Social liberties development assault marchers. I saw Cesar Chavez's Individuals have beaten and chance at," he reviewed. "In any case, what I saw in Dilley will remain with me until the end of time."

Some ICE staff members were becoming baffled with McKinsey's presence inside their central command building. It wasn't simply that destroying painstakingly planned standards was attempting. The McKinsey group had such high turnover that vocation staff members were continually clarifying the organization's internal operations for many influxes of twentysomething advisors. More awful yet, some ICE staff members had started to scrutinize McKinsey's ability.

## [L'influence cache]

One more of McKinsey's "expectations" to ICE was a "authority improvement tool compartment," which came as a 78 page PowerPoint show. It apportioned guidance like proposing administration courses be held at spots like Nationwide conflict front lines or at the 9/11 Commemoration in New York.

By October 2017, McKinsey's agreement was fulfilled for restoration. Regardless of the inside obstruction, an ICE official wrote in a reminder that ERO 2.0 had "quantifiable advantages." Without McKinsey remaining at work, the probability of outcome in owning these changes "is exceptionally low," the update said.

The ICE representative Bryan D. Cox said that McKinsey had saved the organization $16 million on its agreements "without corruption to administration" and that ERO 2.0 had "yielded quantifiable enhancements in mission results."

McKinsey had been attempting to speed extradition, however as it were "when a last legitimate assurance was presented with respect to somebody's defense," the firm said.

In April 2018 the Trump organization carried out its "zero resilience" strategy, promising to criminally arraign everybody unlawfully crossing the boundary. Prior to zero resistance, on the off chance that a family was captured, they would commonly be delivered into the US forthcoming a meeting.

Zero resilience, with guardians in criminal confinement, implied kids must be isolated from them, since they couldn't be held in such offices. Trump migration hard-liners trusted that this draconian step would frighten away the vast majority from attempting to make the intersection. ALL things considered, by mid-June, no less than 25 hundred kids, including in excess of 100 younger than four, had been torn from their folks and now and again moved hundreds or even a huge number of miles from them. The pictures — and the hints of crying kids — stunned a country.

They stunned Individuals inside McKinsey also. However, after the underlying disturbance, McKinsey started working with another migration implementation organization, U.S. Customs and Boundary Assurance.

On the night of Tuesday, December 3, 2019, Scott Elfenbein was in a taxi, going to a supper in Manhattan with his destined to-be parents in law, perusing the ProPublica/New York Times story on his telephone. He thought about how McKinsey's administration would make sense of this. It was difficult to excuse the report's discoveries, upheld as they were by many pages of McKinsey's own PowerPoint slides and messages.

Elfenbein was a brand new McKinsey partner with the exemplary family — a Harvard college degree and a Wharton MBA. The company's new terrible exposure irritated him, but since of the association's attention on client secrecy — even between McKinsey experts — he wasn't mindful of the degree of McKinsey's inclusion with ICE, work that elaborate a portion of his partners.

The new article broke anything harmony he'd made.

# [L'influence cache]

Twelve years sooner, Elfenbein had gotten a bring around midnight from his dearest companion, who he asked not be named.

"Mythical person, I'm being expelled and I needed to call and bid farewell," the companion told him.

Elfenbein hung up, thinking his companion was pulling a downright horrendous prank on him.

Once more, he called: "Don't even think about hanging up on me! Tune in, I've been captured and I'm being ousted. I'm calling to bid farewell."

Elfenbein's companion was a star understudy at their secondary school in Miami, with a close wonderful GPA and the top score on eleven High level Position assessments. Both had recently graduated. Elfenbein was destined for Harvard. In any case, his companion, who came to America when he was two years of age, was undocumented; his Colombian guardians had outstayed their visas. InEligible for monetary guide, he enlisted at the nearby junior college. Presently even that was being removed after ICE specialists struck their home, tossing the family in a confinement community while they anticipated the unavoidable: a one-way pass to Bogotá.

It was, Elfenbein reviewed years after the fact, whenever he first had known about ICE.

Elfenbein and his schoolmates, shocked and sorrowful, got a move on. They conversed with movement attorneys and were told nothing should be possible. They asked their neighborhood delegates to the U.S. Congress for help. Once more, no karma.

In any case, there was this new site — Facebook — that was getting on. They composed posts saying how extraordinary their companion was, and a Fox subsidiary in South Florida got on it. "Obviously a lot of youngsters utilizing innovation to point out a Social unfairness impacted one nearby station," Elfenbein said.

Then, at that point, CNN ran a story. Presently those equivalent Individuals from Congress hit them up. Perhaps there was something his companions could do all things considered. Crisp out of secondary school, they went to Washington, dozing in a confined storm cellar. Their arrangement was straightforward: wander the lobbies of Congress.

They got a congressperson, Chris Dodd of Connecticut, and a Florida senator, lincoln Díaz-Balart, to support private bills, postponing the moment of retribution for Elfenbein's companion and his more seasoned Sibling, however their folks were before long expelled.

His companion proceeded to graduate — with distinction — from Georgetown.

The case stood out enough to be noticed, remembering stories for The New York Times. It likewise assisted with gathering speed for the Fantasy Act — which planned to sanction the a huge number of youngsters the nation over who were

## [L'influence cache]

undocumented simply because of choices their folks made when they were kids. Elfenbein happened to establish a movement support bunch at Harvard.

Perusing the article, Elfenbein realize that McKinsey was in struggle with what was up to that point the characterizing bend of his life. His life partner — Elfenbein was days from his wedding — was obtuse. "On the off chance that you don't stop at the present time, you don't represent anything," she said.

He called his close buddy, presently an effective financier in Brazil, who was similarly gruff: "Don't go screw up your life as a result of me."

That's what elfenbein knew whether he quit, "my little voice wouldn't make any difference."

That Friday, he strolled into the gathering room at the D.C. office. His voice would before long matter without a doubt.

The numerous naval force veterans in the D.C. office had a prepared expression for what was going on: this was an everyone available and jumping into action occasion.

Ordinarily, something like fifty to eighty Individuals would make an appearance at these "city center" gatherings. That day — December 6, 2019 — there were around 200, or close to Half of the McKinsey labor force in the country's capital. They jammed into a space made by Eliminating the dividers between a few gathering rooms.

It was a Drill that was becoming daily practice. At other municipal centers pointed toward countering negative press, the soldiers were definitely informed that the columnists composing the tales had a plan, that the turn out finished for System An or Organization B was genuine, and that the firm was making a move to cure any deficiency.

In any case, this was unique. The work with ICE, first of all, was finished by Individuals in this office. Much more significant, this wasn't whenever the firm first had been faced from inside about its work with ICE. Sneader, the association's overseeing accomplice, had tended to it the prior year.

The new article, upheld by the McKinsey slides, brought up issues about Sneader and the association's administration. Sneader clarified from the very start that his stewardship would be unique in relation to that of Dominic Barton, his ancestor. Barton, tall and urbane, whose first spouse hailed from the labatt lager family, turned into Canada's envoy to China subsequent to venturing down as the company's overseeing accomplice. Sneader, short and confrontational, was from coarse Glasgow — a personal detail he jumped at the chance to specify in TV interviews. He won't love instead of lashing out when his firm got terrible press. Yet, he didn't disregard issues and prior that year had regulated the rollout of another evaluating cycle for potential tasks intended to assist the firm with keeping away from future harming Titles.

## [L'influence cache]

The room topped off. Confronting the group was Nora Gardner, a senior accomplice who drove the Washington office. Additionally present that evening was D'Emidio, the accomplice who had regulated the everyday ICE project, as well as two additional lesser supervisors, Ed Barriball and Jonah Wagner, who chipped away at the Traditions and line Insurance account.

"A large number of us share, areas of strength for extremely and sentiments," Gardner said, starting the gathering. "In the first place, solid enthusiasm, conviction, and regard for outsiders, for basic liberties, for the settle r experience." Recognizing the resentment numerous experts were feEling about the company's work with ICE, she pursued for understanding: "We really do have a common worth framework, and I'd ask us to communicate care in our partners and expect best goal in our associates."

Barriball talked straightaway. He made the purpose in saying that he was an enlisted liberal and "contemplated whether this [ICE] was an office I needed to serve."

Back in the Obama organization, he said, McKinsey had been employed by ICE to assist with further developing a profoundly discouraged Establishment that rEliably positioned close to the base in a review positioning position fulfillment in government offices. Barriball and his partners were investigating ways for ICE to select better Individuals and to quit being "totally gouged by their merchants," Particularly the confidential jail organizations that housed such countless prisoners. McKinsey had never upheld for lower-quality nourishment for prisoners, he asserted. The firm, he said, was just inquiring as to why project workers were charging ridiculously various costs for similar food in various areas.

Notwithstanding obtainment and enlisting, there was a third task. Barriball brushed over it rapidly.

"It was extremely difficult for them to take care of their business on an everyday premise," Barriball said of ICE. He said the vast majority McKinsey worked with at ICE were "concerned essentially with finding and capturing people who had carried out intense violations in the nation" and that this was the sort of thing McKinsey could "assist them with."

"Clear ly the setting changed a considerable amount in the new organization," he added.

Wagner, in portraying McKinsey's work with CBP, said it was "in accordance with things we were actually glad for and I figure we can all vibe pleased."

The accomplices then, at that point, took questions.

For Mobasshir Poonawalla, a lesser expert in the crowd, the remarks by Barriball and Wagner stung. He experienced childhood with government assistance, living in a two-room condo with his folks and four kin. He hit the books with a vengeance and was owned up to Wharton. His more established Sibling wasn't as lucky. He was an undocumented worker who had come to America as a youngster. Under Obama, he had some insurance as a Visionary, however

## [L'influence caché]

Trump's crackdown on migration and his enthusiasm to kill DACA implied Poonawalla's Sibling confronted the genuine possibility being expelled. As far as he might be concerned, McKinsey's public clarification that it was just assisting ICE with removals of Individuals currently on "last lawful assurance" was incensing, on the grounds that that was his Sibling's status. He lifted his hand.

"We've carried on with as long as we can remember concealing him when the doorbell rang," Poonawalla said. Then, at that point, he proposed an idea.

"Rather than refering to bipartisan political help which I especially can't help contradicting, for what reason don't we plainly frame that this is the sort of thing that we never again do, not on account of its political or the optics, but since we are values driven," he said.

That drew some adulation. "Brimming with sympathy," Gardner answered. "Much obliged to you for sharing that. I realize that there are others in the room who are comparatively contacted and having a comparative encounter. Simply a great deal of appreciation for that. I think you'll see the value in that it is difficult for our firm to take a political position on that, on what is an exceptionally charged issue."

Elfenbein, doled out to the Philadelphia office, didn't think it was legitimate to stand up at that point. In any case, the gathering left him upset. He felt that McKinsey had neglected to resolve a profoundly human issue with any feEling of mankind and was incensed that the firm had the nerve to say that aiding what he considered the most polarizing government organization was not political.

Elfenbein and the other McKinsey advisors in the room were being told not to accept what was in the article, however McKinsey's own slides — many them — were additionally distributed as connections, and regardless of the weighty redactions they supported up the article's substance.

Elfenbein found it hard to zero in on his work. The day preceding the municipal event, he was given ideas on the best way to speak with McKinsey enlisting possibilities from Wharton's MBA program in manners that kept away from the ICE issue or soothed them. He was educated not to start conversations concerning ICE with possible enlisted people.

"That is the point at which the non-literal levee broke," he said.

That evening, he sent an email to a portion of his Wharton MBA colleagues who had joined McKinsey as well as a portion of McKinsey's top selection representatives for the school. He called attention to the uniqueness of what McKinsey was talking about openly and the proof accessible inside, remembering project depictions for the true to life pages of a portion of the ICE project specialists.

The Following day he was at the municipal event in D.C. The proud way that D'Emidio and Barriball legitimized the work made him considerably angrier. The Monday after the Washington meeting, Elfenbein added to his underlying email, this time addressing it to undeniably more partners — around twelve hundred — including Sneader and liz Hilton Segel, the head of North America for the firm.

## [L'influence cache]

He was trying the constraints of McKinsey's for quite some time held rule that everybody had an "commitment to contradict."

"I trust you'll peruse my note as coming from a heart in a decent spot while it seems like I'm by and by in an unpleasant spot," he started. He then composed of a "ripped companion was "tore from his bed at 3 AM and set in a terrible ICE confinement focus that actually gives him bad dreams."

"From my perception we have not exhibited authority in emergency nor even showed that Our Qualities turn out as expected under pressure," he proceeded.

He spread out his suggestions in list items. Among them: an interest that McKinsey make a general acknowledgment for working for ICE and "quit saying we could rehash this work." Another: "Quit involving lawfulness as the gauge for ethicality." On this, he was especially gnawing, adding an incidental expression: "In the event that we helped southern states 'further develop farming resource yield' during the 1850s could we actually remain behind that? Our direction so far would demonstrate the response is 'perhaps.' "

He likewise needed to offer back any cash in his check that could be credited to the work for ICE and set up an organization email address, TakeItOutofMyPay@mckinsey.com, for his partners to contribute too.

The email likewise educated McKinsey specialists across the world that the firm as he would see it was not evening out with them on the degree of its work for ICE.

He squeezed send.

"I felt like I planned to hurl."

Elfenbein paused. Two minutes, perhaps three minutes went by.

His telephone rang.

On the line was a very much regarded pioneer at the firm, who let him know how after years at McKinsey he had quit being the individual who supported standards. Elfenbein's email had moved him. Then he said, "Watch this."

He expressed, "I'm with Scott. Remove it from my compensation." And hit answer all.

Hundreds took cues from him, keeping in touch with him from places all over the planet, including Germany, Ireland, the U.K., and Japan. They offered messages of help and sent Elfenbein's email to thousands additional Individuals at McKinsey. "It was a defiance," said someone else who went to the Washington municipal center. "A defiance happened at the firm between junior experts and partner accomplices or more."

A couple of days after the fact, D'Emidio, the accomplice responsible for the ICE project, sent his very own mass email. Subject: "Call for compromise and recuperating."

## [L'influence cache]

In list items, he composed of his profound compassion "for those of you whose families and companions live in anxiety toward my client," as well as responsibility "for having been the reason for such a lot of tension, disgrace, doubt, and outrage for so many of you."

However at that point his email took a turn as he depicted how harmed he was "by the stinging expressions of certain messages blaming me for having pretty much no clue of morals, reason, or values," outrage at the "denunciation" of his partners on the ICE project, in addition to "dissatisfaction" over what he said were "mistaken depictions" of the collaboration. He then, at that point, said he was glad for the "influence " his group had. D'Emidio called for exchange "with the expectation that we can recuperate each other's injuries."

Elfenbein didn't lose his employment, and Sneader even let him in on that his email was "fitting." Yet another senior accomplice called and asked him a very McKinsey-like inquiry: Did he had any idea how much cash in lost efficiency his email had caused?

The experience left Elfenbein, who left McKinsey in late 2021, with an embittered perspective on the firm he had so eagerly joined, floated by the commitment from scouts that he would be "extraordinarily situated to accomplish something that really does every so often assist with pushing society ahead."

"It very well may be oversold," he said.

# [L'influence cache]

## Section 5

### Become friends with China's Administration

In late 2013 an armada of Chinese digging vessels plummeted upon Red hot Cross Reef, in excess of 600 miles south of China legitimate. Among the boats was the Tian Jing Hao, the biggest dredger in Asia, fit for sucking in excess of 1,000,000 gallons of sand an hour from the ocean bottom. More than two years, satellite photographs followed the reef's change from a dreadful offshoot scarcely sticking over the water's surface into a 677-section of land Island.

China's administration demanded that Red hot Cross, and a grasp of adjoining reefs turned Islands in the South China Ocean, wouldn't be mobilized. Yet, on September 25, 2015, the world learned in any case. The regarded Jane's Protection Week by week, utilizing satellite photographs, revealed the finishing of a 3.1-kilometer-long airstrip on the reef equipped for taking care of long-range Chinese planes. Rocket frameworks would before long follow.

That very day, 2,000 miles toward the north, Chen Fenjian, leader of China Correspondences Development Organization, the proprietor of the Tian Jing Hao, accumulated Individuals from his authority group in Beijing for a significant gathering.

China Interchanges is no customary organization. It is one of the 96 state-claimed undertakings that, in view of their significance to China's public safety and financial imperativeness, are overseen by the focal government in Beijing. These organizations make China's weapons, develop and disperse food, work telephone and web organizations, refine oil, produce steel, mine Coal, and, similar to China Interchanges, fabricate scaffolds, streets, and ports all over the planet as an instrument of Chinese international strategy. Chen and other top leaders at these fundamental "focal undertakings" — the zhongyang qiye — are handpicked by the Socialist Faction's Association Division.

To assist with directing him, Chen recruited an American firm, McKinsey. As of late, McKinsey has educated somewhere around 26 concerning the 96 organizations assigned by Beijing as zhongyang qiye.

ALtogether, 702 Individuals partook in the gathering, some through videoconference from the organization's remote workplaces across the globe. Their point: examine how the organization would squeeze into the Chinese government's five-year financial plan. Indeed, even after just about forty years of monetary changes, this remnant from the times of Administrator Mao holds incredible influence , coordinating enormous government assets into inclined toward businesses.

That day, a McKinsey group introduced proposals. However the particulars are confidential, China Correspondences enthusiastically publicized its association with McKinsey — maikenxi in Chinese — where the nation's exceptionally taught tip top longed for finding some work. McKinsey dissected China Correspondences' "market climate" and made proposals on the organization's "by

## [L'influence cache]

and large essential objectives" as well as its "business portfolio system," the state-possessed organization said in a proclamation.

landing China Interchanges as a client was an overthrow for McKinsey. The state-claimed organization had been winning Chinese-government foundation contracts all over the planet as a component of a procedure to polish China's impact. It even thought to be an unfamiliar securities exchange posting for its blasting digging business.

For McKinsey, China Interchanges, one of the world 's greatest designing organizations, implied another income source. Yet, for the US, the organization's Island building had essentially changed the overall influence in the Pacific Ocean.[*]

Nowadays, U.S. warships that pass near the new Islands are routinely followed and pestered by Chinese naval force vessels and helper ships, tremendously improving the probability of a dangerous incident between two atomic furnished powers. In one episode, a Chinese warship came quite close to the bow of a U.S. destroyer close to one of the new Islands, compElling the American boat to move to keep away from an impact. A Washington think tank said the ocean "will be for all intents and purposes a Chinese lake" by 2030. "China, with its dictator framework and its resolved invasion into the South China Ocean and universally, presents a consistent maritime danger," President Biden's naval force secretary said during his affirmation hearing.

McKinsey's work with a Chinese government-possessed organization that constructed Islands in questioned waters clashes with the objectives of an undeniably more significant client: the Pentagon. McKinsey has taken in a huge number of dollars from the Protection Division lately. Inside McKinsey records show that from 2018 until mid 2020, the U.S. Safeguard Division was among McKinsey's top level of clients. No Chinese organization positioned among the company's top income workers during that time.

In 2015, that very year McKinsey was prompting China Correspondences, it was likewise concentrating on how the U.S. Armed force could lessen costs in supporting America's modern base for assembling ammo. McKinsey has likewise worked with the Maritime Surface Fighting Place in Dahlgren, Virginia, which fosters the weapons that would be utilized in a contention with China. In 2019, the naval force granted McKinsey a $15.7 million agreement to deal with its "reasonableness crusade" for the F-35 contender.

The company's specialists likewise routinely take Pentagon posts. One accomplice, Eric Chewning, was head of staff to Stamp Esper, a protection secretary during Trump's administration. In 2020 he got back to McKinsey. McKinsey's Jesse Salazar was named appointee right hand secretary of safeguard for modern approach in the Biden organization.

For McKinsey, it had been a long excursion from educating the commanders concerning American free undertaking to prompting a Chinese state-claimed firm structure army installations for America's boss key and monetary opponent.

## [L'influence cache]

When that South China Ocean airstrip became functional, McKinsey had shown its ability to help clients that others could have stayed away from. Progressive ages of McKinsey's overseeing accomplices had controlled the firm to occupations with different levels of the Chinese government. McKinsey even set up a Socialist Faction cell in its Shanghai office, as per a record in the party's true Individuals' Everyday, as did other unfamiliar organizations. McKinsey says it is "for the most part ignorant about and doesn't follow the confidential political affiliations of its representatives."

Two advancements helped lead McKinsey into the arms of a portion of China's most decisively significant government-possessed organizations. First was the company's rising craving for government work after Nancy Killefer, Recently got back from the Clinton organization's Depository Division, had set up a public-area practice in 2000, opening up another line of income for the firm. Second was McKinsey's steady world wide extension. By the 1980s its non-American accomplices dwarfed the U.S. accomplices. The firm opened new workplaces all over the planet, remembering for Moscow, Dubai, and Johannesburg.

The greatest world wide award of all — basically the one with the most potential — was China. For quite a long time the world's most crowded country had likewise been home to the planet's transcendent economy. It had gone through 150 grieved years, set apart by unfamiliar occupation, unrest, war, and starvation, yet by the mid 1990s, with its economy blasting and its chiefs quick to redesign its sclerotic state-claimed enterprises, China required McKinsey's business ability. ALso, with the association's most rewarding clients, as Volkswagen, marking their prospects on China, McKinsey's chiefs felt that they must be there.

It wasn't generally so. At the point when China was as yet trapped in the communist soil, McKinsey didn't consider the country to be an imperative business opportunity. During the 1970s, Bank of China had moved toward the firm about assist with rebuilding, and in 1985 the Chinese government had requested that McKinsey assist with redesigning its Soviet-period steel industry. In the two occurrences, the firm turned down the work, "for each situation because Firm pioneers didn't completely accept that they could have an effect," as per a record in McKinsey's true history book.

However, China's burning monetary development in the mid 1990s — Gross domestic product developed 14.2 percent in 1992 and beat 13% the accompanying two years — caught the world's consideration. The country's political changes had been set aside momentarily Following the horrendous 1989 crackdown in and around Beijing's Tiananmen Square, yet on the economy Beijing's chiefs were freeing the country up to unfamiliar speculation, enduring the ascent of forceful new privately owned businesses, and hoping to redesign the country's run down state-claimed banks, processing plants, telephone organizations, steel factories, and shipbuilders.

McKinsey had settled in Hong Kong in 1985, and like such countless Western organizations it utilized what was then an English state as a base to wander into the central area. One after another, McKinsey opened workplaces in Shanghai and Beijing in the midnineties. The firm put huge number of dollars in preparing its

## [L'influence cache]

world wide unit of experts for progress in China. Numerous Chinese recruits were shipped off Europe to gain proficiency with the essentials of the art there. In the interim, to dominate Chinese, some McKinsey-bound MBAs from U.S. business colleges enlisted at Beijing's Tsinghua College.

McKinsey's initial work in China zeroed in on assisting its world wide clients with setting up activities there. The 1990s were the point at which the huge multinationals, similar to General Engines and 3M, were scrambling to benefit from the world 's quickest developing significant economy. McKinsey experts were there to assist with directing organizations through the intricacies of carrying on with work in China, reviewed Olivier Kayser, a previous senior accomplice who was situated in Shanghai and Beijing in the last part of the 1990s.

It was a zapping time to be in China. The economy was starting up to Western organizations, and Chinese understudies took off in large numbers of thousands to get a top of the line schooling in the US. China's expanding and generally uncontrolled web was overflowing with innovative ability. Regardless of the political pall that plummeted over the country after the 1989 crackdown, on an individual level Chinese Individuals delighted in opportunities unbElievable only a couple of years sooner. They were presently not attached to a relegated work unit and could rather work and shop where they needed and wed whom they picked. Before long the nation would join the World Exchange Association, and many trusted the monetary progression would prompt requests for additional political privileges.

"The genie of opportunity won't return into the container," President Clinton said in 2000 as he found help for China's promotion to the WTO.

The McKinsey group in China shared that idealism. "There was an inclination that monetary improvement would prompt majority rule government, that the Socialist Coalition would ultimately release its hold on society, and that China would before long become like Hong Kong," Kayser reviewed from his time in China. "The overall course of history was clear ."

Early China-based McKinsey advisors, including Kayser, Gordon Orr, Jonathan Woetzel, and Tony Perkins, an American who is presently a senior in the Mormon Church, knew that for the China practice to succeed, they needed to draw in neighborhood clients, including the state-claimed organizations administered by the Socialist Faction that overwhelm the ordering levels of the economy.

So they set up talks at inn gathering rooms in Shanghai and Beijing for organization chiefs, offering free guidance on organization methodology and association, drawing in enormous groups.

They handled a Shanghai-based government-possessed combination with countless Individuals on the finance. Very nearly 25 year after the work and eighteen years after Kayser left McKinsey, he wouldn't reveal its personality. Be that as it may, the organization, alongside numerous other state-possessed ventures, was confronting oldness. China was opening up the state area to rivalry,

## [L'influence cache]

from both homegrown and global organizations. A great many excess laborers confronted joblessness.

"There was a test of skill and endurance. liberation was coming," Kayser said. "The work misfortunes planned to occur; whether the business gains would compensate for it, you needed to trust."

Kayser and his partners zeroed in on approaches to "ring the sales register" rather than be the unfamiliar counseling firm telling a Chinese state-claimed organization whom to fire. With a feeble communist period deals drive, making a few fundamental upgrades that got new revenue was somewhat simple. "Whenever we had laid out our validity, they could say look, this is the cash we made off of McKinsey," Kayser said.

Following two years on the ground in central area China, McKinsey landed what was to become perhaps of its best client: Ping A Protection.

McKinsey took on Ping An out of 1997 and remained there for the Following 25 years, helping what was a backwater local organization develop to turn into the world 's second-greatest insurance agency by market capitalization. McKinsey advisors loved working with Ping An, in light of the fact that "they just did everything McKinsey said to them to do."

"When the undertaking is finished, they simply execute, no inquiries posed," the previous McKinsey expert, a Chinese public, said in a meeting.

Peter Walker, one of the company's aristocrats who lorded over the world wide protection area, invested a rising measure of energy in China as the relationship with Ping A developed and McKinsey took on more Chinese insurance agency as clients. Louis Cheung, a McKinsey expert who aided lead the Ping A work, moved over to Ping An and was named the organization's leader in front of its 2004 first sale of stock in Hong Kong. Years after the fact he would found a confidential value firm with the grandson of China's previous president Jiang Zemin.

The Ping An Initial public offering additionally showed that even as McKinsey worked with private-area clients in China, the firm — wittingly or not — sought the almighty, unavoidable Chinese government. McKinsey had recruited a top alumni of Harvard's MBA program, liu Chunhang, the child in-law of China's prospective chief, Wen Jiabao. As bad habit chief until 2003, Wen had regulated the monetary administrations industry, including Ping An. Wen's better Half procured a gigantic stake in Ping An in front of the Initial public offering, concealing quite a bit of it for the sake of Wen's older mother. McKinsey has said that it employed liu in view of his capabilities, not his associations. "Any idea that Mr. liu was recruited or utilized for ill-advised design is bogus and very deceptive," the organization said in 2018.

The way that Chief Wen's child in-regulation joined McKinsey shows exactly how esteemed the firm had become to China's Western-taught tip top. The firm moved from one accomplishment to another. From beginning with a couple dozen specialists in China during the 1990s, Following 10 years it had multiple hundred.

## [L'influence cache]

Furthermore, as China's large state-possessed firms ready for world wide securities exchange share deals, McKinsey was there to help them.

Not every person at McKinsey was excited that the firm was committing such a lot of opportunity to working with legislatures and parastatals. To them, a McKinsey expert ought to exhort Chiefs in the confidential area.

Ron Daniel, the company's overseeing accomplice from 1976 to 1988, who a ways into his nineties continued to come into the association's midtown Manhattan office every day, was one of them. At some point, he approached Ian Davis, who drove the firm from 2003 to 2009, let Davis know how he wasn't enthused about this "public area stuff."

Davis' tart answer: "Ron, you mean we ought not be working in China?"

The response was self-evident.

As China's monetary development sped up, McKinsey dove directly into that "public area stuff" — the Socialist Faction controlled zhongyang qiye.

In the main 10 years of this really long period, China's driving state-claimed organizations were shedding long stretches of Soviet-style focal preparation, rebuilding by taking on Western-style "best practices" (a McKinsey strength) and opening huge proficiency acquires that aided prod Chinese development. In 2007 the economy developed at 14.2 percent, matching its sweltering speed from 1992. Organizations like Apple, General Engines, McDonald's, Volkswagen, and Boeing were at long last acknowledging what had been a for the most part unfulfilled dream of Western vendors for a really long time: they were raking in boatloads of cash in China.

For global organizations — McKinsey's center clients — it challenged presence of mind to avoid a market that became, in fast progression, the world 's greatest mobile phone market, the world 's biggest vehicle market, the world 's top exporter, and, by 2010, the world 's number two economy after the US.

McKinsey continued to add marquee state-possessed firms to its client list, including China Versatile, China Telecom, and the oil monsters Sinopec and PetroChina, as well as Coal, steel, banking, groceries, and delivery combinations.

Neighborhood legislatures and Beijing services additionally looked for McKinsey's recommendation. Shanghai employed the firm to assist with metropolitan preparation. In 2009, Ian Davis headed out to Beijing to consent to an arrangement with China's Business Service. That very year, McKinsey was approached by the public authority to assist with arranging its monetary upgrade program to counter the impacts of the world wide monetary emergency. McKinsey's job was little — including sorting out whether or not value slices to TVs would invigorate request — yet Dominic Barton, who succeeded Davis that year as the company's overseeing accomplice, introduced McKinsey's discoveries to the Public Turn of events and Change Commission, the strong arranging office that manages China's modern arrangements.

## [L'influence cache]

One previous McKinsey expert who worked in China said that the company's fruitful push to draw in state-possessed undertakings as clients, at times by offering them limits on counseling expenses, brought about "an exchange of protected innovation from the West" that served "to construct China and fabricate the SOEs."

"Presently we have a major contender. For me actually it was not too motivating to be working for a SOE at cut rates."

As McKinsey's work developed in China, the nation's state-possessed organizations and its administration workplaces anxiously told everybody they had recruited the world's most esteemed counseling firm.

McKinsey's name was so notable that it even pulled in a Chinese copycat, Chengdu McKinsey The executives Counseling Organization. In 2009 the fake McKinsey really won an agreement to exhort the Sichuan common government on its monetary arrangement.

The stratagem tricked the authority China Monetary Week after week, which compared McKinsey — the genuine one — to an octopus expanding its arms of impact. It considered the firm the "unfamiliar mind behind the twelfth Five-Year Plan," featuring the phony McKinsey's work in Sichuan.

While McKinsey and its world wide clients extended in China, the country's basic liberties record drew global judgment. China tossed activists like the Nobel Harmony Prize laureate liu Xiaobo in prison, where he kicked the bucket. The Socialist Coalition got serious about any gathering that could represent a test to its standard. However, Individuals actually trusted, as Clinton did in 2000, that China's period of prosperity would ultimately drain over into the political circle. In 2008, China facilitated the Olympic Games. A huge number of youthful Chinese were finding that they could voice their perspectives on the country's dynamic virtual entertainment stages. Relations between the US and China, however frequently snappy, were on occasion heartfelt.

That would before long change. In November 2012, Xi Jinping, child of one of the pioneers behind Individuals' Republic, took over administration of the decision Socialist Faction.

Xi saw the world uniquely in contrast to the boring apparatchik he supplanted. To Xi, the party was swaying near the precarious edge of breakdown, stumbled by defilement and the convergence of Western thoughts like press opportunity and law and order. Xi would have rather not been China's Gorbachev and direct the death of the Socialist Coalition. Just days into his standard, he gave a discourse rebuking the Soviet party's breakdown in 1991, pinning it on the way that "no one was man to the point of standing up and opposing." Xi imprisoned basic freedoms protectors and women's activists. China's wide open online entertainment stages were gotten control over by forceful restriction. Xi started a heartless crackdown against the Muslim Uyghurs in Xinjiang, including mass confinements and constrained cleansings that the American government would before long mark a slaughter.

*[L'influence cache]*

To support his power, the authority media, constrained by the Socialist Coalition, depicted him in chivalrous terms unheard of since the times of Mao Zedong. Relations with the US crumbled. However, for McKinsey, it was the same old thing.

While the facts confirm that multinationals like BMW, Apple, Boeing, and Starbucks additionally stuck with it in China, the vehicles, telephones, planes, and espresso they sell vary from McKinsey's leader item. By apportioning its expertise to state-possessed organizations, for example, China Correspondences, the manufacturer of the South China Ocean Islands, McKinsey was supporting the force of the Chinese state and the decision Socialist Faction. Xi clarified that there was no distance between the Socialist Faction and driving state-claimed undertakings like China Interchanges, telling party units that "sticking to party administration and reinforcing party building is the wonderful practice of our nation's state-possessed endeavors."

In the fall of 2013, Xi sent off a Maoist-style party "correction" crusade, choking what similarity to free discourse stayed via online entertainment stages. In any case, McKinsey right now not just exhorted state-claimed Chinese organizations and even government offices — it went above and beyond and started to support a portion of Beijing's unmistakable strategies, including a few that put China in conflict with the US and Europe.

One such program was the Belt and Street Drive. Summoning the Silk Street, the train course of hundreds of years past, the trillion-dollar plan looked to broaden China's impact by building ports, streets, scaffolds, railways, and different ventures across Asia, Africa, and then some.

The arrangement immediately brought alerts up in Washington and other Western capitals. Pioneers dreaded China's administration would involve the drive as a covertness intend to grow its own tactical impact, to entangle unfortunate countries by loaning them cash that they couldn't reimburse, and to tie those countries in a Beijing-ruled effective reach. "These streets can't be those of another authority, which would change those that they cross into vassals," France's leader, Emmanuel Macron, said on a visit to China.

McKinsey took an alternate view. Barton, then McKinsey's overseeing accomplice, made Belt and Street the subject of a feature address in Beijing in Walk 2015 at a yearly gathering where organizations looking for business there blend with China's top chiefs. Barton said that McKinsey was extremely amped up for the Belt and Street methodology. He likewise openly excused worries that the drive would be an instrument to extend China's impact.

McKinsey assembled senior government authorities to talk about the drive and intensify the public authority's message that China was leaving on this "not out of personal responsibility, nor out of international goals."

"The world is sitting tight for the 'One Belt, One Street' great outline to move from dream to the real world ," Barton and his partners said in a post on the

## [L'influence cache]

organization's Chinese site in May 2015. "We will work with legislatures, endeavors, and research organizations to direct more point by point research on the above proposition and contribute a little to the extension of the success of human culture!"

Before long, McKinsey advisors started flagellating the significance of China's Belt and Street to clients. In 2015, the Malaysian government employed McKinsey to make a financial plausibility report for quite possibly of the greatest public-work projects at any point imagined in the country: a rail line interfacing the ports on the eastern side of peninsular Malaysia to its prosperous urban communities on the western side.

In a slide show, McKinsey experts composed that Malaysia taking on the undertaking would "construct the country to-country relationship" with China in view of the venture's significance to the Belt and Street Drive. The experts said China had "international reasons" for its advantage in rail lines in Southeast Asia. One more slide brought up that Chinese supporting of a rail line in Indonesia accompanied liberal terms for that country. McKinsey considered it a "unique advantage."

In 2016, China Correspondences Development, exactly the same McKinsey client that was building the Islands in the South China Ocean, won a $13 billion agreement to fabricate Malaysia's railroad. A helper to the head of the state at the time said that Malaysia had offered China Interchanges the rail contract as a feature of a plan to take care of obligations show up to a bad government speculation store.

McKinsey said that its job in the task "was restricted to examining financial effect and monetary practicality" and that the firm played no part in the Malaysian government's choice to employ China Correspondences Development. "To depict us as working in the background to propel any administration's plan — across free client groups and ventures — is essentially false," McKinsey said in a December 2018 explanation Following a New York Times report about its work on projects connected with the Belt and Street Drive.

For McKinsey, promoting the Belt and Street Drive was great business. Nine of the main fifteen Chinese project workers for the BRI have been McKinsey clients.

McKinsey likewise centered around China's disputable modern arrangement, Made in China 2025. First presented in 2015, the arrangement plans to make China the predominant player in businesses like electric vehicles, biopharmaceuticals, and aviation by centering many billions of dollars in state-supported loaning to those areas. China's top exchanging accomplices dread it is a way for China to control whole enterprises and supply chains, sabotaging their own economies and ultimately pushing unfamiliar organizations out of China's own enormous market. In Walk 2021 the Biden organization referred to it one of China's as' "more extensive and unsafe modern plans."

McKinsey delivered somewhere around ten reports in Chinese about Made in China 2025. Be that as it may, in May 2018, confronting a blast of analysis from its most significant exchanging accomplices, China's administration requested the country's media to quit expounding on it. McKinsey likewise quit referencing the strategy.

While dubious in certain areas of the planet, to numerous while possibly not most McKinsey advisors in China this work is typical and satisfactory. By far most of McKinsey's staff in China are neighborhood enlists, and a rising number are becoming accomplices and senior accomplices, empowering them to take on new clients.

A considerable lot of these Chinese specialists have postgraduate educations from places like Harvard and Stanford, however they are important for China's tip top — the greatest recipients of China's one-party rule. Furthermore, they incorporate Individuals like Chen Guang, an accomplice who joined McKinsey in 2007 subsequent to procuring a doctorate in optical designing at Shanghai's Jiao Tong College.

In December 2017, Chen talked at a gathering in Shenzhen of the China Vendors Gathering, one of the greatest workers for hire for Belt and Street and a decisively significant state-claimed firm. The principal focal point of the get-together was "building an excellent expert framework group" — a necessity originating from the equitable completed Socialist Coalition Congress, a once-at regular intervals occasion that blesses the nation's top chiefs. In his discussion, Chen drew correlations between the military and business, and his slide deck showed an image of a warrior holding a rifle.

One more questionable task that McKinsey pushed in China zeroed in on "shrewd urban areas." savvy urban areas is to make metropolitan regions more decent by utilizing arranged cameras to all the more likely oversee traffic, or to lessen water and power use through "brilliant" meters that can send data back to a focal area. McKinsey advanced this thought all over the planet.

McKinsey partook in a 2018 brilliant urban communities gathering in southern China close by an administration commission that dropped from the Mao-period state arranging organization. In 2019 the senior accomplice Sha, one of the company's most memorable nearby recruits, talked at the China Savvy City Exhibition. McKinsey cooperated with its most solid China client, Ping An, to assist the safety net provider with executing brilliant urban areas frameworks in the southern Chinese city of Nanning to screen monetary misrepresentation.

In any case, brilliant urban communities envelops undeniably more than utilizing innovation to more readily oversee traffic or to save money on power and water use. It likewise covers policing and the utilization of prescient examination to assist with forestalling wrongdoing, a reality McKinsey clarified to its crowd in Chinese.

"Police watches can't be all over, for example, yet prescient examination can convey them perfectly located brilliantly," McKinsey wrote in a world wide report about shrewd urban communities, which the firm converted into Chinese. It got broad inclusion in China's state media.

## [L'influence cache]

In a tyrant state like China, where police have not many requirements and there is no law and order, that sentence takes on a totally different importance than it would in London, Tokyo, or New York City. A report gave by a U.S. legislative board on China said that Chinese security authorities are utilizing shrewd urban communities innovation to "grow, improve, and mechanize data assortment and investigation for mass observation."

No place is that more obvious than in China's far west, where the Chinese government has forced the world 's most meddlesome organization of reconnaissance cameras and security designated spots, what the New York Times columnists Chris Buckley and Paul Mozur call a "virtual enclosure" that supplements the huge organization of detainment camps intended to make the locale's Muslim minorities "into mainstream residents who won't ever challenge the decision Socialist Faction."

It additionally is the locale where, in September 2018, McKinsey's More noteworthy China group accumulated for their yearly retreat.

It was a lavish issue. At one occasion, a filigree of red floor coverings bound around sand hills and open tents where the youthful McKinsey people relaxed on supplication carpets and toss cushions. At another, experts ate outdoors in an old Silk Street city and, as the sun set, were blessed to receive a light show highlighting colorful two-bumped camels projected onto the substance of the crenelated city wall.

They likewise accumulated for discourses — and the inescapable PowerPoint slide introductions — at one more setting: this one a lavish dinner corridor looking like a ruler's castle. A sign above caught the state of mind: "I can't resist the urge to panic, I work at McKinsey and Company."

Generally corporate retreats don't stand out as truly newsworthy. Yet, a photograph of this one — complete with the red covers and sand ridges — showed up on the first page of The New York Times on December 16, 2018. The explanation: the McKinsey specialists were celebrating in Xinjiang, only four miles from a confinement camp, one of hundreds in a huge archipelago of gulags in western China lodging as much as 1,000,000 ethnic Uyghur Muslims and different minorities.

When the McKinsey experts accumulated in Xinjiang's antiquated Silk Street city of Kashgar, the detainment camps were notable. In 2016 the Socialist Faction manager in the locale, Chen Quanguo, had forced a cruel arrangement of mass observation and designated spots over about portion of Xinjiang's 25 million Individuals after a flood in savagery between the Muslim minorities and greater part Han Chinese. Specialists, artists, educators, business leaders were undeniably trapped in the trawl, which by 2018 had metastasized into the mass confinement framework. Days before the McKinsey Xinjiang assembling, a Unified Countries board approached China to "promptly discharge" Individuals who had been improperly kept.

Youngsters, whose guardians were kept in the camps, were dispatched to teaching schools that imparted compliance to the Socialist Faction. ladies were confined for

## [L'influence cache]

the wrongdoing of having such a large number of kids and dependent upon compulsory sanitizations and even early terminations. As the remainder of China loosened up conception prevention measures, in Xinjiang birthrates plunged as the public authority made "an environment of dread around having kids," as per a Related Press examination.

The US says this adds up to decimation. A Walk 2021 U.S. State Division report said that annihilation and violations against humankind, including assault, torment, and constrained work, had been committed against the Uyghurs and other minority bunches in Xinjiang by the Chinese government.

Everything that was lost on the McKinsey experts, who caught their Disney-like insight on Instagram. A couple — garbed like additional items from the surprisingly realistic Aladdin film — posted a photograph of both of them jumping off the peak of an ideal sand hill. Many rode camels in the desert, one glimmering the gesture of goodwill. The head of McKinsey in the district, the Harvard-taught Joe Ngai, postured for a preview with his representatives — behind the scenes, female Uyghur entertainers in streaming yellow outfits, moving under a sign decorated with the gathering's subject: "Interfacing Together."

While McKinsey isn't liable for the Chinese government's activities in Xinjiang, facilitating a gathering there put McKinsey on edge. "I'm shocked they didn't get on to the horrendous optics," said James Millward, a teacher at Georgetown College who concentrates on the locale. "Someone ought to have been perusing the information and said, Stand by a moment, we don't need our corporate logo there."

Peter Walker, the previous McKinsey senior accomplice who presently depicts himself as a specialist on U.S.- China relations, attempted to make sense of Beijing's strategy toward the Uyghur minority in an April 2020 meeting on Fox News.

Walker told Exhaust Carlson that in spite of mass confinements a great many people in Xinjiang "are physically in an ideal situation regarding the personal satisfaction," he expressed, making sense of in his view Chinese pioneers' thought process. "Do I concur with that? No, I disagree with it," he said.

In light of the Times record of the Xinjiang retreat, McKinsey said it would "be more smart about such decisions later on."

In an indication of how significant McKinsey considers China to the company's future, two of its new overseeing accomplices — Barton and Kevin Sneader — both headed the Asia practice prior to being raised to the top post. Barton lived in Shanghai, and Sneader, even subsequent to taking the association's top work in mid-2018, based himself in Hong Kong.

In Hong Kong, huge supportive of a majority rule government fights emitted in 2019, going on into 2020, frequently occurring close to McKinsey's office in focal Hong Kong. A large number of Individuals rampaged to exhibit against Beijing's undeniably weighty hand over the previous English province, which up to that point had delighted in freedoms not accessible to Individuals in central area China,

# [L'influence cache]

including opportunity of gathering, opportunity of the press, and opportunity of rEligion.

McKinsey didn't take out promotions or sign any letters on the side of the Hong Kong demonstrators, and moreover mentioned no open criticisms when Beijing doused Hong Kong's vote based system development, and with it the city's thoughtful freedoms, with a draconian new public safety regulation.

Conversely, when gigantic fights emitted across the US after the homicide of George Floyd, McKinsey rushed to align itself with the reason. The firm was among the signatories of a full-page promotion in The New York Times devoted to Floyd's memory. Sneader's name showed up under the organization's logo.

It was an irregularity not lost on a youthful McKinsey partner in the US who had invested energy in China.

"Kevin Sneader is situated in Hong Kong," the advisor said. "In one occasion he can talk energetically about racial equity, yet aren't there people outside his front entryway who could likewise profit from a similar directness?"

As relations among China and the US spiraled descending during the four years Donald Trump was president, McKinsey's work in China pulled in bipartisan examination. In a June 2020 letter to Sneader, Representative Marco Rubio, a Florida conservative, requested that the firm distinguish its work with the express, the Socialist Faction, and any organizations in China in "areas of basic public interest to the US," which he characterized as covering a wide scope of enterprises, including medical services, media communications, drugs, and military or common guard.

Rubio's office said that McKinsey returned to the congressperson however declined to unveil the names of its Chinese clients.

Had McKinsey unveiled its Chinese client list, this is the thing Rubio would have learned: From 2018 to mid 2020, among McKinsey's 54 central area Chinese clients that could be distinguished, nineteen were state claimed, as per inward organization records and declarations by Chinese organizations. One of them, the State-Claimed Resources Management and Organization Commission, is the public authority office that regulates the state's possession stake in organizations. Chen Guang, the McKinsey accomplice who addressed the China Dealers Gathering meeting about the Socialist Coalition Congress, was one of no less than two accomplices overseeing that work, the records show. McKinsey says it has not served SASAC and says that China's focal government "isn't a client of McKinsey, and as far as anyone is concerned, has not at any point been a client of McKinsey." That assertion doesn't specify McKinsey's work with lower levels of China's administration. In 2020 McKinsey was welcomed by SASAC in southwestern China's Yunnan territory to offer vital guidance to a portion of the district's greatest state-claimed organizations, nearby media detailed.

The clients incorporate the large state-claimed business moneylenders China Development Bank and Modern and Business Bank of China, Shandong Steel, and the petrochemicals creator Shanghai Huayi Gathering. likewise on the

## [L'influence cache]

rundown, China Telecom, Sinopec, First Auto Works, and the Coal organization Shenhua, which are all among the 96 key state-possessed firms: the zhongyang qiye.

Directly Following detailing in the Times about McKinsey's work in China, Saudi Arabia, Russia, and other nondemocratic nations, the firm reported an adjustment of the manner in which it would Acknowledge new clients. Each new planned client would now be assessed by a board comprised of McKinsey staff members and outside specialists. Accomplices requesting new clients were told to prescreen them to ensure they were fitting. ALso, the firm said it would never again Acknowledge work exhorting the military, knowledge, police, or equity authorities in dictator states, nor would it take care of business for ideological groups or political support gatherings, and it wouldn't participate in campaigning. McKinsey says that strategy applies to China on the grounds that the nation has a place with a gathering of countries that scored six focuses or underneath on a majority rule government list distributed by The Financial specialist magazine, which positions nations on a ten-point scale.

A few current and previous McKinsey representatives said they were distrustful that McKinsey would completely finish this new strategy, refering to the generous amount of space the senior accomplices all over the planet have in taking on new clients and the disappointment of past screening endeavors to keep the firm from taking on questionable work, for example, with the drugmaker Purdue Pharma.

Furthermore, two previous senior accomplices said the actual outcome of such a strategy gambled subverting McKinsey's plan of action, which they expressed rElies upon putting a huge measure of trust on its corps of accomplices to go with significant choices.

"The renumeration is you had respectability," said George Feiger, a previous senior accomplice in the London office.

# [L'influence cache]

## Section 6

## Watching the Entryways of Gehenna

**Tobacco and Vaping**

The retribution was quite a while in coming. For almost 50 years, the cigarette business had involved falsehoods and trickery to get away from responsibility for selling the most deadly purchaser item in American history. Many years, a large number of studies, proof mounted that cigarettes dependent and killed smokers. Oppressed parties documented claims and lawmakers proposed regulations — all fruitless — as tobacco legal advisors and cordial legislators guaranteed that the ones who ran tobacco organizations remained in the shadows, noting just to investors.

On April 14, 1994, that generally different inside room 2123 at the Rayburn House Place of business. A House board did the beforehand unfathomable: it called chiefs of the seven greatest tobacco organizations to remain before them and interestingly answer inquiries having sworn to tell the truth about their items. The consultation followed new disclosures that tobacco organizations were planning cigarettes to support enslavement.

No longer would the discussion over smoking place simply on whether cigarettes caused coronary illness or malignant growth — an assault makers parried by saying assuming grown-ups knew the dangers yet smoked, that was their decision. New divulgences brought up issues about whether smokers truly had a decision. Imagine a scenario in which producers controlled a habit-forming drug in cigarettes — nicotine — to keep Individuals smoking.

Witnesses blamed cigarette organizations for basically dosing their item with enough nicotine to guarantee dependence. ALkali was added to improve the medication's effect. High-nicotine tobacco plants were developed, and various leaves were mixed to accomplish wanted nicotine levels. One significant cigarette producer composed that it was in the organization's drawn out interest "to have the option to control and successfully use each pound of nicotine we buy."

Tobacco organizations had furtively concentrated on the pharmacology of nicotine and knew that without it Individuals wouldn't smoke. "Consider the cigarette pack as a stockpiling compartment for a day's inventory of nicotine," one Philip Morris specialist composed. "Consider the cigarette a distributor for a portion unit of nicotine. Consider a puff of smoke the vehicle for nicotine." Tobacco stocks plunged in the midst of stresses of an out and out prohibition on smoking. Philip Morris attempted to scare the media by recording a $10 billion claim against two correspondents and their manager, ABC News, for their milestone examination of nicotine control in cigarettes. However, it was past the point of no return. The tide had changed.

The April hearing, broadcast live to the country, arrived at a close to home peak when seven tobacco leaders remained close to one another, hands raised, promising to come clean. They denied what the majority of America knew to be valid — that cigarettes were habit-forming and destructive. The conference

## [L'influence cache]

"played to a profound well known outrage about corporate deceitfulness and covetousness," ALLan M. Brandt, a Harvard history teacher, composed. Tobacco organizations out of nowhere started losing legal disputes, preparing the table for the business 10 years after the fact to pay more than $200 billion in what was then the biggest common prosecution settlement in U.S. history. "The conference introduced a general wellbeing triumph for the ages," The New York Times editorialized. Enormous Tobacco had become one of the country's most castigated businesses.

McKinsey and Company watched this rising tide of judgment, realizing beyond any doubt that for quite a long time the association's experts had been helping the greatest tobacco organizations sell more cigarettes. It was taken care of in average McKinsey style — covertly. McKinsey's name didn't figure in the legislative hearings on tobacco, or in two significant books adding up to fourteen hundred pages, or in media examinations of the business.

Mystery benefited both McKinsey and its tobacco clients. Cigarette creators didn't need specialists sharing showcasing procedure, and McKinsey didn't need notoriety soiled as an empowering influence of organizations sold a lethal item. Were that to occur, imminent recruits could consider how cigarettes squared with the company's "esteems," a word frequently utilized among new workers and clients.

Cigarette organizations, in spite of their standing, were appealing clients for one explanation: they had piles of money. As the financial backer Warren Buffett once said, "I'11 explain to you why I like the cigarette business. It costs a penny to make. Sell it for a dollar. It's habit-forming. What's more, there's awesome image rEliability." like so many chain-smokers, McKinsey couldn't avoid the draw of cigarettes. The benefits were excessively habit-forming.

The account of McKinsey's broad work for large Tobacco has never been told, the subtleties covered somewhere down in fourteen million pages of industry records. That relationship can be followed back to no less than 1956, when McKinsey did a one end to the other assessment of Philip Morris' activity. Advisors visited its plants, talked with chiefs, and concentrated on marketing projections. Among McKinsey's suggestions: take out positions and extend research offices to profit by quickly changing innovation in assembling. After a year McKinsey delivered another report, this one stamped "profoundly secret," that suggested how the examination office, including a trial pilot plant, ought to be organized.

In any case, the report likewise accomplished something different: it foreshadowed the business' change from selling a generally farming item into one that logically designed cigarettes through science, nicotine control, and smoke examination. McKinsey referred to, for instance, the presentation of "reconstituted tobacco," an interaction that transforms tobacco scraps into paper-like sheets, which are then hacked up and added to the cigarette. En route, nicotine is Eliminated with different substances. Be that as it may, altogether, nicotine is subsequently added to accomplish the ideal nicotine content.

## [L'influence cache]

By the mid-1950s, cigarettes were at that point under attack after a flood of upsetting reports connecting smoking and cellular breakdown in the 1ungs. As specialists, specialists, and general wellbeing authorities attempted to caution Americans that smoking can be deadly, Philip Morris joined an industry-drove disinformation crusade pointed toward ruining pundits. No proof can be found in industry records showing that McKinsey assumed a part in this double dealing, however for an organization so profoundly engaged with Philip Morris' business, it strains validity to accept the experts didn't know about it.

One truth is certain. McKinsey realized about the wellbeing hazard of smoking since it suggested that Philip Morris assign a unit to do two tasks: "coordinate all exploration that bears on the issue of smoking and wellbeing," and suggest concentrates on "the physiological impacts of cigarette smoking." In the wake of perusing McKinsey's 1956 report, the cigarette organization's VP for assembling, Andrew C. Britton, composed this in an inward organization reminder: "I figure persistent endeavors ought to be made by exploration to find out precisely exact thing the smoker dEliberately or unknowingly may need that we can give to him." One joy smokers "unwittingly" needed was nicotine.

Any waiting questions about the wellbeing of cigarettes were dispersed one Saturday morning in 1964, when the U.S. top health spokesperson, Dr. 1uther Terry, detailed that various investigations had affirmed the connection between cellular breakdown in the 1ungs and smoking. Perceiving the effect of such a declaration, Terry held his public interview on an end of the week to limit its impact on stock costs. And keeping in mind that smoking was not yet generally disregarded — that would come later — it is improbable that McKinsey, known for its thorough exploration and business shrewd, would neglect to get a handle on the reputational chance of taking on or keeping such a client.

In the event that McKinsey experts were concerned, they worked effectively of concealing it. As admonitions about cigarettes increased, McKinsey took on new tobacco clients, including R. J. Reynolds, lori1lard, Brown and Williamson, English American Tobacco, and even Japan Tobacco World wide. The firm additionally looked to help cigarette deals in Germany and latin America.

Tobacco organizations didn't employ McKinsey to put a beam on their corporate logos. They saw the firm as a significant partner and specialist. In 1985, McKinsey composed a secret 36 page update to William Campbe11, prospective leader of Philip Morris, proposing how the organization could stay cutthroat when tobacco use had crested because of wellbeing concerns. It was a significant second for both the organization and Campbe11. Philip Morris had Recently surpassed its long-term foe R. J. Reynolds as industry pioneer, and Campbe11 was in line for an advancement. (He later became one of the tobacco chiefs who affirmed that nicotine was not habit-forming.)

A few choices for helping or possibly supporting cigarette benefits were not accessible. Philip Morris would not depreciate its item by offering steep coupon limits. Publicizing, especially for its leader image, Mar1boro, had arrived at an immersion point. What's more, the organization's assembling plants were at that point effective and current. McKinsey told Philip Morris that the last choices were

## [L'influence cache]

to grow, pull together the deals force, and move along "the marketing and show programs." Philip Morris spent more than $80 million on item shows and rack space, however that was still substantially less than its central rival, R. J. Reynolds.

Tracking down ways of stimulating a deals force played to McKinsey's solidarity. "Over the most recent three years we have served most of the main 25 U.S. bundled merchandise producers and a portion of the main retailers," McKinsey bragged. To lead its group, McKinsey offered one of its stars, Andrew John Parsons, an English conceived overachiever who, after two degrees at Oxford, enlisted at Harvard Business college and turned into a Dough puncher researcher. The firm added two senior accomplices — Charles Shaw, who fostered McKinsey's South American business, and Tom Wilson, who drove its North American purchaser products practice. McKinsey likewise wanted to add research examiners and frameworks advisors. "We propose to utilize three authoritative gadgets that we have tracked down helpful in comparable ventures," McKinsey said. "Specifically a team, a guiding council and continuous studios."

Mark leDoux, a youthful McKinsey specialist doled out to the tobacco group, had the occupation of managing more modest retailers who had started to address whether selling cigarettes merited the problem. Organizations continued to add new brands to currently jam-packed show racks, and a few clients had a problem with any cigarette deals whatsoever. What's more, hoodlums were shoplifting cigarette containers, or in any event, severing into stores during hours to take them, coming down on their razor-dainty overall revenues. McKinsey told retailers not to stress. "We did the math and found that cigarette deals represented 40% of a run of the mill store's benefits," leDoux said in a meeting. "They didn't understand that." truth be told, cigarettes kept a few stores above water.

The amount McKinsey charged Philip Morris is secret, yet the firm lifted the cover marginally when, for another cigarette client, the firm framed its way of thinking and expense structure. "We put client interests in front of firm or individual interest," McKinsey guaranteed. "We enthusiastically safeguard client classification." And the firm just embraces projects "that have a critical various of worth creation to charges — regularly no less than multiple times." obviously, "esteem creation" can be characterized in numerous ways. ALso, McKinsey's promise to put client intrigues over all else sounded sensible, yet not so much for this industry. Besides, how should McKinsey legitimize encouraging clinics and government organizations on the most proficient method to decrease medical services costs while their tobacco clients were occupying emergency clinic rooms with the wiped out and passing on?

McKinsey stayed with cigarette clients even as inside industry reports surfaced in judicial procedures that cast Huge Tobacco as a hunter keen on tricking the general population about the wellbeing of its items. In 1992, the government judge H. lee Sarokin turned out to be so shocked perusing industry updates in an obligation claim that he cast to the side legal restriction when he stated, "Quite frequently in the decision between the actual strength of buyers and the monetary prosperity of business, covering is picked over revelation, deals over wellbeing, and cash over ethical quality. Who are these people who intentionally and covertly choose to jeopardize the purchasing public exclusively to create gains and who

## [L'influence cache]

accept that ailment and demise of customers is their very own suitable expense thriving."

For his solid words, Judge Sarokin was Eliminated from the situation. Be that as it may, they would be repeated 10 years some other time when one more administrative appointed authority communicated a similar end in the wake of directing the public authority's Mobster Impacted and Degenerate Associations Act (RICO) body of evidence against Enormous Tobacco.

Anybody looking to legitimize taking cash from cigarette organizations could constantly track down a way. large Tobacco utilized huge number of laborers. In 1990 a Fortune magazine overview of top chiefs, outside chiefs, and experts positioned Philip Morris as America's second most respected organization, to a great extent since it had satisfied financial backers. A clinic and a youngsters' zoo bore the name of the Tisch family, proprietors of lorillard, a significant McKinsey client. Furthermore, opposite New York's Great Focal Terminal, Philip Morris' corporate central command included a part of the Whitney Gallery, which the organization referred to for instance "of how private endeavor can address the public interest to the improvement of society."

Murray H. Bring, a senior Philip Morris legal counselor, said the business had no reason to feel sorry. "We realize that we are fabricating a legitimate item," Bring said. "We likewise realize that we are good and legitimate Individuals." Geoffrey Book of scriptures, a senior Philip Morris chief, forewarned against forbidding cigarettes, utilizing words not liable to wind up in a McKinsey slide:

> What how about smokers do on the off chance that they didn't smoke? You get some joy from it, and you get another valuable things, like pressure help. No one understands what you'd go to on the off chance that you didn't smoke. Perhaps you'd beat your better Half. Perhaps you'd drive vehicles quick. Who can say for sure what in the world you'd do.

The homegrown cigarette industry was under attack, however a great many Americans actually smoked, and new clients were expected to supplant the ones who quit or kicked the bucket. This implied cash stayed accessible for specialists. lorillard's CEO, Andrew Tisch, actually beseeched his representatives to help out McKinsey on the grounds that contenders and government controllers had changed market elements. lorillard expected to reconsider system, he said, and McKinsey experts were "famous for their capacity to tackle issues and set out freedom."

Any effective McKinsey system needed to include lorillard's Newport image, the country's second most famous cigarette behind Marlboro. With one of the greatest nicotine yields available, Newport was Particularly famous with Dark clients, to a limited extent since it was promoted forcefully where they resided. In 1978, lorillard utilized James Earthy colored's hit single "Daddy Has a Shiny new Pack" for its showcasing message that "Newport is a totally different sack of menthol smoking." More than 66% of youthful Dark smokers favored Newport's menthol cigarettes. Blacks additionally experienced excessively tobacco-related ailment. Whether by plan or chance, McKinsey in the mid 1990s sent Pamela

## [L'influence cache]

Thomas-Graham, the association's most memorable Dark female accomplice, to assist with driving its lori1lard group.

McKinsey's a lot greater client R. J. Reynolds — run for a period by a previous McKinsey accomplice, lou Gerstner — was battling under obligation from a utilized buyout made renowned in the book Savages at the Entryway. To support productivity, McKinsey proposed two of its number one perennials: offshoring and paying specialists less. "Offshoring parts of items could bring about tremendous investment funds," McKinsey told the organization. "Implanted work — combined with low work rates in developing business sectors — drives reserve funds a valuable open door." Reserve funds for investors, maybe, yet a possibly destroying blow for the uprooted laborers. As confirmation of its capacity to press benefits from work, McKinsey referred to its "world wide organization" of seaward assembling specialists.

RJR's large gold mine, Camel, engaged more youthful smokers for the most part as a result of a publicizing effort that highlighted an animation character, Joe Camel. Utilizing an animation to sell cigarettes chafed tobacco pundits since, supposing that smokers didn't begin youthful, they in all likElihood wouldn't begin by any means. RJR pessimistically showcased Camel as extraordinary for Individuals who do "common decency" and embrace a "desire for living."

McKinsey circled back to RJR's subjects by conjuring a method called "channel examination" to arrive at possible clients in specific socioeconomics, including "popular 20s in metropolitan regions or African Americans." (Pipe investigation outlines cooperations customers have with an organization prior to purchasing their items.) The firm likewise slipped by into very much worn McKinsey-talk, proposing to p1unge into its "strong too1 stash of imaginative thoughts," including an unexplained "executioner thought approach," an expression either rash or ideal for a cigarette organization.

Global business sectors were likewise a developing worry for Enormous Tobacco. With the antismoking development on full bubble in the US, cigarette organizations stressed that opinion could spread abroad. By and by, McKinsey stepped in to help. In Germany, where RJR's Camel was losing piece of the pie, McKinsey advised the organization to empty every one of its assets into renewing the brand. However, RJR needed to move quickly, McKinsey prompted, before new guidelines, pointed for the most part at decreasing underage smoking, could impede specific advancements and publicizing.

In the last part of the 1990s, Philip Morris chiefs engaged a more aggressive global methodology. They joined two other tobacco goliaths, English American Tobacco and Japan Tobacco Global, on a mysterious mission to develop an overarching set of rules that would persuade the world that Enormous Tobacco could se1f-direct and stop youth smoking. Thusly, they would have liked to bypass a significant danger — the World Wellbeing Association's most memorable world wide general wellbeing settlement. Since the three organizations controlled around 41% of the world market, they had the assets to employ McKinsey as well as different specialists, legal counselors, and even Kissinger Partners, the firm established in 1982 by the previous U.S. secretary of state.

## [L'influence cache]

The organizations called their endeavor Venture Cerberus, after the three-headed canine that monitors the doors of Abbadon in Greek folklore.

From 1999 through 2001, the Cerberus group worked through their arrangement in a progression of gatherings in London, Geneva, and New York City. These were not thrifty issues. The tobacco chiefs met in London at the noteworthy Grosvenor House lodging, sitting above Hyde Park and Mayfair, the very good quality shopping, eating, and craftsmanship locale. McKinsey coordinated procedure meetings and suggested ways the three contending organizations could make progress toward a common objective.

After a gathering in London, McKinsey composed a secret outline of what the gathering expected to achieve, including finishing the business' separation, recapturing its voice in tobacco control conversations, and accomplishing a steady business climate. To seem trustworthy, the gathering at first considered employing an autonomous review body to guarantee that the organizations satisfied their commitments. In any case, that arrangement was disposed of in the midst of disunity over how the oversight ought to function.

Project Cerberus' excellent desire was rarely understood. At the point when the business' proposition was at long last uncovered to general society, it pulled in essentially no consideration, on the grounds that on that day, September 11, 2001, psychological militants crashed seized planes into the World Exchange Place and the Pentagon, killing thousands.

Project Cerberus didn't stop the WHO antismoking effort, however the cigarette organizations didn't give up. ALL things being equal, they tried to debilitate tobacco control estimates in nations all over the planet. An examination of Venture Cerberus, distributed in the American Diary of General Wellbeing, reasoned that the task showed once more that wellbeing experts shouldn't confide in the business. "This illustration is especially significant in non-industrial nations, where state run administrations, policymakers, and the overall population are powerless against the tobacco business rehearses and frequently ineffectively ready to challenge their impact," the writers composed.

By the last part of the 1990s, the U.S. Equity Division had at long last started preparing its firearms on large Tobacco, blaming it for disregarding RICO by falsely concealing the dangers of smoking. After a severe fight that brought about six years of case and a nine-month prEliminary, the government judge Gladys Kessler settle d the issue for the last time.

In August 2006, Judge Kessler gave a decision of in excess of sixteen hundred pages that gave voice to wellbeing authorities who for a really long time battled to uncover the business' untrustworthiness. Four significant McKinsey clients were respondents. Kessler's finding cast Huge Tobacco organizations as mobsters, a term generally connected with coordinated wrongdoing. Then in words that repeated Appointed authority Sarokin, she composed that the business had "showcased and sold their deadly item with enthusiasm, with misdirection, with a determined spotlight on their monetary achievement, and without respect for the human misfortune or Social costs that achievement claimed." She likewise shut

*[L'influence cache]*

down the idea that tobacco leaders didn't have a clue about their items were habit-forming and lethal. Kessler composed,

litigants have known a significant number of these realities for something like 50 years or more. In spite of that information, they have rEliably, and more than once, and with colossal ability and refinement, denied these realities to people in general, to the Public authority, and to the general wellbeing local area.

An entire decade after the court's overwhelming takedown of the business, McKinsey was all the while attempting to help Philip Morris, presently called ALtria, to sell more cigarettes, as indicated by inside organization records. "We are one group, working one next to the other," McKinsey said in a strategic plan. As a tobacco colleague, McKinsey communicated its "profound responsibility" to convey "a practical, noteworthy steadfastness program that works for ALtria" — at the end of the day, a program that rewards clients for purchasing a greater amount of their cigarettes, including the organization's famous Marlboro brand.

McKinsey is likewise a partner of the FDA, which beginning around 2009 has had the power to manage tobacco items, including ALtria. As such, McKinsey plays both offense and safeguard, a questionable practice that has extended stayed secret. Starting around 2009, the FDA has granted McKinsey more than $11 million for guidance on managing tobacco and for sorting out the FDA office that incorporates tobacco guideline. During quite a bit of that time, McKinsey likewise counseled for the world 's greatest cigarette organizations without revealing this expected irreconcilable circumstance to the FDA, two senior previous authorities of that office said.

Starting around 2019, McKinsey's tobacco clients included ALtria, Philip Morris World wide, Majestic Tobacco Gathering, English American Tobacco, and Japan Tobacco Inc. For ALtria alone, McKinsey charged more than $30 million of every 2018 and 2019. Serving the controller and the managed has been a vital part of McKinsey's business as usual, Particularly in the national government.

"We have served the FDA on north of 30 drives," McKinsey sent in winning $1.1 million in agreements to exhort the organization's Middle for Tobacco Items. McKinsey's undertakings included "risk ID and moderation" as well as "affecting the ways of behaving, conclusions, and practices that are in opposition to the objectives and goals" of tobacco controllers. Probably, that incorporated McKinsey's cigarette clients.

Eric N. lindblom, previous overseer of the FDA's Office of Strategy for the Focal point of Tobacco Items, said he was "alarmed and amazed" to learn of McKinsey's long record of counseling for cigarette organizations. "We didn't think, duh, they are additionally going to serve the business," lindblom said. "I simply don't recall this approaching up or discussing it."

Dr. lawrence Deyton, the middle's most memorable chief, said he was likewise ignorant that McKinsey had served tobacco interests. "That ought to have been uncovered," Dr. Deyton said. "Assuming that one of those potential merchants has a relationship that could affect their work, I would trust that would be essential for the conversation for capabilities."

## [L'influence cache]

For 50 years, McKinsey experts helped tobacco organizations hawk their poisonous items without punishment and made a fortune doing as such. The executives specialists face moral inquiries all the time about whether to take on a hazardous client, and they handle these issues in an unexpected way. At McKinsey, individual representatives can turn down tasks on the off chance that they have moral hesitations about a specific client. However, assuming an accomplice actually needs that client — and they are feEling the squeeze to find new income streams — then gathering a group of willing representatives is normally simple. The association's decentralized administration structure gives accomplices tremendous scope in simply deciding. Individual specialists can mollify their inner voices, yet the firm actually benefits. (McKinsey said it currently screens clients all the more cautiously and that inside the most recent two years it has quit counseling on tobacco issues.)

The firm likewise realizes there is no lack of suspect organizations looking for a convenient solution to their concerns, once in a while without regard to people in general. Before long, nicotine would come calling once more, this time in an alternate item. What's more, by and by, McKinsey was there to open the entryway.

The tobacco business was bloodied yet scarcely crushed. A huge number of Americans kept on purchasing cigarettes, however not even close as numerous as in earlier many years. The level of youthful smokers, so basic to the business' proceeded with benefit, was plunging, in the end arrival in the single digits. Recent college grads had an alternate arrangement of values from their folks , and standing outside to fill their lungs with disease causing smoke held little allure.

President Obama looked to expand on these changing perspectives by marking regulation in 2009 that expressly gave the FDA the position to control cigarettes, tobacco, and any new item that the organization "considered" a tobacco item. The law would be upheld through another office, the Middle for Tobacco Items, with nicotine a significant concentration. To assist the workplace with working all the more really, the FDA decided to patch up its administrative way of thinking. No longer would the office simply respond to occasions; it would proactively look to recognize wellbeing takes a chance before they turned into an all out emergency. Considering this basic change in technique, the tobacco office concluded it required an external counsel talented in completing significant government rearrangements.

The FDA went to a natural name — McKinsey and Company. In getting the FDA contract, McKinsey recognized the significance of taking on a proactive mentality, as opposed to "the more receptive type of the executives that is excessively normal among comparative associations in the national government." The names of McKinsey's senior chiefs dealing with the agreement were redacted in government records because they were proprietary advantages, a sweeping if problematic utilization of that exception.

McKinsey's work got an early test with the presence of electronic cigarettes, handheld gadgets that conveyed nicotine fume through battery-created heat, not burning. For grown-up smokers, e-cigarettes gave a more secure method for fulfilling their nicotine habit without the unsafe impacts of smoke. Under the law,

## [L'influence cache]

the FDA might have rapidly "considered" e-cigarettes another tobacco item and done whatever it takes to control them. Yet, it didn't. ALL things considered, the organization held up six years before starting the cycle, a choice that would have serious ramifications for teens and bring up issues about the FDA's new "proactive" outlook.

E-cigarette producers couldn't hope to transparently advertise their nicotine gadgets to nonsmoking youngsters, however offering them to grown-ups as less hurtful than cigarettes could accumulate wide help. However, e cigarette organizations dealt with two significant issues. Their items needed to convey consistently elevated degrees of nicotine without an unforgiving taste, something they couldn't yet do, and they expected to fall through or around a probably more watchful FDA. The primary issue involved innovation and science. The second was political.

It was only after 2015 that another item tackled the specialized issues and in the process changed the business. It was called Juul. With a smooth plan, and a battery that could be re-energized in a PC gateway, Juul became known as the iPhone of vaping. This innovative item spoke to twenty to thirty year olds and, surprisingly, more youthful likely clients. It was likewise strong, conveying probably the most noteworthy nicotine yields in the business — what could be compared to twenty cigarettes. As a little something extra, the nicotine taste could be veiled in fruity, youngster engaging flavors. Its little size made it simple to stow away from guardians and instructors, and dissimilar to cigarettes it left no obvious smell of smoke on their garments.

Juul keenly spread the word of its new e-cigarette through a web-based entertainment crusade, stressing way of life, a methodology tobacco organizations had utilized effectively to catch youthful smokers. Juul likewise purchased eye to eye access with teens, paying $134,000 to a sanction school gathering to set up a day camp, as indicated by The New York Times. "Different schools the nation over were offered $10,000 from the e-cigarette organization for the option to converse with understudies in homerooms or after school," the Times detailed.

In only a couple of years, the vaping business had planted the seeds of a young nicotine pestilence — the very kind of danger that the FDA's patched up tobacco unit should recognize early and address.

The Illinois representative Richard Durbin, a veteran of the tobacco wars returning many years, was among the primary Individuals from Congress to raise cautions over vaping. Durbin's dad, a two-pack-a-day Camel smoker, passed on at an early age from cellular breakdown in the lungs, and the representative hadn't failed to remember it. "losing valuable piece of the pie, Huge Tobacco set their specialists and advertisers to work," he said. "They required another item that didn't convey the ethical impurity of malignant growth causing tobacco — stunningly better assuming it seemed to be a USB streak drive and could undoubtedly plug into a youngster's PC."

Had Durbin and his associates inspected the program of Juul workers, they would have found a multitude of previous cigarette organization representatives — 39 of them — from five tobacco organizations, all previous McKinsey clients.

## [L'influence cache]

Clinical experts communicated profound worry about vaping's unexpected prominence with young people. Dr. Jonathan Winickoff, a rehearsing pediatrician at Massachusetts General Medical clinic, expressed a significant number of his young patients knew nothing about "JUU1's monstrous nicotine content and don't grasp the risks of nicotine." When his patients began vaping, Dr. Winickoff expressed, a significant number of them tracked down it "almost difficult to stop."

Congressperson Durbin answered by testing the Establishment on which Juul was fabricated — as a smoking discontinuance item for grown-ups. "In excess of 20% of kids younger than 18 are utilizing e-cigarettes, contrasted and under 3% of grown-ups," Durbin said. "JUU1 knows precisely where their benefits are coming from and it's not from grown-ups hoping to stop smoking... it's from our kids."

Where could the FDA have been? he needed to be aware.

In 2013, two years before Juul even hit the market, five U.S. congresspersons had previously kept in touch with the FDA encouraging the office to state its administrative power over vaping. Nothing was finished. legislators would compose more letters; wellbeing authorities would raise more cautions — once more, without result. Through everything, Juul continued to sell enhanced nicotine, which engaged its young clients. "Pediatricians are detailing their teen patients are putting e-cigarettes under their pads so they can vape short-term," Dr. Sally Goza, leader of the American Institute of Pediatrics, said.

Regardless of their prevalence, little was had some significant awareness of e-cigarettes. Might underage vaping at some point prepare for smoking as grown-ups? Nobody knew. What different synthetic compounds may be in Juu1's nicotine cartridges or in nicotine vials that clients of different brands stack into their open-framework e-cigarettes? There were reasons in abundance for society to have requested replies to these inquiries, Particularly in light of the fact that the juvenile cerebrum is especially defenseless against nicotine enslavement.

This absence of cautiousness brought about what a previous delegate chief of the FDA, Dr. Joshua Sharfstein, called a "out and out calamity."

The FDA didn't make the emergency, yet it did practically nothing to stop it. Organization authorities said they battled to track down the right harmony between assisting grown-ups with halting smoking — still the country's driving reason for preventable passing — and getting e-cigarettes far from kids. The FDA likewise whined that troublesome legal decisions had sabotaged its oversight, however that disregards the organization's choice to conjure its own "administrative caution" to postpone by years the verifying of e-cigarettes. Representative Durbin faulted the FDA for acting less like a guard dog and more like a willing assistant, "deferring rational guideline of the e-cigarette industry," declining to Eliminate unlawful items from the market, and "remaining quiet despite bogus wellbeing claims."

The Times offered its own brutal evaluation of the FDA:

In many meetings, government authorities and general wellbeing specialists portrayed a lost ten years of inaction, accusing a serious campaigning exertion by

## [L'influence cache]

the e-cigarette and tobacco businesses, fears of a political reaction in tobacco-accommodating states, regulatory postponements, and a late respite by a F.D.A. chief who had Recently served on the leading group of a chain of vaping lounges.

Under extraordinary public tension, the FDA declared in July 2017 that it would put nicotine and dependence "at the focal point of its tobacco guideline endeavors." after two months, the FDA made a nicotine directing board of trustees, set up for the most part with senior pioneers from the FDA's medication assessment office and the Middle for Tobacco Items. The two units were McKinsey clients. Some could say slow on the uptake, but still good enough, yet to the guardians of dependent teens the postponements were unpardonable.

There was a great deal of ground to make up. Toward the finish of 2017 a larger number of than 2 million center and secondary school understudies were utilizing e-cigarettes. That number would develop to 5.4 million of every 2019. Furthermore, McKinsey, with Juul as a client, assumed a part in assisting that organization with making progress.

One truth talked most convincingly about the FDA's administrative record. Not a solitary Juul gadget in the US had been sold legitimately, as per legislative declaration in late 2019. A vaping gadget to be sold lawfully would require pre-market survey by the FDA, and starting around 2019 that had not occurred. In any case, Juul's deals of e-cigarettes added up to $1 billion out of 2018, providing the organization with an expected valuation of $38 billion, a larger number of than Portage Engine Organization. McKinsey's particular counsel to the FDA not entirely set in stone, however the reality stays that the organization neglected to distinguish and "proactively" address vaping as an approaching danger. (Toward the finish of 2021, just three vaping items — none made by Juul — were supported available to be purchased by the FDA.)

While the FDA did close to nothing to stop the spread of underage vaping, McKinsey was occupied with counseling for the two most impressive powers looking to overwhelm the vaping market — Juul and the tobacco monster ALtria. Each organization had its own vaping item, yet ALtria eventually chose to help Juul, the market chief. So in 2018, ALtria put almost $13 billion in its previous rival. To add to the arrangement, the tobacco organization dispersed $2 billion in rewards to fifteen hundred Juul representatives.

Working for Juul demonstrated productive for McKinsey too. In under two years of work, Juul paid McKinsey between $15 million and $17 million, ALfonso Pulido, a McKinsey accomplice, expressed in a statement in an item responsibility case in the U.S. Region Court of Northern California.

Neither the guardians of dependent youngsters, nor government controllers, knew about McKinsey's tangled connections. McKinsey said struggle under the surface of interest rules restrict the dividing of private data among advisors for clients with contending interests. In Pulido's statement, he was asked the way that those rules are authorized, however he evaded the inquiry. "They are authorized by cycles and strategies that direct the way in which we staff our groups and put together our groups and serve our clients," he said.

## [L'influence cache]

McKinsey counseled for Juul on exceptionally dElicate subjects, for example, reviewing which flavor names spoke to thirteen-to seventeen-year-olds, however the firm said that work was on the side of the organization's work to forestall youth vaping. McKinsey even proposed to study the "risk system" of Juul's fostering an item for the maryjane market. McKinsey's exploration raised no warnings inside the firm, one accomplice who chipped away at the Juul account said.

Juul workers saw McKinsey specialists all through the organization's San Francisco base camp on Wharf 70, a reModeled shipyard in the Dogpatch area, a stylish blend of stockrooms and craftsmanship displays. Technique meetings were held in a "war room" with plans for the day and significant issues taped to the wall.

Found out if McKinsey chipped away at FDA issues, a worker with direct information on these gatherings answered: "Wow, McKinsey assisted JUU1 with composing their FDA accommodation — absolutely serious." Pulido in his testimony affirmed that McKinsey arranged Juul's reaction to the FDA's investigation into the organization's promoting rehearses.

McKinsey said it quit counseling for Juul in the spring of 2019 in view of rising administrative vulnerability and "expanded familiarity with youth use."

Juul realized it had a huge objective on its back. So the day after the FDA communicated worry about nicotine flavors drawing in more youthful clients — barely another worry — Juul prevented tolerating orders from its 90,000 retailers for mango, organic product, crème brûlée, and cucumber. Yet, not mint and menthol. The choice guaranteed more than it conveyed, as per Siddharth Breja, a previous senior VP of world wide money at Juul. In an illegitimate end claim, Breja said the organization "consistently realize that its deals couldn't endure on the grounds that the mint cases, given its fruity flavor, could compensate for any absence of deals of the other seasoned units." And how did Juul be aware? "This was affirmed through research directed by McKinsey and Co," the claim asserted. (Juul later quit delivering mint, yet not menthol.)

Juul further reinforced its connections to Enormous Tobacco by lifting K. C. Crosthwaite, ALtria's previous boss development official, to Chief in September 2019. The organization took the place that ALtria, previously considered Philip Morris, was certainly not a troublemaker. Yet, a few workers found the organization's nearby connections to the cigarette organization upsetting. One specialist portrayed the organization's viewpoint as "split among mission and cash." At the most elevated levels, the architect said, "it was development, benefit. Stuff about wellbeing was only a cover."

One of McKinsey's significant rivals in the counseling industry concluded it couldn't work for Juul, an organization selling a habit-forming item preferred by minors. A McKinsey accomplice, Michael Chui, posted a public remark communicating worry about vaping. "In only a couple of years," Chui expressed, "vaping has cleared out twenty years of work getting youngsters to stop (or never start) cigarette smoking." Chui didn't single out Juul or his firm, however he probably won't have referred to that McKinsey had Juul as a client. (Another significant consultancy, Bain and Company, additionally had a few groups working for Juul.)

So for what reason did McKinsey take on this questionable client? As per private inward organization reports, Juul clear ly had a major ally in the firm, a pioneer so powerful and regarded that senior accomplices in 2021 would choose him overseeing accomplice, the top post in the firm. His name: Robert Sternfels, who is recorded on interior reports as McKinsey's overseer of client administrations for Juul. McKinsey said Sternfels knows Juul's previous proprietor, however didn't chip away at any "client commitment" with Juul.

McKinsey likewise counseled for a gathering generally saw as a tobacco industry front gathering — the Establishment for a Smoke-liberated World . Established in September 2017, the charitable association stated that its objective was to decrease passings and illness from smoking while at the same time guaranteeing potential givers that its load up was free without any connections to the tobacco business. That assertion was significant for what it didn't say — that Philip Morris World wide began the gathering with gifts of $8.4 million. Of that, more than $400,000 went to McKinsey. PMI was the gathering's only giver, and McKinsey was the sole advisor.

"Our main goal is to end smoking in this age," the gathering composed on its landing page. "We likewise support the improvement of elective items and strategies that might decrease clients' ebb and flow wellbeing dangers and assist them with halting smoking completely." The Establishment vowed to finance research and advance ways "to speed up progress in diminishing damage and passings from smoking."

Wellbeing authorities weren't getting it. In a letter to the English clinical diary The lancet, specialists at the College of Shower revealed that the Establishment spent more cash on advertising than on research. This use, the specialists expressed, "doesn't match the image the Establishment paints of itself as a logical body, however rather upholds the developing agreement that the Establishment gives a key advertising capability for Philip Morris." For sure, the World Wellbeing Association and "many general wellbeing associations universally have taken areas of strength for an in dismissing joint effort with the Establishment," as per the scientists.

In 2017, that very year McKinsey took cash from the tobacco-supported Establishment, President Trump's FDA granted the counseling firm another agreement, this one for $1.2 million, to patch up employing in the tobacco and clinical items units. After two years, the FDA gave McKinsey a $1.5 million agreement for creating "interest, imagination and development" in the tobacco unit's science office.

Trump by and by said something regarding the risks of vaping in September 2019. Situated in the Oval Office with the main woman, Melania Trump, he reported that his organization was moving to boycott all enhanced nicotine fumes, aside from menthol. "We can't have our children be so impacted," Trump said. After two months, he eased off, saying the issue required more review, in the wake of being cautioned of the political aftermath.

## [L'influence cache]

The reaction against Juul kept on building. In late November 2019, ALtria said it had downgraded its interest in the organization by $4.5 billion, refering to prohibitions on vaping in specific regions and the rising probability that the FDA would boycott nicotine flavors.

Then, on January 2, 2020, Trump switched himself once more and declared a restriction on most nicotine flavors. Menthol was excluded. The request likewise didn't make a difference to vape shops, which made the majority of their cash selling vials of nicotine for purported open-tank gadgets, where buyers add their own nicotine. Habit analysts censured the declaration, Particularly the choice to leave menthol available, since they said menthol improved nicotine's effect, making stopping more troublesome. Its cooling sensation additionally veiled the brutal taste of nicotine, making it more interesting to kids, said Dr. Goza of the American Foundation of Pediatrics. "The possibility that menthol is a grown-up flavor is messed up."

The FDA didn't openly dissent. After fourteen days, the New York Times Publication load up proclaimed the office to be in trouble and needing fixing or chance turning into a controller without impact. The article didn't make reference to McKinsey's in the background work for the FDA.

The firm had quietly benefitted in the help of tobacco and vaping as well as, as proof would show, narcotics. McKinsey even wandered into one more area of possibly habit-forming conduct — betting — when it encouraged a significant club on the most proficient method to keep players at the table when they were going to leave.

As McKinsey found, compulsion offered huge prizes — and risks — contingent upon whether you were selling or purchasing. Furthermore, McKinsey accomplices were undoubtedly selling.

# [L'influence cache]

## Section 7

### Turbo charging Narcotic Deals

It was 2002, and McKinsey was on the chase after new clients, this time in the objective rich field of drugs, currently a significant pay hotspot for the firm. McKinsey wanted to invigorate revenue by distributing an article fighting that Huge Pharma had been overlooking cash by misusing its deals force in the field.

While most clients enlist McKinsey on account of notoriety or references, the firm likewise looks for new business by composing thought pieces recommending that organizations have issues needing fixing. The article's lead writer, Martin Elling, a Harvard regulation graduate, would turn into a significant power in McKinsey's drug practice.

Elling's article advised drug organizations for depending on "the 'pinball wizard' deals Model," where drug reps skip starting with one specialist's office then onto the next. The best dealers procured generally equivalent to the less useful ones for a straightforward explanation: their managers couldn't recognize the two. McKinsey referred to it as "equivalent compensation for inconsistent execution," which reared thwarted expectation and confidence issues.

McKinsey composed that medication organizations could fix the issue just by improving at of investigating remedy information. "At the point when a patient fills a medicine, the request is put away in a data set that can be matched for medication, maker, and doctor," the firm made sense of. This data could then be utilized "to target doctors who are probably going to endorse to a greater extent a given medication over the long run, regardless of how much or how little they recommend right now." It likewise permitted organizations to recognize high-performing agents and prize them.

The article didn't be ignored. One ruthless medication organization, Purdue Pharma, clear ly preferred McKinsey's thoughts. From 2004 to 2019, Purdue paid McKinsey $83.7 million in expenses for showcasing counsel that made its tycoon proprietors much more extravagant by stirring up the country's hunger for the painkilling drug OxyContin.

McKinsey collected an impressive group to prompt Purdue, including Elling and two clinical specialists, one of whom likewise had a PhD.

OxyContin had first stirred things up around town in 1996. Since the medication could consistently treat extreme torment, patients were presently ready to stay asleep for the entire evening with an okay of fixation, the organization said. The two cases were before long uncovered to be exaggerated or bogus. A few patients tracked down that the medication, a strong narcotic, quit working sooner than promoted, inciting them to take a greater amount of it. Purdue additionally began offering OxyContin in higher dosages, expanding the gamble of habit.

The medication delivered a few clients euphoric, sending them on a compound high that they needed over and over. Deals hopped. An ascent in wrongdoing followed. At the point when junkies couldn't get OxyContin, they took it or in

## [L'influence cachè]

later years went to heroin and fentanyl, a manufactured narcotic like morphine with the exception of dramatically more impressive.

By opening the force of information examination to find specialists probably going to recommend the narcotic, Purdue had made a beast that would tear openings through families, schools, and networks. Numerous passed on. Notorieties were destroyed.

Eventually, the losses included Elling and his partner Arnab Ghatak, a clinical specialist — both terminated by McKinsey after inward records showed they had examined cleansing records to conceal the company's contribution. The consultancy, which for a really long time had for the most part kept its name out of the news, out of nowhere found it on the front pages of America's papers, leaving a terrible and enduring reputational scar. To settle government examinations concerning its part in aiding Purdue "turbocharge" narcotic deals when large number of Individuals were passing on from gluts, the firm consented to pay more than $600 million even as it denied any bad behavior.

Purdue declared financial insolvency, subsequent to consenting to pay $8 billion to settle government examinations. Its proprietors, the Sackler family, consented to pay $4.5 billion in return for a lawful safeguard against any further narcotic prosecution. A government judge later decided that the insolvency court coming up short on power to give that insurance.

The genuine washouts, obviously, are the 750,000 Individuals who passed on in a plague launched, the public authority said, by the offer of OxyContin. Actually 2021, narcotic passings gave no indication of lessening.

Thinking back, perceiving how this misfortune unfolded is simple. The FDA endorsed OxyContin without a legitimate survey. Purdue overstated its advantage and made light of its gamble. The drugmaker purchased specialist dedication by facilitating in excess of forty torment the executives preparing gatherings, some at warm-weather conditions resorts. As much as 5,000 doctors, drug specialists, and medical caretakers went to these all-cost paid gatherings where Purdue enlisted and prepared them to talk on issues critical to the organization, as indicated by the American Diary of General Wellbeing.

Purdue likewise profited from a development that it helped finance, pointed toward persuading specialists that their uncalled inspired by a paranoid fear of narcotic compulsion made them undertreat torment.

OxyContin initially sank its teeth into the more unfortunate networks. "According to a deals viewpoint, OxyContin had its most noteworthy early progress in rustic, modest community America — currently loaded with covered production lines and Dollar Corner stores," Beth Macy wrote in Dopesick, her strong record of narcotic fixation and misuse. Inside the initial two years of the medication's delivery, 24% of secondary school youngsters in a little western Virginia town said they had attempted OxyContin alongside 9% of seventh graders.

Specialists were being captured for inappropriately recommending pills that were exchanged in the city and in schoolyards. The U.S. lawyer in Maine developed so

## [L'influence caché]

worried that in February 2000 he made the remarkable stride of cautioning the state's PCPs of this get-together threat. Different organizations, rather than seeing the potential for misfortune, saw a way to greater benefits. The narcotic market was growing, and they needed a piece of it.

Still OxyContin stayed a dominatingly neighborhood story, yet not for a really long time. Bounce Cole, a specialist for the Province of Ohio leading group of Drug store, called a proofreader he knew at The New York Times with a story tip: region clinical inspectors along the Ohio Waterway were finding the equivalent narcotic — OxyContin — in an amazing number of dead bodies got for post-mortem examinations. The manager asked a journalist, Barry Meier, to explore, and in the spring of 2001, Meier co-created a first page story that aided transform OxyContin into a public story.

Purdue didn't keep down in safeguarding its turf. As Meier revealed in Pain rEliever, his fundamental book on OxyContin, Purdue "utilized cash, propositions for employment, and different blessings to co-pick, impact, or rout its faultfinders or likely rivals."

With Purdue progressively under a magnifying glass, the drugmaker recruited McKinsey to assist with safeguarding its narcotic Establishment, not an outlandish assumption given that McKinsey calls itself the main consultancy for clinical item organizations, taking care of upwards of 45 hundred tasks in a solitary five-year time span.

Similarly significant, McKinsey knew the narcotic business.

McKinsey had previously been exhorting a Purdue contender, Johnson and Johnson, a vital player in narcotic creation and perhaps of McKinsey's most rewarding client as the years progressed. Most popular for its child items, J&J additionally sold its own narcotic medication.

However, J&J's greatest commitment in the field of torment treatment came from responsibility for organizations handled the beginning material for narcotics, which came from a freak type of Tasmanian poppy plants. J&J offered the item to narcotic makers, including Purdue, inciting policing consider J&J the narcotic "head boss," a humiliating moniker for an organization that constructed its standing as a family-accommodating organization.

McKinsey assisted J&J with selling its mark narcotic, an opiate fix called Duragesic. In PowerPoint slides, McKinsey suggested that J&J target "high maltreatment risk patients (eg guys under 40)" and move doctors who were "stuck" in recommending less intense narcotics into endorsing more grounded plans. Another slide inquired, "Would we say we are appropriately focusing on and impacting remedy conduct in torment facilities?"

The McKinsey slides gave ammo to a claim the Oklahoma principal legal officer documented years after the fact against J&J — however not McKinsey — blaming the organization for "leaving on a guile, negative and underhanded plan to make and take care of the requirement for narcotics, engineer a freak poppy to enhance

## [L'influence cache]

the need they made, exaggerate the viability and limit the gamble of these medications."

In the main prEliminary of a narcotic claim, a J&J witness two times attempted to remove the organization from McKinsey's slides, saying they were "McKinsey's words," not J&j's. Found out if the organization terminated McKinsey, the observer said no and recognized that McKinsey kept on counseling for the organization. The appointed authority decided for the state and requested J&J to suffer a $465 million consequence, refering to the organization's "bogus, misdirecting, and hazardous promoting effort" that prompted fixation and go too far passings. The Oklahoma High Court at last tossed out that decision, saying the state's legitimate methodology in seeking after the case as a public disturbance was imperfect.

J&J and McKinsey could appear to be probably not going to have wound up in the seamier side of the opiates business. Both looked to permeate their journey for benefits with a higher reason — McKinsey through its "values" and a commitment to disagree and J&J through its corporate "philosophy," which held that its most memorable obligation was "to the patients, specialists and medical caretakers, to moms and fathers and all other people who utilize our items and administrations." Representative grumblings and ideas, the philosophy expressed, ought not be deterred.

McKinsey's work lessly affected J&J than on Purdue Pharma.

When McKinsey took on Purdue as a client in 2004, the drugmaker definitely realized it was powerless. The organization's lawful group had educated its agents to try not to utilize terms, for example, "enslavement" and "misuse" in their reports. That very year, the FDA sent Purdue a harsh admonition letter that said its promotions "terribly exaggerate the security profile of OxyContin by not alluding in that frame of mind of the ads to serious, possibly lethal dangers."

McKinsey's counseling group at Purdue Pharma had the sponsorship of three senior accomplices — the most noteworthy position shy of overseeing accomplice. Every one of the three had broad involvement with drugs. Their achievements mirrored McKinsey's commendable characteristics as well as its inconsistencies, from serving the less 1ucky to assisting organizations with benefitting to the detriment of the wellbeing and security of their clients.

McKinsey's group included Arnab Ghatak, a cum laude move on from Princeton, who likewise procured a joint clinical and MBA degree at the College of Pennsy1vania. Ghatak's inclinations included further developing medical care in emerging countries, a mission that didn't square with assisting Purdue with pushing more opiates out the entryway amidst a narcotic scourge. He wedded a lady of comparable scholarly hau1 who directed generosity projects at McKinsey's other narcotic client, J&J. Their association justified a b1ustery article in The New York Times telling how they met.

The other senior accomplices in the group were Elling, the Harvard Graduate school graduate and a head of the company's North American drug practice, and Robert Rosie1lo, who sat on McKinsey's Accomplice Pay and Client Hazard

## [L'influence cache]

Boards of trustees. Rosiello would later turn into the CFO at Valeant, the previous McKinsey client blamed for cost gouging on lifesaving drugs.

No less than 24 different accomplices counseled for Purdue. To have seven accomplices on a similar agreement, notwithstanding a care staff, flagged this wasn't a maverick unit going unnoticed of the company's gamble chiefs. The size and term of the gig ensured the firm consistent income, not something the higher-ups would be leaned to disturb.

McKinsey started counseling for Purdue when J. Michael Pearson drove the company's drug practice. A serious, now and again profane senior accomplice, Pearson didn't fit the generalization of lean and restrained McKinsey experts. However his record at the firm was noteworthy. In his almost quarter of hundred years at McKinsey, he counseled for a considerable lot of the top medication organizations, directing them through unions, consolidations, and different issues. Pearson, who turned into Valeant's President, came to accept that medication organizations spent too luxuriously on new medication advancement without receiving a lot of consequently.

McKinsey's first class list of corporate clients and preeminent certainty persuaded Purdue its narcotic Establishment was safe and sound. But since the firm works stealthily, the medication organization couldn't openly shroud itself in McKinsey's decency.

With government specialists surrounding, Purdue required a stabilizer, somebody sufficiently significant to give it cover. That somebody ended up being the previous New York City chairman, Rudy Giuliani. "We accept that administration authorities are more open to realizing that Giuliani is exhorting Purdue Pharma," one senior Purdue official said.

"America's city hall leader" had a troublesome task. Government examiners in Virginia had arranged a cursing arraignment reminder of in excess of 100 pages that the writer Patrick Radden Keefe portrayed in his book Realm of Torment as "a combustible list of corporate misbehavior." Examiners needed crime accusations brought against three Purdue leaders.

Purdue employed Giuliani to make those charges vanish, and they did, Keefe revealed. In 2007, a Purdue member consented to pay a $600 million fine to settle government charges originating from its initial tricky promoting rehearses. Three Purdue chiefs likewise conceded to a solitary "misbranding" charge and consented to pay $34.5 million.

The shortfall of prison sentences chafed Purdue's faultfinders, Particularly families who lost kids to the scourge. The adjudicator himself communicated lament that the details of the supplication bargains blocked jail terms.

Purdue's advertising issues were not disappearing, nonetheless. The moms of youngsters who passed on from narcotic excesses were revitalizing public help. So in June 2009, Purdue's future CEO, Craig landau, requested that McKinsey track down ways of countering these close to home messages. One potential arrangement: gather together OxyContin clients to stand up for the medication.

## [L'influence cache]

To keep down the tide, Purdue utilized a two-section promoting technique: make seemingly sensible concessions to the general wellbeing local area while proceeding to place pills in the possession of however many Individuals as would be prudent. The organization Eliminated its most impressive portion, the 160-milligram pill. It upheld remedy observing and suspending shipments to Mexico since those pills frequently wound up back in the US. What's more, under tension, Purdue chose to reformulate OxyContin so fiends couldn't pulverize it to deliver the dynamic fixing at the same time, instead of gradually over a drawn out period.

The reformulation, be that as it may, required FDA endorsement, so McKinsey loaned its mastery, setting up for the company's "FDA master" to represent two hours with a top Purdue official. "It was very useful to get experiences on how they are creating the reaction," Maria Gordian of McKinsey kept in touch with her associates in an email.

On January 20, 2009, Gordian detailed that McKinsey and Purdue "had a generally excellent FDA practice yesterday," went to by a few Individuals from the Sackler family. "The group worked effectively on the review, setting up the client and executing the fake gathering. We are headed toward DC today for the really [sic] FDA meeting tomorrow."

Purdue in the end got FDA endorsement for the reformulation, however it didn't change the way that the medication remained profoundly habit-forming and was being recommended to Individuals for whom safer choices were accessible. "The genuine issue with narcotics from the general wellbeing viewpoint is fixation," said Dr. lewis Nelson, an expert in crisis medication and a FDA guide. "These pills in the reformulated rendition never really diminish the probability or size of habit."

Fiends who could never again acquire OxyContin went to the road. 100 tablet bottle bought at a drug store for $400 sold for $2,000 to $4,000 on the bootleg market. As pills turned out to be significantly more scant, fiends went to heroin, setting off what became known as the second flood of narcotic maltreatment. Profoundly habit-forming and unregulated, the opiate was in some cases spiked by road vendors with a manufactured narcotic, fentanyl, which is fifty to a hundred times more impressive than morphine. Clients didn't necessarily in every case realize that fentanyl had been added or in what sum, and numerous passed on from accidental excesses.

To battle a decrease in remedies, Purdue extended its deals force, provoking one of Purdue's proprietors, an individual from the Sackler family, to inquire as to why the organization had anticipated a decrease in OxyContin deals, when he figured they ought to rise. At minutes like this, Purdue chiefs again went to McKinsey.

To help deals in the midst of the reinforcing narcotic scourge, McKinsey needed to concoct extremist novel thoughts. One idea was to advance OxyContin as a medication that gave patients "opportunity" and "true serenity," alongside the "most ideal opportunity to carry on with a full and dynamic life." OxyContin could likewise decrease pressure, making patients more hopeful and less disconnected, McKinsey said, an idea wellbeing authorities called preposterous.

## [L'influence cache]

McKinsey additionally proposed that Purdue focus closer on nurture professionals and doctor associates, who are not specialists yet can impact recommending rehearses. "They have the best agent access and are progressively significant in huge gathering rehearses," McKinsey said. The two gatherings enrolled twofold digit expansions in OxyContin deals, one more objective of chance.

Purdue, in the mean time, coordinated a business challenge to recognize and remunerate its top salespeople — not another idea, but rather in accordance with McKinsey's suggestions from years sooner.

OxyContin use was all the while ascending in pieces of the nation, giving Purdue trust. "Regardless of a public downfall, miniature market examination recommends significant pockets of development that Purdue ought to zero in on," McKinsey wrote in 2013. "It is empowering that at a postal district level, generally 40% of zips are really becoming their OxyContin remedy volume."

One development pocket was Stronghold Wayne, Indiana. However, an assessment of those "uplifting" marketing projections uncovered a path of misuse and wretchedness. Narcotic related passings were flooding in the Stronghold Wayne region, with heroin and fentanyl adding to that ascent.

At a Stronghold Wayne torment center, Dr. Michael Cozzi composed more narcotic contents than any specialist in the state, in the end driving the state to suspend his clinical permit. Seeing up to 120 patients each day, Cozzi composed 64 thousand solutions for controlled substances in two years. Of those, just about 3,000,000 dose units were for oxycodone, the narcotic and primary fixing in OxyContin. At the point when patients didn't have cash, Cozzi Acknowledged weapons as installment. In one month, he recommended controlled substances for 1,700 patients.

The deals blast helped something like one Purdue field rep also. In 2012, during what the Indiana head legal officer called the pinnacle of narcotic endorsing, that agent positioned first among 525 agents cross country in selling the organization's aggravation medication. She alone represented $2 million in OxyContin deals during the principal quarter of 2012. Her prize: a get-away to Aruba and a first-quarter reward of $36,000.

Purdue might have involved this deals information for more than Aruba excursions. Indiana specialists said in lawful papers that the drugmaker "knew the characters, rehearses, and endorsing volumes of each and every medical services supplier the organization visited, and consequently was all around arranged to recognize dubious recommending. However Purdue didn't utilize this data to safeguard patients and people in general." McKinsey could likewise have utilized its business information to caution Purdue of perilous prescribers.

ALL things considered, OxyContin deals stayed a worry for Purdue. Higher-strength pills, the organization's most productive ones, were in decline, just like the quantity of pills per remedy. Purdue's problematic standing made it feasible for contending organizations to sell their narcotics by simply saying their medications were not OxyContin.

## [L'influence cache]

The circumstance had crumbled to where in the late-spring of 2013, Purdue taught McKinsey to figure out how to stop the discharging. Shallow advertising tricks be doomed.

This was war, and McKinsey started seeing the Individuals who tested Purdue as the adversary. Endeavors to check the pestilence had gone excessively far, the firm affirmed, making it hard for patients who really required rElief from discomfort to find support. To fix this, McKinsey expected to plunge into Purdue's motor room, sort out what was broken, and think of an arrangement — a significant endeavor, in view of client assumptions, yet additionally due to the mission's direness.

Known for its insightful abilities, McKinsey requested that Purdue purchase more information, directly down to the number of milligrams of OxyContin each prescriber composed. The specialists didn't simply lounge around their PCs and accounting sheets; they wandered into the field, talking with doctors, nurture experts, and drug specialists. They rode alongs with agents and read up procedures for keeping patients on narcotics longer, as indicated by policing.

The specialists utilized McKinsey-address convey, examining "field force execution," benchmarks, and the association's exclusive "corporatized supplier network connector." Probably, Purdue understood what all that implied.

"Ultimately our work expands upon our related involvements serving Purdue that return 10 years," McKinsey composed. This institutional information gave the firm the validity that other counseling firms needed. McKinsey consoled Purdue by saying it was "seeking after 20+ unmistakable open doors" to support deals.

On July 18, 2013, McKinsey introduced the Purdue Pharma board with its eagerly awaited market investigation. It was fundamental however sobering. A few issues were self-evident. To stem the progression of narcotics, the Medication Requirement Organization and the Equity Division had started constraining various connections in the production network, including wholesalers and drug stores. That prompted patient grievances about issues filling their narcotic remedies.

"The retail channel, the two drug stores and wholesalers, is under extreme examination and direct gamble," McKinsey composed. "We see clear interruption affecting patients and it is spreading. The scope of obstructions incorporate whole drug stores being stopped by merchants, drug stores themselves forcing tablet cutoff points... and drug stores deciding to not stock OxyContin." These actions represented a "reasonable and direct danger to patient access," McKinsey finished up. "This requires a pressing reaction."

The most exceedingly terrible access issues were at retail drug stores, Particularly Walgreens, which had unexpectedly changed strategies subsequent to letting it be known penniless the law by not appropriately observing solutions. The pharmacy chain's new protects hailed dubious patients and forced portion limits.

McKinsey suggested a counterattack. The firm proposed campaigning Walgreens pioneers "to relax." The most daring suggestion was to make an elective

## [L'influence cache]

medication conveyance framework. The arrangement, McKinsey expressed, was to convey OxyContin straightforwardly to patients through mail-request drug stores to evade retail drug store limitations on high-portion, dubious remedies.

Another choice, McKinsey expressed, was to "retaliate" against steps that the DEA, the Branch of Equity, and others were taking to address narcotic abuse. Purdue likewise required an unmistakable procedure to answer compElling gatherings like Doctors for Capable Narcotic Endorsing.

The time had come, McKinsey said, to "turbocharge" Purdue's deals motor.

McKinsey's proposals were generally welcomed by the organization. In any case, Russell Gasdia, Purdue's VP of deals and showcasing, secretly addressed something like one of the ends in an email to Arnab "Arnie" Ghatak at McKinsey. "Arnie, some venting.... I have a few genuine worries with the prospect that our issues place on a need to turbocharge deals."

Ghatak messaged one more McKinsey accomplice and attempted to reassure him about Gasdia's second thoughts. "FYI... think it is simply pressure, will attempt to see him live tmw."

McKinsey actually needed to introduce its turbocharge plan to Purdue's proprietors — Individuals from the Sackler family. After the gathering, Ghatak revealed that the executive gathering "went well overall — the room was loaded up with just family.... We went through show by display for around 2 hrs. They were incredibly strong of the discoveries and our suggestions." Elling concurred: "The discoveries were completely clear to everybody and they gave a ringing underwriting of 'pushing ahead quick.' "

The main focal point from McKinsey's July 2013 investigation was this: while pharmacies and policing were attempting to restrict the amount OxyContin was flowing through the country's circulatory system, McKinsey was doing the exact inverse, in any event, recommending ways of getting around those security measures.

Then, at that point, somewhat more than seven days after McKinsey proposed ways of helping deals of OxyContin, the FDA — the organization most liable for guaranteeing the security of the nation's medication supply — compensated McKinsey with a $2.6 million counseling contract with the Middle for Medication Assessment and Exploration, which manages remedy and conventional medications, including OxyContin. The FDA contract called for McKinsey to "work with the workplace initiative, the program chiefs, and other key staff to configuration, create, and carry out a working Model that guarantees great correspondence both inside and remotely."

Before very long, McKinsey carried out ever-more grounded suggestions to keep the OxyContin pipeline streaming, for example, focusing on the heaviest prescribers, pointedly expanding prescriber visits by agents, utilizing patient promotion gatherings to stand up against endeavors to restrict "suitable" access, speeding up endeavors to set up an elective medication circulation channel, and taking part in significant level discussions with Walgreens.

## [L'influence cache]

"As opposed to tending to the pieces separately," McKinsey expressed, "we prescribe you make moves to 'Turbocharge Purdue's Business Motor' and streamline across all components of the triumphant deals Model — from focusing, to regions, to motivator remuneration." The firm summoned words from the Vietnam War, focusing on the significance of "winning the hearts and brains" of the deals force and forever changing how the organization works. Purdue later rebranded its "turbocharge" crusade, acknowledging it probably won't agree with families that lost youngsters to narcotics. The new name: "Develop to Greatness."

In 2017, McKinsey made an idea that staggered the medical care local area when it later became public. The firm figured Purdue ought to consider giving wholesalers a discount for each OxyContin glut inferable from pills they sold. As an aide, McKinsey assessed the number of clients of these organizations that could go too far. It extended that in 2019, for instance, 2,484 CVS clients would either go too far or create a narcotic use issue. A discount of $14,810 per "occasion" implied that Purdue would pay CVS $36.8 million that year. CVS is likewise quite possibly of McKinsey's greatest client. McKinsey said that Purdue never executed the discount program.

As the ten years came to a nearby, McKinsey reported that it would never again take on narcotic makers as clients. By then, at that point, 400,000 Americans had passed on from mishandling solution or unlawful narcotics. En route, Purdue's proprietors had Eliminated $10 billion from their organization.

Should there be any waiting inquiry regarding the significance of McKinsey's work, one of its accomplices, Maria Gordian, a lead "guide" to the medication organization's CEO, addressed it obviously and strongly in an inner notice she wrote in 2009.

At the point when McKinsey showed up, Gordian made sense of, Purdue was confronting "a shaky and testing circumstance." luckily for the medication organization, McKinsey acted the hero. "Through a progression of endeavors, we got the future of the critical OxyContin Establishment" (italics added).

Dubious she'd put that on her list of qualifications now.

Other humiliating reports surfaced as government specialists shut in, including this email that Elling sent on July 4, 2018, to one more senior accomplice on the Purdue case, Dr. Ghatak: "It likely checks out to have a fast discussion with the gamble council to check whether we ought to do something besides disposing of every one of our records and messages. Suspect not yet as things get harder there somebody would go to us."

"Gratitude for the fair warning," Ghatak answered. "Got it."

"Have an extraordinary fourth," Elling answered.

McKinsey terminated the two men without indicating an explanation, but to say they disregarded the company's proficient norms.

## [L'influence cache]

On February 4, 2021, Kevin Sneader, the association's overseeing accomplice, conveyed a broad notice declaring that McKinsey had arrived at a settlement with 49 state lawyers general. "To be sure, while our past work with narcotic makers was legitimate and never planned to cause damage, we have held ourselves to a higher bar. We missed the mark concerning that bar. We didn't satisfactorily recognize the pandemic unfurling in our networks or the awful effect of narcotic abuse and dependence, and for that I am profoundly grieved."

Sneader made no notice of McKinsey's counseling work for the various connections in the narcotic production network, similar to the retail pharmacies and the significant medication merchants. A portion of those elements wound up paying great many dollars to settle government examinations concerning their treatment of narcotics. The idea of McKinsey's recommendation to these organizations not set in stone.

By August 2021, McKinsey had paid about $641 million to settle claims from states and U.S. domains, however that didn't end the case. A McKinsey legal counselor said at a government trial in California that the firm was confronting fifty extra claims documented by urban communities, regions, local American clans, association medical advantage plans, and schools, among others.

McKinsey likewise set off on a mission to moderate the issues it assisted with making.

In 2018, Tom latkovic, a senior accomplice in Cleveland, co-wrote an article named "Why We Want Bolder Activity to Battle the Narcotic Scourge." latkovic likewise co-created a McKinsey article that offered ten "bits of knowledge" into the narcotic emergency. One cautioned that narcotics are as often as possible recommended to patients "with known or potential gamble factors for misuse."

McKinsey likewise upheld a philanthropic gathering, Shatterproof, committed to finishing the disgrace of chronic drug use. Its organizer, Gary Mendell, whose child committed suicide in the wake of battling with dependence, gives profound talks, including one at a McKinsey medical care gathering, about how the shame of narcotic habit deferred the mission to overcome the pandemic.

latkovic offered a comparable message: "As we've accomplished more work on narcotics, we have come to see the value in the profound and truly detestable job that disgrace plays in the emergency."

latkovic's endeavors to battle the disgrace of chronic drug use were excellent. Yet, an assault on disgrace considers society capable. An assault on narcotic makers, merchants, and doctors is unique: it is awful for business. For a really long time nobody at McKinsey considered freely scrutinizing the firm for assisting Purdue Pharma with selling more narcotics.

McKinsey did, in any case, gloat about making the Middle for Cultural Advantage Through Medical services. The firm stated, "We have respected that mission by serving our clients successfully and putting resources into issues profoundly pertinent to society, like Social determinants of wellbeing, provincial wellbeing,

## [L'influence cache]

maternal wellbeing and conduct wellbeing — including psychological well-being, substance use and the narcotic emergency."

Purdue isn't exclusively to fault for the narcotic pandemic. Specialists overprescribed OxyContin, drug specialists gathered rewards for filling solutions they shouldn't have, the FDA and DEA permitted the scourge to come to fruition, and administrators neglected to authorize regulations to shield people in general.

"We didn't advance beyond it. No one advanced beyond it," the FDA chief, Dr. Scott Gottlieb, said at a clinical meeting in October 2017. The FDA ought to have restricted OxyContin's utilization to just certain patients, however it didn't, nor did it issue solid early admonitions of the medication's high gamble for fixation. The FDA official who drove his organization's survey of OxyContin's medication application accepted a position at Purdue two years subsequent to leaving the FDA.

Dr. Michael Carome, head of Public Resident's Wellbeing Exploration Gathering, said the FDA time after time simply decided "that set the monetary interests of narcotic producers over safeguarding general wellbeing."

A New York Times Title offered this cruel judgment: "As Several Thousands Kicked the bucket, F.D.A. Neglected to Police Narcotics." The organization should supervise a program that necessary the producers of OxyContin and other long-acting narcotics to back the preparation of doctors on their protected use and afterward assess whether the program worked. Be that as it may, the FDA failed, a clinical report closed.

"In any event, when lacks in these endeavors ended up being clear through the F.D.A's. own survey cycle, the office never demanded enhancements to the program, called a gamble assessment and rElief technique, or REMS," The New York Times composed. The senior creator of the review, Caleb Alexander, said he was shocked that "the plan of the program was insufficient all along."

Here again McKinsey's double job as a counselor to the directed and the controller became an integral factor. In 2011, the FDA granted McKinsey a $1.4 million agreement to revamp the workplace directing the defective projects that were the focal point of the review.

Informed that McKinsey had counseled for the FDA while prompting Purdue, Dr. Andrew Kolodny, a senior researcher and co-overseer of narcotic strategy research at Brandeis College, communicated shock. "It is an impossible to miss irreconcilable circumstance," he said in a meeting. "That never ought to have been permitted, never ought to have occurred."

On legislative center Slope, congresspersons wanted to find out whether McKinsey's cozy relationship with the FDA had added to the public authority's inability to perceive and get control over the narcotic pestilence. On August 23, 2021, a bipartisan gathering of six representatives kept in touch with the FDA, getting some information about the organization's broad agreements with McKinsey.

## [L'influence cache]

"While working with the FDA, McKinsey likewise worked for a large number of entertainers in the narcotic business, including a considerable lot of the organizations that assumed a vital part in powering the narcotic pestilence that our nation currently faces," the letter said.

No less than seventeen of the agreements granted to McKinsey by the FDA somewhere in the range of 2008 and 2021 — worth more than $48 million — required the firm to work with the Middle for Medication Assessment and Exploration, the letter said. That division was answerable for endorsing specific medications, including so1ution narcotics.

In 2010 and 2011, the legislators noticed, the FDA had granted more than $2.4 million in agreements to McKinsey to plan a framework called "track and follow" to improve the organization's capacity to recognize drugs destructive to customers. Those agreements "firmly recommend that McKinsey, while addressing the FDA, was effectively captivating with its private-area clients that were the objectives of this new administrative interaction — an undeniable irreconcilable circumstance," the letter said.

McKinsey's connections to government wellbeing authorities went further than the legislators understood. In Walk 2022, New York Times correspondents were the primary co1umnists to get another store of McKinsey records that showed how the firm unobtrusively sought the one who turned into the country's most powerful medical care official, Alex Azar, Trump's secretary of Wellbeing and Human Administrations.

After Azar left Eli lilly, where he filled in as president, he asked McKinsey for guidance in getting a new line of work. His fundamental contact there was, who, alongside Ghatak, was instrumental in encouraging Purdue Pharma to turbocharge OxyContin deals amidst the narcotic plague.

"I'd truly esteem sitting with you folks and talking through thoughts you might have and guidance on the best way to check out and for valuable open doors," Azar told Elling in an email.

Elling answered right away. "We'd very much want to sit and learn of your goals and give any considerations that may be useful."

"Awesome," Azar answered. What precisely was examined when they got together isn't known, yet seven months after their gathering Azar landed the position as HHS secretary.

"Much appreciated folks ," Azar kept in touch with Elling. "Exceptionally thankful for all your assistance. Allow me to find my sense of balance around there and we can visit about the training and association with HHS."

long before Azar's Senate affirmation, a break created in McKinsey's office over what to educate him in a notice concerning the narcotic emergency. Ghatak tried to minimize the risk, in any event, venturing to such an extreme as to say that the words "emergency" and "pestilence" were poetic overstatement, a partner said.

## [L'influence caché]

Tom latkovic, a senior accomplice, needed to fortify the advance notice. "I'm attempting to feature the hornet's home you are entering," he wrote in an inside notice.

With brief period to determine the contention, McKinsey Eliminated an emphatic segment that Ghatak saw as shocking.

A representative for Azar rejected that McKinsey assisted him with landing the HHS position.

While narcotic fixation and deadly goes too far impacted wide areas of society, they fell heaviest on the functioning poor, attempting to get by in rust-belt urban communities where processing plants shut, compensations deteriorated, and occupations were re-appropriated. The pestilence added to the further cracking of the working class while reducing the possibilities of those seeking to go along with it.

In a survey of the book Passings of Sadness and the Fate of Private enterprise, Atul Gawande composed that the writers, two Princeton financial experts, investigated a vexing inquiry: why such countless Individuals from the regular workers without higher educations were kicking the bucket from medication and liquor misuse or self destruction. The numbers had arrived at such a level that future in the US overall dropped three years straight.

Narcotics assumed a part, however as Gawande noticed, they didn't make the circumstances that generated the misery.

We as a whole yet load the weapons of implosion for Individuals in wretchedness. The U.S. has... embraced robotization and Globalization with more prominent energetic willingness and less limitations than different nations have. Dislodged laborers here get generally minimal in the method of assurance and backing. Furthermore, we've empowered money to take a bigger portion of the financial increases.

Gawande composed that the book put numbers "on a long-stewing however undeveloped sense among many Individuals that something had turned out Badly with the Pursuit of happiness."

As narcotic maltreatment tore through America, a considerable lot of its empowering influence s — specialists, merchants, and controllers — were openly uncovered. However for quite a long time one imperative player figured out how to get away from public examination in legislative hearings, books, papers, narratives, and clinical diaries. That player was McKinsey, the consigliere of medical organizations and their controllers, a textual style of business college insight that vowed to rethink the eventual fate of clinical consideration to serve all.

It was only after 2019 that Maura Healey, the Massachusetts head legal officer, uncovered that her office had been digging through the drugmaker's private records and found McKinsey's profound contribution with Purdue. Healey was the primary principal legal officer to sue Purdue's proprietors, and her staff's

## [L'influence cache]

examination of McKinsey drove the way for other state lawyers general to consider the firm responsible.

The states are presently ready to utilize their portions of the $600 million settlement to pay for treatment, counteraction, and recuperation. McKinsey likewise consented to restrict its work with makers of habit-forming opiates and promised to put huge number of pages of records connected with its narcotic work into a public data set.

Regardless of weighty media inclusion of McKinsey's part in stirring up the narcotic plague, numerous administration authorities stay faithful to the firm. In Healey's own state, lead representative Charlie Cook recruited McKinsey to deal with a review into the "fate of work" while McKinsey was paying the state for the damage it caused from narcotics. Healey called the lead representative's choice to recruit McKinsey "absurd."

The Boston Globe revealed that the state's wellbeing division had proactively paid McKinsey more than $18.6 million starting from the start of 2020.

Only hours after The New York Times distributed an article about Healey's discoveries, a confidential discussion channel for present and previous McKinsey laborers enrolled their responses. A few were swearword bound articulations of shock. Others discussed the obligation to serve the client's primary concern inside moral and moral limits. One more composed that it was fine to expand investor esteem "yet not the slightest bit costs, not at the expense of our virtues and our general public's prosperity."

After the Times distributed those reactions, the site was closed down.

## [L'influence cache]

### Section 8

### "Transforming a Coal Mineshaft into a Precious stone"

The loot is plentiful. Accuse your wireless of an ExxonMobil-marked battery. Spread out in the cool Colorado mountain air on a sweeping that folds into its own conveying case, graciousness of the Mount Sinai clinic framework. Get your free Cotopaxi rucksack from the organization whose proverb is "Stuff for Good." Make the world more gorgeous with "wildflower seed bombs" from Standard Businesses, the structure materials organization that established 35 hundred trees to pay tribute to this yearly Celebration of the incredible and the upside. Welcome to the Aspen Thoughts Celebration .

At Aspen, and its Swiss cousin, the World Financial Discussion in Davos, a greeting approves your significance, an acknowledgment that you have something wise to say, that you have a place in the organization of the rich and the strong. Imperatively significant issues get broadcasted here in affable board conversations frequently directed by noticeable writers who treasure the spotlight. Facebook's Imprint Zuckerberg talked there in 2019 to a crowd of people liberated from naysayers blaming him for sabotaging a vote based system.

The year Zuckerberg talked, participants were blessed to receive an occasion by the rapper Normal, who wore a white Shirt decorated with the trademark "let love Triumph ultimately the Final Word." The Aspen Thoughts Celebration is Halfway guaranteed by Paul E. Vocalist, pioneer behind the mutual funds Elliott The board, blessed "the world 's most dreaded financial backer" by Bloomberg News. Another guarantor is ExxonMobil. Tossing leaders, researchers, VIPs, and columnists into a similar room "can produce thoughts equipped for changing our reality," Exxon Mobil spouts.

Sporadically, a blasphemer sneaks through on the rundown of invitees. Such was the situation with the Dutch student of history Rutger Bregman, who broadly pierced the Davos participants in January 2019 for flying many carbon-dioxide-regurgitating personal luxury planes into an occasion "to hear David Attenborough talk about how we're destroying the planet." He immediately turned to the subject of rich Individuals not covering an adequate number of expenses, an issue he believed was vital to tackling a large group of society's concerns in any case, he said, got sparse consideration at Davos. "It seems like I'm at a firemen meeting and nobody's permitted to talk about water."

Bregman wasn't welcomed back in 2020.

McKinsey, another Aspen financier, has no such concern. The company's accomplices are welcomed back a large number of years. It's their night at the Oscars. Institutionally disinclined to exposure, McKinsey sees Aspen and Davos as any open doors for its experts to meet possible clients, flaunt their examination, and play out the unpretentious craft of persuading corporate supervisors and government organizations that they have issues they may not understand. ALso, McKinsey can address them.

## [L'influence cache]

In June 2019, the last pre-Coronavirus meeting of the Aspen Celebration , McKinsey came in force. André Dua, a senior accomplice from the Chicago office, talked about robotization in the work environment. Iareina Yee, the company's central variety official, zeroed in on ladies in senior corporate positions. Michael Chui, a McKinsey World wide Establishment accomplice, emceed a board on innovation and trust.

Then, at that point, there was Dickon Pinner, a senior accomplice and fellow benefactor of McKinsey's manageability practice. He was the principal fascination on a three-part board called "Environment limits: Business Systems to Relieve Financial and Social Dangers."

lean, energetic, and inclined to outlining chats with three list items like so many of his McKinsey partners, Pinner burned through the majority of his profession in the company's semiconductor practice. He likewise was a previous specialist at Shell, the goliath oil and gas organization. Another specialist, a previous McKinsey expert and Oxford researcher, Cameron Hepburn, serves on a warning board for Shell and is a senior exploration individual at an oil-industry-supported think tank. The third speaker, Phil Waldeck, a protection chief, has no obvious foundation in environment studies. However, his organization, Prudential, has a $5 million association with Aspen. In the event that he needed world -evolving thoughts, Waldeck filled in as the Greek melody. "Double tap on that," he'd say to underline a discussion point.

Pinner came furnished with PowerPoint slides outlining carbon dioxide levels and temperature returning 350,000 years. It showed emotional swings, with both moving couple. Then, around quite a while back, the line leveled out. What followed was the blossoming of human civilization, which, he said, "was predicated on environment dependability." Over the most recent 40 years, that security finished, with carbon dioxide levels taking off to levels not found in multiple million years. Indeed, even with the development of sun oriented and wind power, world wide temperatures are set to rise 3 to 4 degrees Celsius (5.4 to 7.2 degrees Fahrenheit) under current approaches.

"We are not on the correct way at the present time," he said.

Pinner was making a relevant and dire case for activity, playing to one of McKinsey's assets — its capacity to measure issues.

Gillian Tett, the Monetary Times columnist directing the meeting, referred to his show as "totally chilling," adding that she would challenge anybody "to simply get out, 'whatever' " and leave.

The world was using up all available time. Months after Pinner's discussion, climbing temperatures and dry spell powered huge out of control fires that crushed pieces of Australia. Then, as the seasons turned, the flames moved toward the Northern Half of the globe, inundating the American West and turning the sky over San Francisco a Martian orange. Multiple million sections of land consumed. The California fires were limited scale contrasted and the hellfires that emitted in Siberia in 2021. It was Russia's greatest fire season ever, consuming a region about the size of Tunisia.

## [L'influence cachée]

With hotter air ready to hold more dampness, tropical storms came to New York City. Focal Park recorded its most hourly precipitation ever between 10:00 p.m. also, 11:00 p.m. on August 21, 2021, a record that was crushed just eleven days after the fact as the leftovers of Typhoon Ida overwhelmed the city. Researchers said that Greenland's kid ice sheet was dissolving so quick it could have passed the final turning point, significance regardless of whether a dangerous atmospheric devation halted, it would keep on liquefying, taking steps to immerse the world's beach front urban communities.

Anybody perusing the blast of critical calls from McKinsey to lessen fossil fuel byproducts could get the feEling that the firm is a Bright Green Organization. It conveys "green groups" in its workplaces across the world, ferreting out ways of diminishing the association's carbon impression, from decreasing paper use to scaling back movement through really videoconferencing. The firm puts resources into activities, for example, sunlight based cookstoves in China and tropical jungle conservation in Panama to balance its outflows. McKinsey even ascertains its own absolute fossil fuel byproducts, which consider the air travel logged by McKinsey's street fighter advisors.

Being green is essential for McKinsey's true mantra, memorialized in its set of principles: "As a firm, we view in a serious way our obligation regarding the natural manageability of our tasks and our workplaces do whatever it may take to diminish our ecological impression. We likewise serve private, public, and Social area clients across the world on advances they are taking to address environmental change."

The message McKinsey needs to pass on is plainly spread out on its site: "We are focused on safeguarding the planet."

McKinsey is an evangElist — out in the open — on the requirement for its clients to make a pressing move on environmental change. In one year, from August 2019 to August 2020, the firm put out no less than 56 reports or messages on the point. Titles included "Earth to President: Your Organization Is Now In danger from Environmental Change," "Maintainability Under the Ocean," and "Design on Environment: Take a gander at How the Style Business Can Desperately Act to Decrease Its Ozone depleting substance Outflows."

Those McKinsey reports don't make light of the emergency. In one slide deck from 2019, McKinsey predicts that environmental change is "expected to be as serious in influence as weapons of mass obliteration."

One explanation McKinsey is so energetic in broad daylight about environmental change is that the large number of youthful, especially knowledgeable, and earth cognizant Individuals it initiates anticipate it. Their kids will probably live into the Following hundred years, while the dissolving ice covers in Greenland and Antarctica could lower numerous seaside urban areas, while the Center East and portions of the Indian subcontinent might turn out to be excessively hot for human home.

McKinsey believes that planned recruits should accept that they are joining an organization that thinks often about the environment. Its web based testing

## [L'influence cache]

framework provokes candidates to pursue the right ecological choices in a virtual experience. "You are the guardian of an Island where plants and creatures reside in different assorted environments" was one late situation. The test taker is then entrusted with building a solid coral reef and tracking down the right immunization to fix a group of birds from a "revolting infection."

In its numerous public reports, McKinsey is clear -looked at and suitably scaremonger about the approaching natural danger. In 2020, the year after Pinner's appearance in Aspen, he co-wrote a McKinsey Quarterly article that spread out the manners in which the world could restrict the world wide temperature climb to 1.5 degrees Celsius above preindustrial levels. That is the level set by the UN's Intergovernmental Board on Environmental Change, past which, the board closed, it will turn out to be progressively challenging for people to adjust.

Pinner and his associates contended that the world was using up all available time to arrive at that objective, and delineated three situations on the best way to arrive, all requiring decreases in discharges from the oil and gas industry, electric utilities, agribusiness, and the tailpipes of vehicles and trucks.

"Fortunately a 1.5-degree pathway is in fact feasible," the McKinsey specialists composed. "The awful news is that the math is overwhelming. Such a pathway would require sensational outflows decreases over the course of the Following decade — beginning at this point."

What organizations can't do, McKinsey expresses, is to take part in advertising, zeroing in on "warm hearted drives" without truly changing the way of behaving of an organization, from environmental change to tutoring ladies and minorities. "Our test to our clients is: how might you go from words on a page to realities on the ground? How would you move from marking and trademarks to something lived in the everyday?"

That was the test Gillian Tett, the mediator in Aspen, presented to Pinner. Given the criticalness of the emergency, she posed a sensible inquiry: "Have you attempted to take this to Washington? Have you attempted to take it to the White House?"

Pinner said no, rehashing the line McKinsey uses to legitimize working with disputable clients like ICE and the Saudi government.

"I think according to our perspective, we don't actually play a part to play on the strategy side," Pinner said. "Where we want to add esteem is by changing over the science into numbers that uncover the gamble and put them in a structure that chiefs can decide." Furthermore, he suggested, government wasn't the response. "We think the large issue here is around capital arrangement and allotment," he added.

That was Pinner's large concentration: to show how markets weren't as expected representing the gamble of putting resources into seaward oil apparatuses, pipelines, and, surprisingly, beach front land in Florida, resources sure to endure a

## [L'influence cache]

top dog as temperatures and ocean levels rose and the world created some distance from non-renewable energy sources.

When squeezed at the board for something — anything — he would be happy with prescribing to strategy creators, the furthest he would go was this idea: "How should you boost the confidential area to divert capital streams into resources that are safer." He wasn't requesting explicit arrangements that could influence oil or Coal creation yet rather calling for business sectors to some way or another do something amazing.

Regardless of Aspen's grand yearnings, the "arrangements" that generally arise have a typical topic: they include practically no penance from the world's tycoons or huge partnerships. ALL things considered, they center around the confidential area "doing great by accomplishing something useful" — with little measures to resolve squeezing issues that frequently call for aggregate activity. It's great PR.

That is the investigate presented by Anand Giridharadas, a previous McKinsey specialist and a previous Aspen individual. In a 2015 discourse to his kindred colleagues, he scrutinized the whole reason of the association, saying it causes the rich and strong to have an idealistic outlook on the gradual great deeds their organizations do under the standard of "corporate Social obligation" while their center organizations keep on incurring hurt.

Giridharadas referred to it as "the Aspen Agreement," a conviction that "the champs of our age should be tested to do all the more great." Yet there was a proviso, he said. "Never at any point advise them to cause less damage. The Aspen Agreement holds that private enterprise's harsh edges should be sanded down and its overflow organic product shared, yet the basic framework should never be addressed."

Take ExxonMobil. At the 2019 Aspen gathering, Vijay Swarup, the oil organization's head of innovative work, praised the excellencies of "carbon catch," an innovation that can siphon smokestack discharges once more into the ground. ExxonMobil said it was "all the buzz." Yet ExxonMobil had been humming about carbon catch for over 10 years by this point, and the innovation stayed buried in the pilot stage. Yet, carbon catch never really addresses ExxonMobil's greatest commitment to an unnatural weather change, specifically the huge number of vehicles and trucks all over the planet consuming its fuel. Months before he spoke, Exxon Mobil estimate that its outflows by 2025 would be 17% higher than in 2017, adding 21 million tons yearly of carbon to the climate, about what Greece emanates every year. The organization stayed quiet.

Three weeks after Pinner talked in Aspen, the leaving McKinsey partner Erik Edstrom targeted the "vibe great drives" that organizations use to give the presence of being earth centered without going to the excruciating lengths important to have an effect, as a matter of fact. However, the focal point of his rage wasn't an oil organization, or a Coal excavator, or an automaker: it was McKinsey itself.

In numerous ways, Edstrom fits the profile of an ideal McKinsey employ. In the same way as other of the company's specialists, he is a tactical veteran, having

*[L'influence cache]*

driven a U.S. Armed force detachment in Afghanistan and served on the ceremonial group at Arlington Public Burial ground. In an organization that values actual ability, he was among the fittest of all — a marathon runner and, at West Point, the top scorer in the military's actual wellness test. After the military, he went to Oxford, institute of matriculation to a large number of McKinsey's top chiefs.

However, Edstrom's time in Afghanistan drew out one more side of him, one that scrutinized the insight of the senior military and regular citizen pioneers who saved America in a battle for an age: a conflict that carried untold enduring to Afghan regular citizens and killed or injured a huge number of American fighters. "On the off chance that a thousand years of the dead could speak: no selling out more cozy than is being shipped off kill or pass on for no good reason, by your own comrades," Edstrom wrote in a book about his conflict insight.

While in the military, Edstrom was impacted by the previous VP AL Carnage's mission to bring issues to light about man-made environmental change, covered by the 2006 Oscar-winning narrative, A Badly arranged Truth. He maintained that his expert life should zero in on assisting with taking care of this existential issue. At Oxford, Edstrom procured an expert's in natural change and the board, as well as getting a MBA. Edstrom at last got comfortable Melbourne, turning out first for Boston Counseling Gathering and afterward, beginning in mid 2018, for McKinsey.

like every new partner, Edstrom was given two books. One was Marvin Grove's Viewpoint on McKinsey, written in 1979, which explains fundamental beliefs and rules that formed McKinsey. The other was A Background marked by the Firm, a clear interior organization history.

From the set of experiences book, Edstrom discovered that McKinsey owed a lot of its prosperity to counseling for Petroleum product organizations.

Mobil Oil was McKinsey's first super client in the mid 1950s, when it likewise served Association Oil and Sun Oil. During the 1950s, at the proposal of Texaco, McKinsey took on work with Imperial Dutch Shell, first in Venezuela in 1956. Shell was so satisfied with McKinsey that the next year it requested that the firm direct a world wide rebuilding, assisting McKinsey with establishing roots on the European mainland, as indicated by the company's true history. By 1960, Texaco was McKinsey's greatest client.

McKinsey then took on work with government-possessed oil monsters like Pemex in Mexico, PDVSA in Venezuela, and Saudi Aramco. Coal-mining clients likewise came from the beginning. At the point when the firm opened its office in Melbourne in 1963, the spot Edstrom would work the greater part a century after the fact, among its most memorable clients was Broken Slope, presently BHP, the world's biggest mining organization by market capitalization, which mined Coal in Australia. The top of the Melbourne office during the 1960s, Bar Carnegie, proceeded to head the Australian part of Rio Tinto, presently the second-greatest mining organization. The two organizations are McKinsey clients right up 'til now, and a large number of Edstrom's partners in Melbourne were dealing with those records.

## [L'influence cache]

McKinsey's initial work with oil organizations needs authentic setting. The information that rising carbon dioxide levels can warm the air was not well known during the 1950s, when Mobil and Texaco were driving the association's incomes. In any case, very much like with tobacco, any turn out finished for Petroleum derivative organizations throughout the past 25 year by the exceptionally taught unit of McKinsey experts was finished with the full information that the item their client sold was hopelessly hurting the world.

Despite the fact that Edstrom had expected to take care of on ecological problems, that demonstrated troublesome in Australia, where huge, politically powerful mining organizations have turned the nation, and Indonesia, into the world's two greatest exporters of Coal. In an asset ruled society, where per capita fossil fuel byproducts surpass even American levels, there wasn't a lot of interest for generously compensated natural specialists. At BCG and afterward McKinsey, Edstrom prompted a confidential value organization, a bank, a telecom supplier, a brew advertiser, and a childcare organization. He likewise read up jail bed the executives for the Australian territory of New South Grains.

While natural work was scant, Edstrom before long found that there was work galore in the Coal business, and in spite of the association's public line that it was "focused on safeguarding the planet," McKinsey invested heavily in aiding Coal organizations become more beneficial.

At some point, the Australia office sent around an email with a joined video. The Title: "What we do matters: See a motivating client influence story."

Edstrom clicked play, and a slide sprung up named "Transforming a Coal mineshaft into a precious stone in a Half year." Set to enthusiastic music, the video, since brought down, depicts a new McKinsey work for what had all the earmarks of being an Asian client that brought about a Coal mineshaft expanding creation by 26%, he said. Notwithstanding the world wide environment emergency, in spite of the way that consuming Coal for power contributes almost 33% of energy-related fossil fuel byproducts, somebody at McKinsey thought this work was commendable.

This was "perhaps of the most productive task in our organization," the top of the Coal-mining organization said on the video cut, as per Edstrom.

Mark Shahinian had a comparable encounter. like Edstrom, he had a postgraduate education in natural science and expected to tackle those abilities at McKinsey. He worked out of the Boston office, ascending to turn into a commitment director — the mid-level supervisors who play out a job likened to a unit sergeant in the military.

Shahinian is pleased with the naturally engaged work he did at McKinsey, Particularly a persuasive learn about how the cost of lithium-particle batteries — the sort that power electric vehicles — was set to decisively drop. Yet, he said, McKinsey and its rivals rely upon huge world wide organizations doing projects that keep going for years or many years. Oil organizations fit that bill. Sun oriented gear new businesses by and large don't, and there simply wasn't that much work for him in efficient power energy. McKinsey follows the cash.

## [L'influence cache]

McKinsey says it is working with its clients all over the planet to "address environmental change," yet starting around 2020 there was no efficient power energy organization among any of its greatest clients, however it exhorts sans carbon electric utilities like Mercury in New Zealand, and ALbemarle, which mines lithium, the vital part in batteries. Vestas, a breeze power organization, is likewise a client, yet little contrasted and the large oil and Coal organizations.

"They can't concoct billable hours that don't exist," Shahinian said of McKinsey. In any case, there are billable hours at the huge oil, gas, and Coal organizations, work that offers open doors for junior advisors to propel their vocations.

Australia is one of a handful of the created nations that is effectively wanting to open new Coal mineshafts, Particularly in the tremendous Galilee Bowl in the northeastern territory of Queensland. A partner accomplice welcomed Edstrom to deal with a Coal project in Queensland, yet he declined, with regards to the McKinsey strategy that permitted specialists to turn down tasks assuming that they had moral second thoughts. In any case, in passing on the task, Edstrom lost an opportunity to construct attaches with ranking directors, and that at last prompted additional time "near the ocean," McKinsey-represent an expert with no client work.

Edstrom accepted the strategy of allowing specialists to quit projects on moral grounds was a cop-out, liberating McKinsey in general from standing firm.

In the event that he was unable to work in his picked field, basically Edstrom could bring issues to light among his partners of the approaching environment danger. He joined the "Green Group," where specialists around Australia examined ecological issues, and searched for ways of impacting the executives' reasoning regarding the matter.

On a corporate retreat to the Incomparable Obstruction Reef, he and his kindred experts saw firsthand the desolates of rising carbon dioxide levels. "It was ceasing to exist staggeringly quick," Edstrom said. "It seemed to be the ashy logs from an extra pit fire." Inside, the Green Group raised the likElihood that the withering reef was expected, to some degree, to McKinsey's support of Petroleum derivative clients. "Yet, that message failed to receive any notice. After the excursion, Individuals returned to their ordinary client work, including working for Coal mineshafts with unsurprising results for the climate."

Edstrom examined his bosses regarding the distinction between McKinsey's public explanations about controlling fossil fuel byproducts and its work with Coal organizations. Accordingly, he was told, "In the event that we don't serve Coal clients, BCG [Boston Counseling Group] will."

Edstrom was turning out to be progressively baffled. The mental disharmony came from client function as well as at corporate get-togethers, for example, the 2018 Australia Values Day, held in the leader meeting rooms ignoring Sydney's head horse-racing track.

After the standard motivational speeches and the corporate holding games, for example, a putt golf contest on a course produced using durable food (gave to the

## [L'influence cache]

poor, obviously), the specialists were blessed to receive the night's diversion — McKinsey's own Australia-based band, the Marvins, named after the company's unbElievable true pioneer, Marvin Nook, renowned for placing the company's advantages over his own.

For a band named after such a compelled by a sense of conviction and closefisted man, the center Individuals from the Marvins — an accomplice and two senior accomplices, moguls many times over — decided to play a surprising arrangement of melodies. There was "Ordinary citizens," a 1995 hit by the English band Mash, about a rich young lady who needed to encounter life among Britain's regular workers.

> You won't ever live like average folks
>
> You won't ever do anything that average citizens do
>
> Never bomb like commoners.

Then, at that point, there was "Killing in the Name" by the elective metal gathering Fury Against the Machine, sung by a band comprised of the whitest of white-shoe counseling firms, whose accomplices consistently cycle all through government. The tune closes with this line: "Screw you, I will not do everything that you say to me" (rehashed multiple times) trailed by a "Mother lover."

The next year, the Australian office's Qualities Day went down market — part of an extensive response to the 2018 New York Times report on McKinsey's luxurious corporate retreat in western China, only miles from a rambling detainment place lodging Uyghur Muslims. In light of far and wide analysis, McKinsey had said the firm "would be more smart about such decisions later on." In 2019, the accomplices' discourses were weighty on values and morals. Be that as it may, after the Australia overseeing accomplice, John lydon, had gotten done with talking about how, at the very least, McKinsey didn't serve clients who hurt Individuals or conned clients, Edstrom felt he needed to stand up. Somebody gave him the amplifier.

Consider the possibility that, Edstrom asked, McKinsey served arms creators who made weapons used to bomb the nation of origin of other McKinsey experts. Was that with regards to the organization's qualities?

Before long thereafter, his position at McKinsey reached a conclusion. His absence of good tasks — exacerbated by his turning down the Coal project — added to a terrible showing survey. He was, as McKinsey puts it, "guided to leave." He thinks his frankness was likewise a variable.

Not long before he was approached to leave, Edstrom at last accomplished get to deal with an ecologically engaged project. It was for the New Zealand electric utilty Mercury, which utilizes just efficient power energy. Assisting the organization with holding clients and get new ones was fruitful and fulfilling. In any case, by then, at that point, his destiny was fixed.

## [L'influence cache]

As he was going out the entryway in mid-July 2019 — three weeks after Pinner talked at Aspen — Edstrom conveyed what became the mother of all goodbye messages. It deflected around McKinsey workplaces across the globe.

There's the same old thing about a representative, at McKinsey or any organization, sending around an email after leaving. An epistolary structure seldom cuts off ties. At McKinsey that is doubly in this way, on the grounds that a McKinsey specialist never truly leaves the firm. The imposing graduated class organization, systematized at McKinsey, keeps Individuals fastened to the firm for a really long time after they leave, with messages, reunions, and, generally significant, work possibilities. Stand in opposition to the firm and you risk being cut off from a long period of systems administration open doors.

That is precisely exact thing occurred with Edstrom.

A couple of sections into his email, it was clear Edstrom wasn't staying on track of offering thanks for the distinction of working at McKinsey and trouble at the possibility of leaving it. Thus, after momentarily expressing gratitude toward a few partners, his email took a sharp turn, striking at the core of McKinsey's moral Establishment — its qualities.

"My brief time frame at the Firm," he expressed, "has shown me how much effect McKinsey can accomplish in a short measure of time. I'm massively pleased with having had a tiny impact in that. In any case, making influence is certainly not a flat out great." And accomplishing great work, he added, doesn't compare to accomplishing something useful. "I trust it's the ideal opportunity for McKinsey to make a point of reference setting move around client choice. As an association, McKinsey appears to jabber about values and standards without taking an esteemed or principled represent quite a bit of anything."

Then, to ensure his message wasn't lost, he utilized words seldom coordinated at McKinsey's chiefs. "To me McKinsey is a flippant foundation." He said McKinsey consistently took on clients who carried mischief to other people. "There are many situations where I trust this makes weakness society, McKinsey's standing, and the planet."

Edstrom targeted two areas specifically, McKinsey's work with the military, the focal point of his Qualities Day evaluate, and its work with Coal-mining organizations. "Coal kills," Edstrom composed. "The more drawn out Coal organizations stay operating at a profit, the more unsalvageable harm will be finished to the climate."

Yet, that is precisely exact thing McKinsey was accomplishing for its many Coal clients, he composed, making them more effective and beneficial, putting off the day when the market influence s depicted by Pinner would at long last shut them of down. A lot of organizations are "flippant," he said, yet McKinsey's irreverence doesn't simply influence itself. As the world's most compElling counseling firm, it shapes the acts of thousands of clients.

"There is a usually involved express for two-faced eco-promoting used to cause a business or item to show up more 'reasonable' than it really is: 'greenwashing.' "

## [L'influence cache]

Edstrom referred to the case of McKinsey helping creation at a territorial Coal organization by 26%. As verification, he joined a connection to the video. A little gathering of McKinsey specialists were empowering this single client — not distinguished in the video — to supply the world with Coal that would add megatons of carbon dioxide.

"Consider it," he proceeded. "Is there a more regrettable client to serve than those straightforwardly liable for putting us on the inconceivable quick track to planetary omnicide?"

In the hours after he sent the email, many McKinsey specialists from around the world composed back to him. One partner, likewise in Australia, said that when he had protested working with a Coal client, he was told "it was alright, there were a lot of different partners who might finish the work."

One more expressed, "Time and again we become reso1utely visually impaired for mental soundness, yet over the long run that is not alright." Still another: "Everything being equal I really do think we have a great deal of reflection to do."

Edstrom wasn't the main McKinsey expert in Australia standing firm on the climate. A couple of years sooner, a few specialists had left a task with a Canadian gold-mining organization in neighboring Papua New Guinea that for quite a long time had been the focal point of protests in light of the fact that the mine unloaded its waste, or tailings, straightforwardly into waterways, one previous McKinsey representative said.

Since McKinsey savagely monitors its insider facts, even inside, Edstrom didn't have the foggiest idea about the genuine degree of McKinsey's work with the world's greatest polluters. In the association's almost century of presence, no journalist has gotten admittance to McKinsey's client list. Be that as it may, throughout announcing this book, we have.

For a firm "dedicated to safeguarding the planet," McKinsey counts no less than seventeen mining and Petroleum derivative organizations among its greatest clients. By and large, those clients acquired McKinsey countless dollars as of late, as per interior records.

Starting around 2010, McKinsey has worked for something like 43 of the hundred organizations that have siphoned the most carbon dioxide into the environment beginning around 1965, in view of a rundown of polluters gathered by the Environment Responsibility Establishment, a charity that brings issues to light about how partnerships are adding to environmental change. Those 43 organizations, while representing the clients who utilize their items, were answerable for in excess of 36% of the planet's ozone depleting substance outflows from non-renewable energy sources in 2018.

Number three on the noteworthy polluter list, Chevron, quite possibly of McKinsey's greatest client, created no less than $50 million in counseling charges in 2019. Saudi Aramco, number one on the rundown, has been a McKinsey client since basically the 1970s.

## [L'influence cache]

During that 50 years, Chevron's all out discharges came to 43.7 gigatons (43 billion tons) of carbon dioxide. In 2019, energy-related outflows for the whole planet added up to around 33 gigatons, as per the World wide Energy Organization.

Other top McKinsey non-renewable energy source clients incorporate ExxonMobil, BP, Imperial Dutch Shell, Russia's Gazprom, and Qatar Petrol.

Assuming that McKinsey was encouraging these organizations on the best way to lessen their fossil fuel byproducts, the work would mirror McKinsey's corporate qualities. However, that doesn't necessarily have all the earmarks of being the situation. Undertakings, or "studies," that McKinsey has as of late finished for Chevron demonstrate that diminishing fossil fuel byproducts was not the focal point of its work. There was, for instance, the "Upstream Oil and Gas — Computerized Guide." The greatest undertaking fixated on a "item arrangement" for Chevron's Mid-landmass Specialty Unit, a district enveloping oil-creating regions in the southern US, remembering the Permian Bowl for Texas, where Chevron is the top maker.

A case can be made that oil organizations like Chevron need the shrewd unit of McKinsey experts to direct them through an existential danger to their plan of action: the world wide push to create some distance from non-renewable energy sources. BP and Shell, for instance, are scrambling to grow their perfect energy organizations.

So with a multitude of McKinsey advisors prompting them on procedure, what approach did Chevron pick? Drill, child, Drill.

In July 2020, similarly as the world wide pandemic was obliterating interest for Chevron's fuel, the organization's President, Mike Wirth, addressing the Texas Oil and Gas Affiliation, said that the world wide push for clean energy "doesn't spell almost certain doom for oil and gas," Bloomberg Businessweek announced. Wirth said that Chevron would "track down ways of making oil and gas more proficient, all the more earth harmless."

The differentiation with the European oil organizations couldn't be more sensational. Half a month after Wirth's comments, BP said it would diminish oil and gas creation by 40% in 10 years. BP and Shell have sliced their profits to help pay for their progress away from Petroleum products.

As of mid 2022, McKinsey said it had attempted multiple thousand "manageability commitment" with clients. One Model McKinsey referred to was helping a "significant energy supplier" that it didn't distinguish cut its carbon dioxide outflows by 82%.

However as of late, McKinsey kept on getting new Petroleum product clients, making them more beneficial and more proficient at extricating carbon from the beginning.

## [L'influence cache]

Similarly as Edstrom was expressing farewell to his partners in Melbourne, McKinsey specialists in Canada were documenting into the corporate central command of a major new client: a Vancouver-based Coal-mining organization.

The Elk Stream goes through the flawless wild of the Canadian Rockies as it winds its direction south. Upriver, somewhere down in the mountains close to the English Columbia-ALberta line, the untrampled landscape gives way to what looks like a disaster area. A portion of the taking off tops have been impacted away, filling the encompassing valleys.

This is the Greenhills Mine, one of the top-creating Coal mineshafts of Teck Assets, the greatest maker in North America of metallurgical, or coking, Coal. Steel factories utilize this Coal in shoot heaters to Eliminate the oxygen from iron mineral, delivering the metal used to make steel yet additionally creating huge amounts of carbon dioxide, to such an extent that steelmaking represents around 7% of the world's ozone depleting substance discharges.

Teck, one of the world's greatest exporters of steelmaking Coal, sells quite a bit of what it mines to Asian clients. What might be compared to around one-10th of Canada's complete carbon dioxide outflows that year.

The open-pit mining strategy at Greenhills, much the same as the mountain ridge evacuation mining in the Appalachians, uncovers normally happening poisons, for example, selenium, which saturates the upper Fording Waterway, part of the Elk Stream watershed. Researchers say the spillover is killing and distorting fish downstream as far south as the Montana line and debasing drinking water, as indicated by a 2019 article distributed by the Yale School of the Climate. At high focuses, selenium can cause sickness, weakness, skin sores, and neurological problems in people.

In the fall of 2018, Teck got another administrator, conceivably the most noticeable Canadian in world wide business: Dominic Barton, who until July of that year filled in as overseeing accomplice of McKinsey, where he promoted the company's green accreditations. Preceding Barton joined Teck, McKinsey seemed to do almost no work for the organization, as indicated by inner records. After Barton became administrator, that changed. In 2019, McKinsey, by one interior measure, took in about $20 million in expenses from Teck, making the Coal organization perhaps of McKinsey's greatest client.

A survey of work McKinsey accomplished for Teck secured one position that zeroed in on "Coal Handling Streamlining" at the Greenhills mine. One more was "Pit-to-Port Model and Focal Help." Another McKinsey project took a subtle approach with close to nothing: "Drill and Impact."

Following a year at work at Teck, Barton was designated Canada's representative to China, which delivers Half of the world's steel, and with it critical contamination. A portion of that steel is made with Teck Coal. China's sovereign abundance store claims Teck stock, and a previous senior Chinese representative sits on its top managerial staff. Teck says it is expecting to be carbon unbiased by 2050.

## [L'influence cachée]

Barton left Teck, however McKinsey specialists remained and kept on gathering a huge number of dollars in charges.

In 2021, as the world economy recuperated from the Coronavirus actuated stoppage, fossil fuel byproducts returned quickly too. The main polluter, producing in excess of a fourth of the world's aggregate, was China. The organizers in Beijing animated the economy by stirring up a development blast, prompting huge expansions in steel creation and power age, both exceptionally Coal escalated.

In China, McKinsey was educating some with respect to its greatest steelmakers, hungry for coking Coal from its huge Canadian client, Teck. Among the company's client program, Hebei Jinxi Steel, the state-possessed Shandong Steel, and Shanxi liheng Iron and Steel. The firm as of late has likewise prompted the two greatest oil organizations, China Public Petrol Enterprise and Sinopec, and in August 2019 McKinsey introduced a report to the leading body of the third greatest, CNOOC.

A large part of the Coal fuEling Chinese industry came from Southeast Asia, where McKinsey was working with a portion of the locale's greatest Coal-mining organizations. One of the association's significant clients lately was Banpu, a Thai energy organization with mines across the locale.

In Indonesia, the world's second-greatest Coal exporter after Australia, McKinsey has as of late counted two significant Coal excavators as clients, and the firm likewise works with PT Pertamina, Indonesia's second-greatest oil maker.

The work, in conflict with McKinsey's public assertions on the desperation of fighting environmental change, addresses the idea of the actual firm: at McKinsey, the senior accomplices, dissipated across the globe, have given orders on business in their space.

By 2021, Dickon Pinner's postulation on the enchantment of the market cutting contamination, contended so powerfully at Aspen two years and more than sixty gigatons of ozone depleting substance discharges prior, was demonstrating horribly insufficient. American Coal trades, both for power plants and for steel heaters, were taking off. So too were Coal costs, which dramatically increased from August 2020 to August 2021.

McKinsey's own Coal nobles — the accomplices directing work in the business — were not just compensated; they were commended. In Indonesia, Vishal Agarwal won an advancement to senior accomplice. An interior declaration for the World wide Energy and Materials group respecting him accompanied a realistic that seemed to riff off the Stranger TV series. Agarwal was the "Outstander."

"Vishal the Incomparable, the account of the pioneer that transforms Jewe1 enterprises in Indonesia into the heroes that take on the world," it read.

Behind the scenes of the realistic — eating into a mountainside — an open-pit mine.

## [L'influence cache]

Outrage and dissatisfaction were mounting among McKinsey's majority, more youthful experts confronting a long period of progressively critical environment calamities. Among 465 Individuals answering an inside review on need issues for McKinsey to address, 369 named "environmental change and fossil fuel byproducts," by a wide margin the a large portion of any issue. Interestingly, just 79 picked "remuneration and advantages."

On Walk 23, 2021, a gathering of around twelve junior and mid-level specialists sent an open letter to the company's initiative. A few Individuals from the gathering had perused Erik Edstrom's 2019 goodbye note and were motivated by it. Their letter based on a portion of his thoughts, taking it to another level.

"The environment emergency is the characterizing issue of our age," they composed. "Our positive effect in different domains will amount to nothing on the off chance that we don't go about as our clients adjust the earth unalterably."

The gathering cautioned that McKinsey's proceeded with work to assist polluters with benefitting "presents serious gamble to our standing, our client connections," and the association's capacity to draw in gifted Individuals. "For quite some time, we have been advising the world to be striking and adjust to a 1.5C outflows pathway; it is very much past due that we take our own recommendation," they composed.

The gathering expressed that by 2030 McKinsey ought to Eliminate all the carbon the firm has transmitted since its establishing in 1926, by purchasing carbon balances. Significantly more significant, the gathering said McKinsey ought to reveal data regarding its clients' complete outflows, push its clients to line up with the UN's all's pathway of 1.5 degrees Celsius, and utilize the company's standing and impact "to meet wide alliances and guide the dEliberate progress from a carbon-driven economy."

In something like two weeks, in excess of eleven hundred McKinsey workers had marked the letter. Pinner and one more senior accomplice, Daniel Pacthod, the co-heads of McKinsey's manageability practice, set up a call with the letter essayists.

Pinner was thoughtful. He upheld finishing McKinsey's work with Coal organizations, in any case, given the association's strong provincial senior accomplices, he had minimal possibility redirecting the firm. "Without senior accomplices from the Center East, focal Asia, Africa, Australia, and South America this discussion is disproportionate," one of the members on the call said.

Pacthod said, "We must be practical, I mean, we're not a charity."

Pinner had one, earnest solicitation: "Kindly don't take this to The New York Times, we are so close."

Fourteen days after the letter emerged, Sneader and his Recently chosen replacement, Bounce Sternfels, answered, let the gathering know that they "share your view that the environment issue is the characterizing issue for our planet and

## [L'influence cache]

all ages" and planning an "ask me anything" organization meeting on the point for Earth Day, April 22, 2021.

Two days before Earth Day, McKinsey declared the development of "McKinsey Maintainability," a stage expected to assist its clients with meeting the objective of slicing the world's fossil fuel byproducts down the middle by 2030 and accomplish net zero discharges by 2050. "Our point is to be the biggest confidential area impetus for decarbonization," Sneader said.

The Earth Day talk by the association's chiefs repeated that thought. Sneader, then, at that point, actually heading the firm, and Sternfels, joined by a couple of other senior accomplices, including Pinner and Pacthod, responded to questions. The message from the company's initiative was obtuse: McKinsey would keep on serving the enormous polluters since, they said, the firm couldn't assist them with decarbonizing on the off chance that they didn't have a relationship. "How could we not serve Petroleum product clients in the event that we will be applicable?" There was no obligation to public revelation of McKinsey's work with polluters. It was a key interest. Without exposure, McKinsey "had permit to drag out environmental change since they can take cover in the background of classification," the member said.

After two months, on June 30, a gigantic fire destroyed to the town of lytton in English Columbia. The other day, the temperature flooded to 121 degrees Fahrenheit, breaking Canada's intensity record and outperforming the untouched high temperature in Las Vegas.

Half a month after the fact, Sreevatsa Praveen, a mid-level McKinsey expert in Dubai, put out a call for help. An Asian power organization was intending to fabricate a 800-megawatt Coal-terminated power plant and was searching for project workers to supply gear, like boilers and coolant frameworks. Might anybody at any point share a few contacts?

Rizwan Naveed, a mid-level McKinsey expert who assisted with drafting the environment letter, set free in a goodbye email to partners on the yawning hole between what McKinsey was talking about openly and how it was doing clients, all under the shroud of secrecy. "Simply perusing our own distributing on the point clarifies that by proceeding to assist our most contaminating clients with extending discharges unabated, we are active supporting and abetting the annihilation of our current circumstance," he composed.

"Any world wide discussion about maintainability at McKinsey that doesn't represent our work with polluters adds up to greenwashing, with our supportability clients, partners, and their effect being utilized as the cleanser," he wrote in the email, dated July 30, 2021.

Naveed, who noticed that his work at McKinsey zeroed in on estimating the discharges of the company's clients, composed of his disappointment that senior accomplices, who tuned in with a thoughtful ear, said the right words regarding checking outflows, then eventually abstained from successfully change McKinsey's work with huge polluters.

## *[L'influence cache]*

In late October 2021, The New York Times distributed a record of the letter and the inner discussion it had started. The compassion senior McKinsey accomplices had shown was for the most part gone: in its place, an unashamed guard of the association's work. Composing his rejoinder in The Money Road Diary, McKinsey's new overseeing accomplice, Sway Sternfels, said, "Organizations can't go from brown to green without getting somewhat messy. What's more, assuming that implies some mud gets tossed at McKinsey, so be it.

"As far as we might be concerned, the case is clear: The greater the player, the greater the potential decreases," he composed. "leaving those that are contributing the most to emanations doesn't propel the reason."

One of the essayists brought up that Sternfels was making a misrepresentation: they were asking not that McKinsey leave these clients yet rather that the firm unveil the complete fossil fuel byproducts from these clients and that it center around assisting them with cutting those discharges. Sternfels didn't address the way that McKinsey made a large number of these organizations browner, not greener, and that they got countless dollars for the firm.

One resigned McKinsey senior accomplice, Carter Bundles, saw things in an unexpected way. In a meeting very nearly three years before the letter was drafted, he foreshadowed their alert over always rising outflows and McKinsey's part in exhorting polluters.

Barely any McKinsey veterans adored the firm more than Parcels, quite possibly of the best expert the organization at any point created. A vigorous traditionalist, Bunches established the company's ecological administration practice. A year prior to his demise in 2019 — his voice desolated by throat disease — Bunches considered McKinsey's choice to exhort significant polluters.

"It's a drawn out horrible thought."

# [L'influence cache]

## Section 9

### Poisonous Obligation

### McKinsey on Money Road

The monetary delayed bomb that would annihilate the American economy was at that point ticking when Chairman Michael Bloomberg and Congressperson Throw Schumer showed up at New York City Corridor on the morning of January 22, 2007. They had come to the Blue Room, standing side by side before an oil representation of Thomas Jefferson, to caution that a lot of unofficial law compromised thriving on Money Road. Both political pioneers had long profited from their relationship with the city's monetary business sectors. As they talked, certain Money Road rehearses were beginning to create Titles — rehearses that would before long cost huge number of families their homes, their positions, their investment funds, and their working class lifestyle.

To put forth their defense, Bloomberg and Schumer introduced a review they had dispatched from McKinsey. Since the 1930s the firm had worked intimately with probably the most weighty forerunners in finance: men like Walter Wriston of Citibank and David Rockefeller of Pursue Manhattan. McKinsey, the highest quality level of the executives counseling, said the economy was compromised by a lot of guideline, not excessively little.

McKinsey cautioned that without changes in approach New York could lose its remaining as the monetary capital of the world . Should that occur, ability and capital would move to Europe — London specifically — and occupations would be lost, with outcomes undulating the country over. "I'm fixated on this issue," Schumer told columnists.

As a matter of fact, guideline of monetary foundations and markets had really facilitated as of late. The Downturn period rules isolating protections firms and business banks — intended to hold loan specialists back from making dangerous ventures with contributors' cash — had been thrown to the side almost 10 years sooner. Monetary business sectors were allowed to try different things with extraordinary new items, producing gigantic benefits. Contract moneylenders could now effectively auction the credits they made, opening up funding to make even more advances. Home advances were packaged, then, at that point, sold and exchanged. This securitization of credit prodded private getting yet had a huge drawback. Since Money Road profoundly wanted to purchase home loans and vehicle credits, particularly higher-yielding subprime credits, advance officials progressively didn't mind whether a borrower was trustworthy.

Pain free income governed the day. FICO scores that should give a beware of untrustworthy loaning rather erroneously guaranteed high-risk venture items as protected. The world's greatest safety net provider, AIG, anxiously sold monetary instruments, called credit default trades, planned to safeguard financial backers against Armageddon misfortunes that its top leaders were persuaded could never come.

## *[L'influence caché]*

As the city chairman and the congressperson spoke, Money Road's change into a monster club still couldn't seem to saturate the public cognizance, however its proof was there for the Individuals who needed to track down it. Home costs in the most sizzling business sectors, similar to California and Nevada, were doing the unbElievable: falling. At 85 Wide Road, a fifteen-minute stroll from city lobby, Goldman Sachs investors were scrambling to decrease the company's openness to what might before long be called poisonous obligation.

However, on this day, Bloomberg and Schumer had different needs, and scrutinizing the monetary business sectors wasn't one of them. Bloomberg, a previous bond broker, became one of the country's most extravagant men by offering monetary data to Money Road. Schumer, as a New York congressperson, addressed not any more remarkable body electorate than the protections business, tapping them for almost a fourth of a billion bucks in crusade gifts for liberals. He upheld an official correction that obstructed the Protections and Trade Commission from directing FICO score organizations. He additionally supported Money Road's solicitation to lessen its subsidizing of the SEC and to permit business banks and venture banks to blend.

By employing McKinsey, Bloomberg and Schumer had chosen a firm talented at exploring Money Road. McKinsey accomplices not just counsel for the greatest banks; they frequently wind up running them. In 2007, McKinsey veterans involved top situations at lehman Siblings, Morgan Stanley, and UBS. McKinsey's previous overseeing accomplice Rajat Gupta had joined the leading group of Goldman Sachs the past November, days in the wake of resigning from the firm.

To show the profundity of its exploration, McKinsey flaunted that its advisors by and by evaluated in excess of fifty Presidents in monetary administrations and overviewed another 300 ranking directors. Work and shopper bunches were additionally reached, however for them no numbers were given.

The firm presumed that Europe was starting "to embrace U.S.- style credit terms," compromising American predominance in the "utilized loaning" and subprime markets. One business pioneer communicated worry that the US was being underestimated in subsidiaries. "The more agreeable and cooperative administrative climate in London specifically makes organizations more agreeable about making new subsidiary items," McKinsey composed.

One brilliant spot: America actually drove the world in securitizing credit, McKinsey said, "yet the seeds of progress are as of now developing" as the idea turned out to be progressively famous in Europe.

The experts suggested debilitating pieces of the Sarbanes-Oxley Demonstration of 2002, a regulation intended to forestall the sort of corporate misrepresentation that brought about the liquidation of Enron, at the time the greatest in U.S. history. Enron's CEO, a previous McKinsey senior accomplice, went to jail for his part in that embarrassment.

## [L'influence cache]

Scarcely a year after Schumer and Bloomberg exhibited the McKinsey report, it vanished. ALso, nobody needed to restore it as Money Road slipped always profoundly into a financial void not experienced since the Economic crisis of the early 20s. News stories, top of the line books, and grant winning narratives have investigated the starting points of this devastating breakdown. The guilty parties are a large number: financiers with a desire for greater benefits, controllers overlooking those they should safeguard, and compromised lawmakers.

These post-mortem examinations only from time to time notice McKinsey.

In its initial years, McKinsey chipped away at the fringe of the monetary framework, doing celebrated middle class snort work. During the Economic crisis of the early 20s, McKinsey procured unassuming expenses from speculation banks by leading what were then called "financiers' investigations," a prerequisite before a bank could endorse bonds for clients. James O. McKinsey saw this direct work — taking a gander at an organization's business, resources, Individuals, and hierarchical design — as key to getting much more business.

Be that as it may, those tasks were never at the center of McKinsey's work, which for quite a bit of its initial history rested solidly with standard American business: organizations like General Engines, U.S. Steel, and Texaco. They could manage the cost of McKinsey's expenses. They were the sorts of clients that produced new work a large number of years. They were the sorts of clients where McKinsey could truly do something worth remembering.

Banks, profoundly directed after their focal job in worsening the Economic crisis of the early 20s, were years from recovering their job as a focal driver in McKinsey's income stream.

American banks were limped by heap state and government regulations that successfully implied that their business finished at state lines. In 1933, another regulation, the Glass-Steagall Act, split business banks and speculation banks. Congress and the new president, Franklin Delano Roosevelt, needed to ensure that frenzies on Money Road at absolutely no point in the future prompted runs on banks the country over. The Government Store Protection Company safeguarded savers' records from bank disappointments. Huge New York City moneylenders like Citibank and Pursue lacked the ability to legitimately open branches in adjoining Westchester Area until 1960.

The banks that endure the Downturn resembled exceptionally managed, exhausting utilities. The joke during those years was that financiers worked on the 3-6-3 rule. Pay investors 3% premium (the public authority controlled loan costs), loan the cash out at 6% (frequently by essentially purchasing Depository bonds), and start by 3:00 p.m. The spread among store and loaning rates ensured that even an ineffectively run bank could turn a little benefit.

With unassuming benefits came humble compensations. In 1980, the most generously compensated broker in the US was Roger Anderson, the executive of Mainland Illinois. He made $710,000 that year, or $2.24 million out of 2021 bucks. In 2021, James P. Gorman, a previous McKinsey senior accomplice who was

## [L'influence cache]

CEO of Morgan Stanley, made $35 million, tied for the best position with David Solomon, the Goldman Sachs President.

This implied that most American banks couldn't advance into the monster enterprises that, in the years after The Second Great War, became trustworthy uber clients for McKinsey. That started to change in the last part of the 1960s. The large cash community banks in New York and Chicago were arising out of their post-Despondency Shell as the world economy kept on blasting, zeroing in on their flourishing corporate clients and pursuing them across the globe.

In 1967, Walter Wriston, the new CEO of New York's Most memorable Public City Bank, reasoned that his Establishment — also called Citibank — had grown out of its old association. He asked his dear companion the administration master Peter Drucker what he ought to do. Drucker said he ought to employ McKinsey, and he did precisely that.

The advisors suggested revamping the bank around business areas, as corporate or retail banking. The McKinsey accomplice Dick Neuschel cautioned Wriston the change would turn the bank's staff against one another. "You don't have the guts to do that," Neuschel said. At any rate, wriston believed that was an unusual and irritating attempt to sell something, yet recruited McKinsey. The day the McKinsey men strolled through the entryways of Citibank at 399 Park Road, the times of the 3-6-3 rule had actually finished.

On Christmas Eve 1968, Citibank began carrying out the McKinsey plan. Fifteen months really taking shape, it coordinated the bank into utilitarian instead of geographic lines, with new divisions for enormous corporate records, little and medium-sized organizations, and retail clients.

The framework was classified "lattice the executives," and Drucker compared it to "attempting to play b-ball, tennis, and soccer on similar court with similar Individuals simultaneously," the financial columnist Phillip Zweig wrote in his 1995 memoir of Wriston.

The thought was to decentralize navigation, much as GE and GM had proactively finished with assistance from McKinsey. In financial that implied empowering lower-level brokers to make greater advances. The objective: to guarantee that Citi's corporate clients were served by financiers who grasped their businesses, not by generalists who dealt with a different arrangement of clients. In a complex hierarchical construction, it seemed OK to sanely convey the bank's assets where and when they were required. As Wriston put it, Citibank needed to have a framework where "when you really want the clarinet player, he's there. In any case, you can't have a clarinet player in 100 nations, so you devise a lattice."

One of the impacts, Zweig composes, is that the McKinsey plan, joined by Wriston's forceful income development focuses for every one of the bank's benefit places, dehumanized the organization.

"Before the progressions that Wriston created, workers felt an affirmation, inferred in the event that not composed, that assuming they performed well, they wouldn't need to stress over their next work."

## [L'influence cache]

Yet, estimated exclusively by benefit development, McKinsey's work was a triumph. In 1972, Citibank, with its McKinsey-planned hierarchical construction, surpassed Bank of America as the most productive American moneylender. McKinsey was before long offering grid the board to banks the nation over, including to David Rockefeller's Pursuit, Wriston's archrival. Wriston terminated McKinsey. He kept the grid.

By the 1970s the financial business was awakening from its agreeable sleep. Wriston's adversaries yearned to match his 15% focuses for yearly benefit development. In any case, to do that, they expected to revamp, declining loaning choices to war zone lieutenants who knew their businesses. Banks the nation over followed the lead of Citi and Pursue, employing McKinsey with the goal that they also could open the privileged insights of the network.

The McKinsey-ization of Money Road was brewing.

Be that as it may, in banking as in effective financial planning, past execution is no assurance of future outcomes. In Chicago, McKinsey's grid helped set off a chain of occasions that added to what was then the greatest bank disappointment in American history and the most obviously terrible monetary emergency since the Economic crisis of the early 20s. At the focal point of this emergency were three major McKinsey clients, Mainland Illinois, Pursue, and Seattle-First, or Seafirst, all of which had anxiously guzzled the McKinsey Kool-Help.

Mainland Illinois was once the biggest bank between the East and the West Drifts. It was a paragon of traditionalism with a lowercase c — run for 25 years from 1934 by Walter Cummings, Another Vendor who had driven FDR's bank adjustment program. The bank's advance book slanted unequivocally to the world 's most secure venture: U.S. Depositories. Correspondents cited Cummings as saying that the main great credit was one that had been reimbursed.

Under his replacements, Mainland turned out to be more ready to embrace more serious gamble, to contend comparable to the large New York banks. So in 1975, a crew of McKinsey specialists — depicted by one bank official as "stony-confronted folks " — slipped past the Ionic sections gracing the entry of 231 South laSalle Road and on to Mainland's financial floors. They would remain for over a year, meeting the bank officials from a pre-arranged survey.

"The McKinsey public appeared to be somewhat contemplative, perhaps exhausted," composed James P. McCo1lom, a bank official at the time who later composed a book about Mainland's ascent and fall. "They thought a ton, going down the rundown of inquiries; they noticed the responses, however more with tolerance than with interest."

"Since clear ly they definitely knew the responses."

By January 1977 the bank — with McKinsey's assistance — was prepared to execute grid the executives. McKinsey required the bank to redesign, giving individual Specialty units, and more junior investors, more ability to approve large advances. This decentralization appeared to work at Citibank, so why not at Mainland?

# [L'influence cache]

For a couple of years, Mainland's McKinsey-drove revamping seemed effective. By 1981 the bank was the greatest business and modern moneylender in the US, its portion cost flooding even as supplies of other enormous banks stayed stale. In 1978, Dun's Audit commended Mainland as quite possibly of the best organization in the country close by stalwarts like Boeing and GE.

Be that as it may, advance notice difficult situations ahead had been disregarded. loaning flooded, yet stores didn't keep up, significance banks turned out to be more utilized, the FDIC composed years after the fact. A significant number of those new credits would go bad, most prominently in what had been called Gathering U, the energy loaning division. In 1977, Mainland's Gathering U turned into the new home of John lytle.

Until McKinsey's framework completely changed him, lytle was everything except a star at Mainland. Following twenty years of scarcely wandering past Chicagoland, he ran an arrangement of about $20 million in the bank's private venture division. Regardless of no foundation in the exceptionally specific field of energy loaning, he before long ended up directing $600 million and Recently engaged to go with huge loaning choices.

In 1978, lytle was acquainted with the head of energy loaning at an upstart Oklahoma City bank situated in a shopping center of a similar name, Penn Square. Attributable to its little size, Penn Square was restricted on how much cash it could loan to the state's thriving oil and gas industry, so it welcomed far greater Establishments like Mainland, Pursue, and Seattle-First to take part in the thing is called upstreaming.

lytle hit it off with the Penn Square chief, and Mainland's work with the shopping center bank took off. En route, he by and by acquired more than $500,000 from Penn Square. In the last part of the 1970s, soaring oil and gas costs concealed Penn Square's disgraceful loaning rehearses. lytle progressed up the positions and continued to get more advances. By 1982, Mainland possessed more than $1 billion in Penn Square-began advances. However, when energy costs dove in the midst of the most keen financial slump in many years, the credits began turning sour, provoking government bank controllers to close down Penn Square that July. Mainland detailed its most memorable misfortune since the Economic crisis of the early 20s.

Mainland had the most openness to Penn Square, yet Pursue and Seattle-First — both McKinsey network clients — were additionally hit hard, alongside numerous more modest organizations. After a year, Seafirst fell and was obtained by Bank of America. Then, in the spring of 1984, Reuters distributed bits of hearsay that Mainland confronted chapter 11. The bits of hearsay turned into an unavoidable outcome as a significant number of Mainland's large corporate clients pulled their stores. By July, the national government rescued Mainland by taking a greater part stake. It was the greatest bank disappointment in American history until 2008. It likewise brought about the "too large to even consider fizzling" convention, which directed monetary controllers in the downturn that would come later.

lytle got three and a Half years in jail for duping Mainland of $2.25 million. The appointed authority said that lytle was "somebody in far over his head." Pursue

## [L'influence cache]

would go through years attempting to remove itself from millions in terrible Penn Square credits.

McKinsey's financial work procured the rage of Paul Volcker, the Fed executive at the hour of the Mainland salvage, who joked to the leader of the Central Bank in Dallas that "in his day he realized a bank was set out toward inconvenience when it became excessively quick, moved into an extravagant new structure, put the director of the board as top of the craftsmanship panel, and recruited McKinsey and Co. to do a motivation remuneration study for senior officials."

The Fed administrator was in good company to scrutinize McKinsey's recommendation. Alerts were coming from inside the firm too. In their book looking for Greatness, Tom Peters and Weave Waterman composed that the best organizations tried not to utilize the framework or had deserted it. Referring to it as "the stylish yet clear ly ineffectual construction of the seventies," Peters and Waterman said the framework simply didn't work since it siphons away imagination and obligation in the help of a numerical Model.

Mainland's McCollom went above and beyond, saying, "McKinsey had sold us framework the board, the very fake rElief that the great organizations stayed away from."

It worked out that one more unmistakable McKinsey specialist reached a comparative resolution.

lowell Bryan had an instinctive comprehension of how an ineffectively run financial framework could hurt Individuals in Center America. At the point when he was a kid, his dad educated him regarding how the disappointment of four banks in dust Bowl Oklahoma had spelled a finish to the family fortune.

A football player and star grappler at Davidson School in North Carolina, Bryan procured a MBA from Harvard in 1970 and invested energy after his graduation preparing the South Vietnamese to run their media communications framework. It was perhaps of the most secure work in the country, he said, "in light of the fact that the North Vietnamese would have rather not obliterated the framework they realized they would dominate."

In the wake of working for a period at State Road, the large Boston-based resource director, Bryan was employed by McKinsey as a financial expert, that very year that the firm started revamping Mainland Illinois. Bryan viewed McKinsey's financial work as "unprofessional." The challenging tasks with Citi, Pursue, Seafirst and Mainland Illinois were done to a limited extent by McKinsey experts who particular not in banking but rather in association and promoting.

"I was Recently stunned that we were attempting to serve clients with as little information as we had," Bryan reviewed years after the fact.

Bryan would before long become one of the scholarly monsters at a firm brimming with Rhodes researchers. At the point when he was employed, the association's financial practice was little, around 3% of its client work in 1975. In any case, that before long different. By 1983, McKinsey's Monetary Organizations

## [L'influence cache]

Gathering, comprised of banks and insurance agency, took up 25-30 percent of the work in New York and London, McKinsey's two greatest centers.

In one sense, McKinsey just rode the wave. The financialization of the American economy was well under way. The Downturn period guidelines that had fixed the business banks and had restrained Money Road started to slacken. Organizations progressively skirted business banks to fund-raise, giving business paper or garbage securities. Savers got much better rates with currency market accounts that put resources into business paper. By 1986, the covers on the premium banks could propose for investment accounts were a rElic of past times.

Financialization implied that the days when the best-paid brokers in the land made under $1 million a year were finished. With Money Road pay rates and rewards increasing ever higher, McKinsey started to lose a portion of its stars. As the company's true history put it, "There was a developing feEling of dissatisfaction among certain accomplices, Particularly more youthful accomplices in the nations with extraordinary monetary focuses, that the potential for abundance creation at McKinsey couldn't match what they could find in vocations like speculation banking."

To make a McKinsey vocation more alluring, the firm upgraded its pay framework, permitting its accomplices to get more cash-flow. In 1985, McKinsey set up its own speculation organization, the McKinsey Venture Office, which oversaw benefits reserves and the speculations of its top advisors. Besides the fact that McKinsey putting was its stamp on Money Road, yet Money Road was putting its stamp on McKinsey. One senior accomplice deplored that these assumptions for more significant compensations were changing the way of life of the firm, "and not to improve things."

There were a lot of chances for McKinsey accomplices to legitimize those more significant compensations. Business banks had lost the comfortable, government-ordered financing cost edges that had for a really long time given their leaders the opportunity to raise a ruckus around town by 3:00 p.m. Presently banks needed to adjust or bite the dust. "They were on an expressway to nothing," said George Feiger, recruited by McKinsey in 1981 as a financial specialist.

Some went to McKinsey for exhortation, be that as it may, progressively, organizations were looking somewhere e1se, Particularly to the upstarts Bain and Boston Counseling Gathering, in light of the fact that McKinsey was presenting cutout recipes and offering them to an endless series of clients. Ron Danie1, the new overseeing accomplice, needed the firm to be a textual style of thoughts that could be utilized to develop attaches with existing clients and attract new ones. "We can't simply be a Firm of takers and appliers," he told his kindred chiefs in Vienna in 1980. "A greater amount of us should be providers and makers of new reasoning and groundbreaking thoughts."

lowell Bryan thought he had an answer, a thought so large that in the chronicles of monetary history it positioned straight up with the creation of twofold section accounting in fifteenth-century Venice. On the off chance that McKinsey could possess this novel thought — he considered it a "innovation" — banks all around the world would racket to enlist the firm.

## [L'influence cache]

Bryan's enormous thought: the securitization of credit. While he didn't develop securitization, he became perhaps of its greatest, most apparent advertiser.

It was additionally the coherent reaction to the influx of terrible credits that McKinsey itself had assisted with making with framework the executives and decentralization. In principle, securitization would empower banks to keep away from that destiny by off-stacking the credits, and the dangers, to financial backers. Be that as it may, similarly as customary bank loaning is laden with chances, so too is securitization.

Until the last part of the 1960s, America's home-loaning industry basically worked the way George Bailey, played by Jimmy Stewart, clarified it for the terrified clients of Bailey Building and Credit in the 1946 exemplary It's a Brilliant life.

"You're thinking about this spot completely off-base as though I had the cash back in the protected," Stewart tells his clients, frantic to pull out their cash when they see a sudden spike in demand for the town bank. "The cash hasn't arrived. Why, your cash's in Joe's home, that is right close to yours. And afterward the Kennedy house and Mrs. Macklin's home and 100 others. You're loaning them the cash to construct and afterward they will repay it to you overall quite well."

like the Bailey Building and Advance, America's banks and frugalities were obliged on the home loans they could issue until they tracked down additional investors. Securitization tackled that issue.

In 1968, Fannie Mae, an organization made by a demonstration of Congress to advance house purchasing, was provided the ability to purchase up regular home loans from banks, pack them into tradable protections, and offer those protections to financial backers. It infused a big cheese of liquidity into the home loan market. Banks, frugalities, and another type of organizations having some expertise in contract starts, for example, Countrywide Monetary could now make home credits from acquired money and afterward auction them to Fannie Mae or its twin, Freddie Macintosh. Flush, rehash.

By the mid 1980s, Money Road firms, drove by First Boston and Salomon Siblings, were quick getting into the matter of advance securitization, applying the plan to large home loans not covered by Fannie, as well as to other obligation instruments, for example, vehicle credits and Visa obligation. However, the thought was delayed to get on. It required a scholarly hero to make it good. lowell Bryan filled that need.

In 1986 he introduced the "Securitization Venture" at McKinsey. The point, he made sense of, was "to work on McKinsey's capacity to serve its broad client base of monetary organizations, including cash focus banks, protections firms, and insurance agency."

McKinsey advisors started producing articles and books that praised the advantages of credit securitization. In 1988, the firm distributed Bryan's Separating the Bank, which put securitization at the focal point of a totally redesignd banking framework. A subsequent book, Securitization of Credit, by the McKinsey

# [L'influence cache]

specialists James Rosenthal and Juan Ocampo, offered a how-to direct for organizations and banks that needed to utilize the "innovation."

The McKinsey triplet of Bryan, Rosenthal, and Ocampo likewise distributed diary articles that would before long be referred to by the Central bank as it investigated the new peculiarity of securitization. The Diary of Applied Corporate Money dedicated its Fall 1988 issue to securitization, with McKinsey advisors composing three of the nine articles.

Securitization, Bryan said, could free organizations — banks, however any organization — from the restraint of their monetary records. An organization need just set up a "specific reason vehicle," infuse the resources — anything that borrowers needed to reimburse after some time, for example, home loans or car credits — then, at that point, offer those resources as a security to financial backers.

For banks, getting advances shaky sheets was Particularly alluring. The more advances on the books, the more money saves they were expected to hold. Securitization opened up capital that could be utilized to make more advances. "Securitization's true capacity," Bryan said, "is extraordinary in light of the fact that it Eliminates capital and monetary records as limitations on development."

Yet, that wasn't all. To McKinsey, securitization was more proficient as well as possibly a more secure method for loaning cash. This was incompletely a direct result of what the business was calling "credit upgrade," basically an assurance on the item given by a bank or an insurance agency. This would permit FICO assessment offices like Moody's and S&P to give ideal evaluations for the item.

These credit ensures "can raise the credit hazard of a pool to venture grade levels," Bryan composed. "This thus permits people, benefits reserves, and different classes of financial backers who have neither the ability nor the longing to survey credit chance to put resources into the protections gave by the particular inspiration vehicle."

To Bryan, a framework where the originator, the "credit enhancers," and the evaluations organizations generally investigated the credits was clear ly better compared to the prior approach to loaning cash.

"In the securitized credit process, three gatherings, as opposed to one, fret about credit quality," Bryan composed.

Rosenthal and Ocampo, working under Bryan, wrote in their how-to book that with credit securitization banks that make all the more terrible credits would normally be disregarded, making an idealistic circle where the framework removes terrible moneylenders or powers them to get to the next level. "After some time this will prompt better credit choices at the place of beginning," they composed.

There were, obviously, the compulsory notes of mindfulness. Bryan recognized that securitization wasn't basic. Its prosperity rElied upon the skill and, somewhat, the completely pure intentions of all gatherings and that "in the event that an excessive number of arrangements are ineffectively endorsed and in the event that

## [L'influence cache]

huge defaults and misfortunes result, this promising new innovation could, to say the least, rush a credit breakdown."

The books and articles by McKinsey's Rosenthal, Ocampo, and Bryan assisted Money Road with selling the possibility of securitization. McKinsey accomplices then, at that point, spread out across the globe, getting out the uplifting news about particular reason vehicles, resource tranches, and credit improvement to the unenlightened.

Since the organized securitization bargains were so convoluted, legal counselors assumed a major part. Few were a higher priority than Jason Kravitt, who established the securitization practice at Mayer Brown. Kravitt read Rosenthal and Ocampo's book and said it gave the thought some scholarly heave.

"Harking back to the '80s and '90s, we were all on a journey of revelation. We assumed we planned to make the world a superior spot," Kravitt said thirty years after the fact. "I think the McKinsey book gave the thought and the item and industry a great deal of bElievability."

For investors, Individuals who required persuading were the backers — organizations that created supposed receivables, for example, GM's car advances or Banc One's Visa accounts. They made the unrefined substance.

"The McKinsey book assisted with validity with backers," William Haley, who worked for Salomon, told Bloomberg's Imprint Pittman in 2008. "It wasn't so natural in the first place. Gatherings currently have great many Individuals, yet I recollect once in Beverly Slopes, I gave a discourse and there were perhaps 25 Individuals in the crowd."

Salomon and First Boston didn't require McKinsey's assistance on securitization. McKinsey began producing charges — the first thought behind Bryan's undertaking in any case — with business banks and protections firms that needed to join the securitization game.

McKinsey's accomplices let clients know that setting up a securitizations division wasn't only a question of poaching ability from rivals. In many occasions, the progressive culture of a fastened down business bank needed to change to oblige the gamble taking society of venture financiers who had some expertise in such credits, reviewed Feiger, a senior accomplice in McKinsey's European financial practice in the mid 1990s who proceeded to head what turned into the speculation banking arm of UBS, the Swiss financial goliath.

McKinsey encouraged the business banks on the most proficient method to change their association to oblige more gamble to get better yields. Once in a while that elaborate setting up an exchange finance division, or a push to internationalization, or a Specialty in resource securitization. "We assisted them with getting into something achievable," Feiger said.

One more previous McKinsey accomplice who chipped away at Bryan's securitization project said that once news spread about McKinsey's work nearby, banks became intrigued. "The biggest banks on the planet came to us and posed

## [L'influence cache]

inquiries about how they could manage it and how they could manage their particular resources."

By 1990, the Central bank, understanding that securitization was clear ing the monetary business sectors, gave a report, the catalog of which is studded with McKinsey references. Of the Rosenthal and Ocampo book, the Fed noticed that while it was "educational in nature, the writers are obviously favorable to securitization."

Since the US had created securitization, it had a major early advantage over rivals in Europe and Asia. McKinsey saw a market an open door in teaching brokers all over the planet about the idea. In mid-June 1991, specialists in the field met in London for a gathering coordinated by the Monetary Times and led by George Feiger.

While Feiger's show put forward the advantages and likely traps of securitization, it clear side of the record the firm he addressed was on. His paper started by making sense of why a monetary foundation ought to need to securitize its resources. He likewise alluded to exactly the way in which profound the idea had entered McKinsey's reasoning, saying the firm has "offered guidance to modern organizations as far as rebuilding monetary records, and furthermore to monetary foundations as far as business system and monetary record procedure, and securitization of resources has been a vital part of these exercises."

Bryan attempted to offer the plan to legislators. As far as he might be concerned, the presentation of securitization was completely an insurgency. Bryan assessed it would require ten to fifteen years for securitized credit to "uproot totally the exemplary financial framework." That wasn't long, he said, since "the basics of the financial framework have remained basically unaltered since the Medieval times." He contrasted the presentation of securitization with the change from vacuum cylinders to semiconductors and afterward to coordinated circuits.

"The more we at McKinsey have mulled over everything, the more persuaded we have turned into that organized securitized credit is a prevalent innovation," Bryan composed.

At that point, the American monetary framework was faltering from numerous emergencies. The breakdown of Mainland Illinois, the disappointments of scores of reserve funds and credit organizations, and billions of dollars in terrible credits made to latin American countries prompted requires a purge. Bryan thought he had the arrangement: putting securitization at the core of another idea for American banks. He proposed parting the financial framework into "center" banks, ones that worked in taking government-guaranteed stores, and "discount" banks that zeroed in on loaning and utilized securitized credit.

Bryan's center bank thought won a few allies in Congress, and in 1991 the idea came up for a vote. A forty-year-old delegate from Brooklyn, Charles Schumer, presented the action and stood up for it at a House Banking Panel hearing that June. Banks commonly abhorred the action, in any case, thus did the 38 year-old Depository undersecretary for homegrown money, Jerome Powell, who, alongside Bryan, likewise affirmed that day. The action was crushed.

## [L'influence cache]

Bryan would keep pushing for securitization well into the 1990s. In 1996 he and a partner, Diana Farrell, composed a book, Market Unbound: Releasing World wide Private enterprise, a paean to showcase matchless quality over government, that prominent the tremendous development of the supply of securitized credits — which had developed from $100 million of every 1980 to $1 trillion out of 1992. The McKinsey team anticipated further development into the new 100 years, Particularly outside the US.

"Proceeding, advance securitization will be more critical to the outright development of the world's fluid monetary stock than it was throughout the last 10 years," Bryan and Farrell composed.

Bryan had valid justification to say that. One of McKinsey's previous experts, Jeffrey K. Skilling, was trying Bryan's thoughts of securitization in Houston, where he was changing a sullen Petroleum gas merchant into an energy exchanging organization called Enron. At McKinsey, Skilling had been "profoundly impacted" by Bryan. Presently, as the Chief of Enron, he had the ability to set Bryan's words in motion. Furthermore, he did.

On December 2, 2001, Enron petitioned for Part 11 insolvency insurance. Outside Houston, hardly any customary Americans experienced the organization's breakdown. However, even as Enron was disentangling, financiers on Money Road were producing changed renditions of securitized contracts that inside a couple of years would ignite the greatest monetary emergency since the Economic crisis of the early 20s.

With loan fees after the 9/11 goes after the least in many years, financiers went chasing after better returns. Working with the huge home loan originators like Ameriquest and Countrywide, they started securitizing home advances that Fannie and Freddie stayed away from — the subprime contracts made to hazardous borrowers. Credit offices, rEliant upon those equivalent Money Road firms for expenses, didn't have the foggiest idea — or couldn't have cared less — that Individuals across America were defaulting on their home loans.

A significant number of those dispossessions included advances to Individuals who were not trustworthy. In any case, Money Road required subprime advances to make contract upheld protections and the perpetually fascinating subsidiaries worked from those protections. To tempt borrowers, they offered contracts with customizable rates, premium just installment choices, and that's what mystery rates, Following two years, rose pointedly.

The "three gatherings" Bryan said would make securitized credits better than regular loaning rather worked in show to siphon increasingly more poisonous obligation into the world wide monetary framework. Somewhere in the range of 2001 and 2008 a larger number of than $27 trillion was securitized, a sum equivalent to two times the U.S. Gross domestic product in 2007.

Trillions of those dollars would before long vanish.

Weeks after Schumer and Bloomberg talked at city corridor, the disentangling turned out to be extremely open with the liquidation of New Century Monetary, a

## [L'influence cache]

subprime moneylender, continued in July 2007 by the breakdown of two Bear Stearns mutual funds that put resources into securitized contract obligation.

By the next Spring, Bear Stearns, America's fifth-greatest speculation bank, was consumed by J. P. Morgan in an administration expedited fire deal. In any case, the dam truly broke in September when lehman Siblings and Washington Shared opted for non-payment. The national government needed to rescue AIG — overwhelmed with billions of dollars of cases for the "credit upgrades" that it couldn't pay — as much as $182 billion. ALso, the long-term McKinsey clients Merrill lynch and Wachovia, both lethally injured by their subprime property, were auctions off to more grounded rivals.

The shared factor: poisonous securitized obligation.

This happened under two years after Schumer and Bloomberg promoted the McKinsey concentrate on that cautioned against awkward guideline and the gamble that Europe could get America on resource securitization.

"In principle, securitization ought to diminish credit risk by spreading it all the more broadly," Secretary of the Depository Tim Geithner and larry Summers, Obama's top monetary counsel, wrote in 2009 as they were presenting the defense for new guidelines. "In any case, by breaking the immediate connection among borrowers and moneylenders, securitization prompted a disintegration of loaning norms, bringing about a market disappointment that took care of the lodging win and developed the lodging fail."

For Money Road investors, it was a game, and their aggravation was fleeting. A couple of months after the total implosion, many Money Road financiers were getting yearly rewards. By 2013, the S&P 500 list hit record highs. Yet, a huge number of normal Americans never recuperated from the Incomparable Downturn. Joblessness moved to the most elevated level in an age. In 2013, the Public authority Responsibility Office said that the slump came about in $22 trillion in misfortunes for the economy.

On the off chance that they hadn't succumbed to savage subprime banks and unrealistic home renegotiating bargains, the cratering economy implied that numerous Americans before long slipped into monetary indebtedness. A large number of dispossessions — lopsidedly influencing minorities — topped in 2010, two years after the business sectors crashed.

In 2018, 10 years after the monetary emergency, The New York Times returned to a portion of Individuals its journalists had talked with at that point.

In Marietta, Georgia, Meg Fisher lost her employment as a legitimate secretary in mid-2009. A college alum, she had forever had the option to track down consistent work previously, yet this time couldn't. She and her better Half sought financial protection in 2009, and they lost their rural home to dispossession a couple of years after the fact. "I likely won't ever be authoritatively full-time utilized from now on," Ms. Fisher, then, at that point, 56, told the Times.

## [L'influence cache]

Guillermo Gonzalez defaulted on some loans and lost his Miami-region home to dispossession in 2008 when the cratering economy cut his payments as an alcohol wholesaler. After 10 years, he was gradually recuperating. "We're doing it slowly but surely."

It wasn't simply America. In China, twenty million transient specialists out of nowhere gotten themselves without a line of work as products fell. Ireland's joblessness took off to 16 percent from under 5% before the accident. Iceland's banks, vigorously put resources into U.S. securitized resources, lost $330,000 for everyone in the country.

"Securitization depended on the reason that a bonehead was conceived consistently," Joseph Stiglitz, the Nobel Prize-winning financial specialist at Columbia College, said in October 2008. "Globalization intended that there was a world wide scene on which they could look for those nitwits — and they found them all over the place."

Assuming McKinsey or Bryan felt any regret for converting securitization for such countless years, they absolutely didn't show it. In 2009, Bryan, who had long pushed for lighter government oversight of the business sectors, said the breakdown happened on the grounds that controllers "fundamentally decided not to direct."

"On the off chance that you take a gander at securitization from the 1970s until approximately 2000, you see generally profits by it," he wrote in the McKinsey Quarterly. "The explanation it became unstable is that we permitted a lot of credit hazard to enter the framework."

McKinsey doesn't reject that it assumed a part in the spread of securitization: "McKinsey fostered the ideas driving securitization, which today stays helpful and generally utilized in the monetary framework and more extensive economy." Yet during the 1980s securitization was a "early idea that looked similar to the perplexing instruments at issue in 2008" and to try and "in a roundabout way trait the 2008 monetary emergency to McKinsey's work" would be "profoundly deceptive," the organization said.

Feiger, the previous McKinsey chief who aided spread the possibility of securitization in Europe, says that McKinsey generally made sense of the general mishmash about securitization to its clients. "What you're managing is a chain of trust," Feiger says of the idea. "To work, all gatherings must have trustworthiness and skill. What occurred in the monetary implosion is that they weren't skillful or legit."

Ocampo, the co-creator of Securitization of Acknowledge, left McKinsey as an accomplice in 1995. like Bryan, he said that the "innovation" had been manhandled.

Bloomberg's Imprint Pittman was one of only a handful of exceptional Money Road journalists to see the approaching of the monetary implosion. In the weeks after the liquidation of Lehman Siblings and the huge bailout of AIG, he expounded on the starting points of the securitization frenzy. That drove him to

## [L'influence cache]

Ocampo's book and to the Enron exceptional venture vehicles set up under Skilling. "A strong innovation has been driven past as far as possible," Ocampo told Pittman in late 2008. "Throughout the previous five years, rather than going 65 mph, they've been gunning it up to 140 mph, 150 mph."

# *[L'influence cache]*

## Section 10

### Allstate's Mystery Slides

### "Winning Will Be a lose Situation"

On a pre-fall day in 2000, Dale Deer was driving west on Highway 70 in focal Missouri when traffic halted in light of development work.

Behind him, Jason ALdridge, a twenty-year-old understudy, was on a crosscountry excursion from Kentucky to Las Vegas with a companion. ALdridge was attempting to change his voyage control and didn't see that traffic had halted. Seconds after the fact, his Mercury Cougar banged into the backside of Deer's Chevy pickup truck, seriously harming Deer's back and neck.

Mishaps like this happen consistently on America's streets, which is the reason drivers are lawfully expected to convey protection. ALdridge's strategy was with one of the country's most popular back up plans — Allstate, a revered organization that gathered his expenses in return for the commitment of shielding him from major, unforeseen monetary misfortune.

Both Deer and ALdridge anticipated that would be the situation here, as well. Confronting a pile of bills, Deer presented a case for $24,000, well beneath the $100,000 greatest on the strategy. Furthermore, that is where the interaction went off in an unexpected direction. The Allstate agent looking into the issue, Mary Greene, mysteriously decided not to handle Deer's case, saying later that she chose to take a "pass." Burnt out on pausing, Deer sued ALdridge.

Back at school in Kentucky, Aldridge opened the entryway one day to a cop serving him a court summons. He was being sued for $2 million. "I truly thought my life was finished," said ALdridge, who had once lived in a trailer park. "I just surrendered." He quit going to classes.

ALdridge ultimately sued Allstate, asserting that the guarantor behaved inappropriately by not paying Deer's case. Really at that time did his legal counselors make a significant revelation: an administration counseling firm, McKinsey and Company, had been prompting Allstate through PowerPoint slides on the most proficient method to get a good deal on claims. So they requested that Allstate produce the slides. After Allstate denied, the adjudicator for the situation, Michael Habits, requested Allstate to turn them over.

Allstate rejected. Judge Habits found Allstate in hatred of court and fined the organization $25,000 every day until it consented to his request. Allstate actually declined. In late 2007, the Missouri High Court followed up by additionally requesting the back up plan to deliver the slides. Again the guarantor declined, and by the center of 2008, Allstate had run up more than $7 million in fines. Habits later said he had seen nothing like it in almost thirteen years on the seat.

What might actually be in those slides that Allstate could disregard court requests and chance huge number of dollars in fines to keep quiet?

## [L'influence cache]

This was likewise an inquiry being posed by David J. Berardinelli, a previous examiner in New Mexico who was the main offended party's legal counselor to expound on the presence of the McKinsey slides. An admirer of Elite execution vehicles, fur garments, and fine wine, Berardinelli had learned of the slides while addressing an older couple — Allstate clients for over thirty years — who were seriously harmed in 2001 when an alcoholic driver constrained them off a cold street and into a gorge.

As a feature of his examination concerning why Allstate dismissed their case, Berardinelli found that McKinsey had assisted the guarantor with updating its cases framework and that a mystery slide deck made sense of everything. He requested it. Allstate denied, asserting the slides contained proprietary advantages. In the end, Allstate was constrained by the court to deliver them to Berardinelli, however just depending on the prerequisite that he not disclose them. Allstate even put a watermark on them, delivering sweeps or copies muddled.

At the point when a New Mexico requests court allowed Berardinelli to freely deliver the slides, he returned the old ones to Allstate, with the assumption that he'd get more intelligible duplicates. Be that as it may, Allstate had sprung a snare. They kept Berardinelli's old slides and afterward would not give him substitutions.

Not prepared to surrender, Berardinelli went into the court record a 300 page rundown of the slides that he had incorporated before. Allstate attempted to have the outline put under Seal, yet the court said no. In the mean time, expression of these inner records — in excess of twelve thousand pages, and slides — spread all through the American legitimate local area, provoking one attorney to depict them as "a sort of sacred goal" for offended party legal advisors.

"They were able to sit tight for quite a long time, tie up our court frameworks, and burn through an over the top measure of cash in legitimate expenses — all to keep this calm," Berardinelli composed.

After becoming aware of Allstate's protection rehearses, the Florida protection chief started an examination, and he, as well, found Allstate reluctant to create mentioned archives. "Assuming Allstate will pay $25,000 each day in fines to a Missouri court for its continuous inability to give comparable reports, it's conspicuous to me that it will take in excess of a financial assent to inspire them to consent to our summons," the chief said.

The chief suspended Allstate's permit to sell accident coverage until the organization delivered the slides. That certainly stood out on the grounds that main California and Texas have a greater number of vehicles out and about than Florida. In 2008, Allstate yielded, momentarily posting the slides on its site.

For what reason did Allstate battle so lengthy thus hard? The most brief clarification comes in the Title of a book composed by Berardinelli: From Great Hands to Boxing Gloves.

Beginning around 1950, "You're well taken care of with Allstate" has been the trademark of the Allstate Company, one of the longest-running and most unmistakable slogans in American business. For quite a long time, under the

## [L'influence cache]

responsibility for, Roebuck and Company, those words implied something: Allstate would, a large number of years, pay out by far most of its superior pay in claims, typically creating an unassuming benefit. The organization's representatives would try and settle on house decisions — called pop-outs (as in "jump out" of the workplace) — to convey claims actually looks at face to face.

That changed in 1995, after Allstate finished its side project from Singes. As another openly recorded organization, its chiefs enthusiastically embraced the undeniably financialized economy where huge expansions in share-based pay turned into a significant objective — unbelievable in the sullen climate at Singes. Fully expecting the side project, a group from McKinsey met with Allstate's administration in late 1992.

After three years, they were good to go out their arrangement to help benefits utilizing the McKinsey slides as a guide. "It worked. It paid off for them," Judge Habits, who directed the ALdridge case, said of McKinsey's work with Allstate. "I surmise they rake in some serious cash doing this."

In one slide, McKinsey advised Allstate to attempt to settle 90% of its cases as fast and as efficiently as could be expected. For the other 10%, policyholders or outsider petitioners who didn't take the Allstate deal or, much more terrible, employed a legal counselor, the "boxing gloves" treatment was all together. They would battle in courts, for a really long time if essential, wearing out any individual who considered suing.

McKinsey planned a framework — the Cases Center Interaction Overhaul — that pushed agents to make speedy, lowball offers instead of permit them to think of settlements that they thought about fair. Agents, presently fastened to a modernized cases framework called Goliath, were decreased to minimal more than call-focus laborers perusing arranged scripts. Pop-outs became interesting. For property holders' cases, it was another PC program — Xactimate. However, the thought was something similar. Push petitioners to Acknowledge not exactly the covered sum. Allstate says this portrayal is "bogus and misdirecting" and that it updated its cases framework during the 1990s to "pay guarantees all the more quickly and precisely." McKinsey declined to remark.

Most McKinsey slides, from the outset, appear to be anesthetic, loaded up with expressions like this: "The manner in which we approach petitioners and foster connections will fundamentally adjust portrayal rates and add to bring down severities." Yet Allstate representatives comprehended what it implied, in light of the fact that it was clarified for them in plain English.

This is the way Maureen Reed, a lawyer for Allstate from 1992 to 2003, depicted a gathering on the subject with senior Allstate chiefs:

> We were told at this gathering that McKinsey had reasoned that Allstate was "paying a lot for claims" which had made a corporate culture of inquirers hoping to be paid for claims. This was introduced as something terrible. McKinsey encouraged Allstate that to increment benefits, Allstate expected to pay less on claims.

## [L'influence cache]

Vital to the objective of diminishing payouts was keeping policyholders from recruiting attorneys, she said, on the grounds that "addressed" clients on normal got payouts on numerous occasions greater than inquirers who didn't enlist lawful assistance.

"We were informed that Allstate planned to fundamentally alter how cases were taken care of so petitioners couldn't get legal advisors," Reed said. ALL in all, beat down the restricting advice by battling each movement in court, working everything out such that tedious and costly that legal counselors would rethink documenting suit against Allstate. This was the "boxing gloves" part of the methodology.

"More Individuals without portrayal would mean bigger benefits for the organization," she said. McKinsey was advising Allstate to transform its cases community into a benefit place.

The words merit italics since what McKinsey did at Allstate on a very basic level changed America's protection industry.

Americans have had an affection disdain relationship with insurance agency for a really long time. They love their neighborhood protection specialist, regularly a mainstay of the local area, a mentor for Youth baseball or Pop Warner football. However, they disdain managing insurance agency that barrage them with desk work demands and here and there deny what they see as genuine cases. Until McKinsey showed up on the scene, the calling was overwhelmed by experienced claims agents limited by regulation to offer fair cases. The "claims man" was a fair and desired calling in after war America.

Protection is totally indispensable to make preparations for startling misfortune, and in some cases expensive recuperation, whether from a fender bender, an overwhelmed home, an unexpected crippling physical issue, or the passing of a family provider. With protection, you're reimburse; there's a grave, exceptionally soothing commitment: you'll be "restored."

Without protection, the monetary defenses that keep a great many Individuals in the working class can rapidly disintegrate. "Protection is the extraordinary defender of the way of life of the American working class," composes Jay M. Feinman, a regulation teacher at Rutgers who concentrates on the business. "Yet, just when it works."

For a really long time in America, it did. Individuals purchased approaches. Insurance agency put away that top notch cash and paid out the cases that the approaches — contracts — specified. The business was beneficial most years however not remarkably so. Gifted Individuals — agents — generally assessed claims on their benefits.

McKinsey had been counseling insurance agency since basically the 1950s. During the 1980s the senior accomplice Peter Walker, who later proceeded to zero in on China, constructed a fiefdom of the company's protection counseling business, distributing an industry book every year that looked at the presentation of every one of the enormous organizations. It made the ideal gift for aggressive protection chiefs.

McKinsey was centered around its conventional job of making organizations more proficient — reducing expenses. For the cases division, that implied controlling the cost of taking care of cases, referred to in the business as misfortune change cost, or laE. This could be anything from winnowing abundance workers, chopping down mailing costs, haggling better costs for copier paper, or diminishing extra time costs.

Yet, fiddling around the edges, smoothing out workplaces, and cutting costs could get the organization just up until this point. What insurance agency spend on claims handling is a little part of what they pay out in claims themselves. In 2018 the property and loss industry paid out $365.9 billion in claims, burning through $64.6 billion in handling charges, meaning guarantors on normal spent around 17% of what they paid out for organization costs.

By the 1990s, with McKinsey-drove financialization clearing the economy and steadily expanding tension from extremist investors for organizations to support benefits, the firm pushed a major novel plan to its clients: decreasing the sum paid out in claims. In McKinsey-speak: "Following quite a while of crushing the expense side, the board perceived enormous open doors to rebalance and put carefully in laE to catch reimbursement reserve funds." The new way to deal with helping benefit was to diminish what insurance agency saw as ridiculously high sums paid out to certain petitioners. To control what it called "spi1lage."

McKinsey was advising Allstate to proclaim battle on a sizable extent of its policyholders basically. One slide declared, "Winning will be a lose situation." as such, Allstate's benefits come to the detriment of its policyholders. One more included a picture of a crocodile. Why? Since, similar to a crocodile, Allstate would just "sit and stand by" for its casualty — the inquirer — to surrender. "The cash came from the main spot it could emerge out of — the pockets of Allstate policyholders and petitioners," Berardinelli composed.

Before McKinsey, there were as yet furious policyholders. Before McKinsey, insurance agency lowballed claims. However, McKinsey organized it. ALso, on the grounds that the firm has no apprehensions about exhorting numerous organizations in similar industry, its thoughts metastasized. As contenders saw Allstate's benefit take off and its chiefs become rich, different guarantors employed McKinsey. This is the McKinsey way and has been since the association's initial days. With McKinsey, there's no commitment of selectiveness. It takes on work with numerous organizations in savagely aggressive ventures, from tobacco to banking to drug makers.

Following Allstate's reception of the McKinsey framework, State Homestead, the greatest property and setback guarantor, pursued a similar sorcery mixture. Its McKinsey-planned "Speeding up Cases Greatness" framework was first acquainted with its field workplaces in mid-1995. AAA followed a couple of years after the fact. Freedom Common likewise turned into a McKinsey client.

## [L'influence cache]

"It has been widely known inside the setback protection industry since no less than 1995 that McKinsey was transparently selling the equivalent update techniques and guarantee taking care of cycles it created in the mid 1990's for State Ranch and Allstate to their rivals," Stephen Strzelec, a previous chief for State Homestead, said in a 2008 testimony.

"They set a precedent," one previous McKinsey accomplice said of the company's work with Allstate. "The cases cycle was simply malevolent, and I believe what's happened now is that more insurance agency have followed that."

At Allstate, benefit took off more than six fold in the 10 years after McKinsey's program was set up. Its portion cost more than quadrupled, helpfully destroying the more extensive business sectors. The compensation of Allstate's main five leaders, attached to the offer cost similarly as the McKinsey accomplice Curve Patton had imagined 50 years sooner, shot up. In 1994 their consolidated remuneration added up to $2.95 million. After 10 years it had reached $19.3 million. In 2020 the main five chiefs made a consolidated $38.2 million, drove by the President, Thomas Wilson. By 2021 the normal compensation of an Allstate laborer was about $62,000, scarcely staying aware of expansion north of a quarter century.

In the mean time, the level of expenses paid out on claims declined. Allstate chiefs and investors were turning out to be remarkably rich by decreasing payouts, keeping numerous policyholders from getting all the cash to which they were enTitled. It was, said Russell Roberts, a previous administration specialist who is spending his retirement concentrating on how McKinsey has changed the protection business, "switch Robin Hood."

The flood in Allstate's portion cost was joined by an emotional fall in the "unadulterated misfortune proportion," the proportion of cases payouts partitioned by premium pay, prior to figuring in working expenses. In 1987, Allstate paid out 70.9 pennies in claims for each dollar it took in. By 1997, two entire years into the McKinsey makeover, the proportion had tumbled to 58.2. By 2006, in the wake of spiking a year sooner in the midst of gigantic cases coming about because of Typhoon Katrina, it was 47.6.

Congress wanted to find out whether policyholders were being hurt by Allstate's journey for higher benefits. In 2007, J. Robert Tracker, a protection master with the Buyer Alliance of America, told Individuals from the Senate legal executive Panel that McKinsey's recommendation was prompting lower claims payouts. Tracker encouraged the board to inspect whether recruiting a similar specialist — McKinsey — was commensurate to deceitful conduct with respect to guarantors, who have a restricted exception from antitrust regulations. Barely any private-area enterprises get such exclusions, likened to those delighted in by Significant Association Baseball.

"The utilization of these items to cut claims payouts might be essential for the explanation that buyers are getting record low payouts for their top notch dollars as safety net providers procure uncommon benefits," he said.

## [L'influence cache]

That was positively the situation at Allstate. Indeed, even as the organization was battling to keep quiet, its chiefs were promoting the outcome of its new cases Model to Money Road. At a 2006 financial backers' meeting, Allstate's then CEO, Ed liddy, expressed that from 1993, when McKinsey previously proposed its Cases Center Cycle Update, to 2005, how much cash Allstate had paid out in substantial injury claims had fallen by 10%.

liddy partook in that riches. In 2006, he was paid $24 million.

Roberts, the previous administration specialist, assessed that the McKinsey framework brought about the exchange of $94 billion from policyholders to Allstate cash safes from 1995 to 2018. Include State Ranch and different organizations that embraced the McKinsey framework, and the absolute methodologies $374 billion, Roberts determined. "Such a large amount this is driven by the entire McKinsey mindset and their steady drive to remove additional cash from people while giving them less worth — taking that cash and diverting it to themselves, and to chiefs and to investors," Roberts said.

Roberts started exploring McKinsey's impact on American culture, Particularly the protection business, in the wake of filling in as a specialist observer in 2009 for Berardinelli, the legal advisor who carried the slides to the public's consideration. ALL things considered, the adjudicator decided for Berardinelli's client, referring to a limited extent Allstate's maltreatment of the overall set of laws. Allstate refers to Roberts' examination as "shortsighted and invalid," saying it is difficult to extrapolate figures from the hour of McKinsey's work during the 1990s on the grounds that the cases processes have changed over the long haul. Allstate says 95 pennies of each and every dollar it takes in goes to pay guarantees or working expenses.

The McKinsey claims framework reached out a long ways past Allstate and a long ways past private physical issue claims.

In 2007, Bloomberg Markets magazine distributed a singing examination concerning how Allstate, State Ranch, and different guarantors, utilizing the McKinsey strategy, were regularly low balling offers to mortgage holders whose homes had been harmed or obliterated by cataclysmic events. The most well known furious inquirer: the Mississippi conservative representative Trent lott, who sued State Ranch when the organization wouldn't pay for harm to his home from Tropical storm Katrina. State Ranch said the harm was from water (not covered), as opposed to wind (covered).

A 2003 fire in the San Diego region obliterated multiple thousand houses, however guarantors, including Allstate and State Ranch, would not repay policyholders for the sum expected to supplant their homes, in some cases countless dollars underneath substitution esteem, Bloomberg revealed. They were not being restored.

Under state regulations the nation over, insurance agency are committed to pay the fair worth of anything benefits their policyholders are qualified for. An insurance strategy is, all things considered, a policy. In any case, what makes the obligation of insurance agency significantly more squeezing is the way that

## [L'influence cache]

numerous sorts of protection aren't discretionary. Each driver is legally necessary to have collision protection. Contract organizations expect Individuals to purchase mortgage holders protection. An industry where the public authority constrains Individuals to purchase their item is particularly committed to do its guardian obligation.

"Delay, deny, guard disregards the standards for dealing with claims that are perceived by each organization, educated to agents, and encapsulated in regulation," Feinman, the Rutgers regulation teacher, said.

Shannon Brady Kmatz comes from an Allstate family. Her dad worked at the organization for 37 years. As a young lady experiencing childhood in New Mexico, she would some of the time follow along on pop-outs, particularly in the event that it included an excursion to Ruidoso, a mountain town and ski region a couple of hours southeast of ALbuquerque. She was pleased with her father. At the point when somebody asked where her dad worked, she'd push her palms out and say two words: "Great Hands."

Be that as it may, in 1997, when Brady chose to follow her dad's strides and acknowledge a bid for employment from Allstate, he advised her to reevaluate. He had resigned a year sooner in light of the fact that the organization had changed, and not to improve things.

She endured three years. During that time, she met a great complete of two policyholders up close and personal. Then there was the third one, who visited her office in Albuquerque. He dashed into the second-floor meeting room taking a cut away shotgun, furious that Allstate was slow-strolling his case. "You realize that stuff could happen in light of the fact that you have a great deal of furious petitioners out there," she said.

Brady doesn't put up with imbeciles. Subsequent to leaving the protection business, she turned into a cop. She addresses inquiries with "indeed, sir" and "no, sir." However her three years at Allstate tried her. The spot was far unique in relation to where her dad had spent his functioning lifetime.

Brady portrays the existence of a McKinseyfied Allstate agent in Hobbesian terms: frightful, brutish, and short.

The ten agents were stuck into a second-floor room, contending with one another for rewards, and in any event, for the opportunity to keep their positions. Every agent was evaluated for the number of cases they that shut for low dollar sums. Brady's gathering was known as the "unrepresented unit" on the grounds that the petitioners hadn't recruited attorneys. It was her work, in accordance with McKinsey's proposals, to keep it that way.

Brady, who turned into a specialist observer for lawyers suing Allstate, said in a sworn proclamation that it was "widely known at Allstate" that Individuals who employed legal counselors got settlements that were on normal a few times those of Individuals who weren't addressed.

## [L'influence cache]

So Brady said she deceived the policyholder. It wasn't her words; it was from a McKinsey script they called "lawyer financial matters." "Certain Individuals decide to recruit a lawyer, however we would truly like the chance to work straightforwardly with you to settle the case," the content read. "lawyers regularly take between 25-40% of the all out settlement you get from an insurance agency in addition to the costs caused. Assuming you settle straightforwardly with Allstate, notwithstanding, the aggregate sum of the settlement is yours."

Or on the other hand, as a McKinsey slide expressed in all covers, "WIN BY Taking advantage of THE Financial matters OF THE Act OF Regulation."

There's no time to waste. The McKinsey framework spread out severe standards for finishing off cases — most in something like thirty days, even more inside sixty, and every one of them by ninety days — or giving them to the "addressed" unit, or to the misrepresentation division. What's more, do it for as minimal expenditure as could really be expected. Close them quick, close them modest, and rewards and advancements were available for whoever gets there first. Fall behind, give the policyholders more cash, and you'd before long end up being placed in JIJ — Occupation in Risk — by the director.

Every Monday morning, Brady and her partners would track down a printout of their 30/60/90 advancement on their work areas. A whiteboard on the wall followed the workplace progress, permitting everybody to perceive how they estimated facing their partners.

Agents realized that their most prominent partner in gathering their 30/60/90 objectives were poor people and uninformed policyholders. The ones with unfortunate English, the older living on Federal retirement aide, or the ones needing the cash to cover bills. "In the event that you realized they were living check to check, they were a practical objective," Brady said. Assuming that Allstate sent them a lowball check via the post office and they changed out it, that was equivalent to settling. "Assuming that they cash the check, it is full and last. Sort of unnerving, right?"

The objective was to settle whatever number cases as could be allowed, even before the cases had been assessed, and do it for not exactly the approved sum.

The protection agent's job had been enormously lessened. During her dad's time, setting an incentive for a case had been an expertise. Under Allstate's new framework, the PC would let out a gauge. This was Goliath, a program that broke down many various wounds entered by agents like her. As Brady before long scholarly, Monster had been changed to lowball claims sums. It was then her responsibility to convince the policyholder to acknowledge a case even lower than the one ejected by Mammoth.

Mark Romano, one Individuals liable for tweaking Giant with the goal that it leaned toward the safety net provider, worked out of Allstate's central command in Northbrook, Illinois. "I could turn the handle, as it were, and increment the upsides of cases, or I could turn the handle down and lessening the worth," he said.

## [L'influence cache]

When payout information showed something was awry, Romano took to the street to figure out what was happening. He and his partners found that agents were entering a strange measure of herniated plate wounds into Goliath, a definitely more significant case than a "delicate tissue" guarantee like whiplash. Romano was told to "adjust" the cases groups the nation over, advising them to decrease the quantity of herniated circle claims "notwithstanding on the off chance that a nervous system specialist or a muscular specialist or a radiologist or whomever said it was a herniated plate."

For Romano, who previously had extreme qualms about his work, this was, in the most natural sounding way for him, "the absolute last thing that could be tolerated." He had voiced his interests about Mammoth to Allstate legal counselors who were setting up a safeguard against a legal claim. He started encountering serious migraines. Specialists couldn't sort out why. He went on inability. At the point when he returned, he was reassigned and actually told he had no future at the organization. Romano took exiting the workforce in 2009. "I had turned into a risk," he said.

The cerebral pains disappeared. The next year, he joined the resistance: the Purchaser league of America, where he attempted to illuminate shoppers about the new reality in America's protection industry.

At the point when he began in protection, back in his local Florida, he considered it to be a method for making a good living while at the same time assisting Individuals with adapting to monetary misfortune. "I felt significantly better about the thing I was doing."

To start with, he said, the cases division wasn't seen as an expense community, simply an important piece of the business. "It was one of a handful of the chances to really connect with your client, thus they needed to ensure it was a positive encounter," he said.

"It developed throughout that chance to turning into a benefit place, as it were, which it never was planned to be," Romano said. "Furthermore, a ton of that, as I learned close to the end, was a consequence of a great deal of these projects that were being established by McKinsey."

Allstate says courts "didn't recognize institutional issues including underpayment of cases" from the Goliath framework, adding that "McKinsey was not associated with the execution of Giant."

Following quite a while of fights in court, both Dale Deer and Jason ALdridge won settlements from Allstate. Deer was granted $750,000 in addition to intrigue, which Allstate paid in October 2007, over seven years after the mishap. The next year, ALdridge won his own settlement against Allstate. The terms were classified.

## *[L'influence cache]*

### Section 11

**"The Enron Astros"**

At 7:08 p.m. under a cloudy sky, Octavio Dotel of the Houston Astros tossed the game's most memorable throw, denoting the authority opening of Houston's eccentric new baseball arena. It had the association's most memorable retractable rooftop with an enormous glass window that provided fans with a perspective on the city's office towers. Within highlighted a real train and a counterfeit Slope somewhere down in focus field with a flagpole that defenders needed to explore in the uncommon examples balls were hit that far.

On this early April day in 2000, with the temperature in the high seventies, the rooftop stayed open, permitting the sellout horde of 41 thousand to encounter baseball how the stars have aligned just right played — outside.

The arena's inventive plan imparted metro honors to one more Houston organization that likewise looked to be changed: Enron Partnership. Settle d in a fifty-story fabricating a little excursion from the ballpark, Enron had in no time turned into a Money Road number one, riding an updraft of groveling articles and flooding benefits. The organization embraced the in vogue new idea of imaginative annihilation, where enterprises are urged to reestablish themselves occasionally. Under this way of thinking solidness and cooperation become less significant in a commercial center that prizes risk today, not tomorrow. The individual as opposed to the company presently rules, with remunerations going to those most un-terrified of disappointment, a way of thinking portrayed in the generally lauded book on Enron, The Savviest Folks in the Room. These people required no gathering approval, just the boldness to act.

It appeared to be fitting that this creative organization, an image of blasting Houston, would be associated with the shimmering new arena. So on first day of the season, baseball fans watched their most memorable game in an arena called Enron Field. The naming freedoms cost Enron $100 million, a reasonable total for America's seventh-biggest public company. A while later, Enron stock hit an untouched high of $90.56.

The association, be that as it may, didn't stand the test of time. late the next year, Enron fell into what was then the greatest chapter 11 in U.S. history. Enron signs, abruptly a humiliation, were eliminated from the arena. The organization's two chiefs went to jail, and a third was going there when he passed on. As Enron's stupendous arrangement disentangled, its evaluators, the respected Arthur Andersen, were found destroying organization records, driving the organization to give its permit over to work. By and large, in excess of 70,000 Individuals lost their positions, the vast majority of them at Andersen. Numerous Enron workers lost their retirement reserve funds also.

The Astros experienced an alternate sort of shame. Years after the fact, the group cheated to win the World wide championship, bringing about baseball's greatest outrage since White Sox players took cash a century sooner to toss the World wide championship. The Astros' senior supervisor and field administrator were terminated.

## [L'influence cache]

Enron and the Astros were finished in by exorbitant arrogance, yet additionally by their unquestioning confidence in the matchless quality of innovation. Enron involved it to shroud deceitful movement in manners that people in general couldn't comprehend, permitting it to report bogus benefits and keep its stock cost rising. The Astros utilized innovation to take signs and transform players — and the actual game — into bloodless informational collections, adjusting the excellence and show of the country's most cherished sport. "The most brilliant folks in the clubhouse," is the manner by which one magazine alluded to them, a sign of approval for the Enron team. Their conceited egotism transformed the Astros into the most despised group in the majors.

Enron and the Astros shared another significant bond. They put their confidence in McKinsey and Company. The two associations were controlled by a previous McKinsey expert, helped by a stable of specialists still at the firm, a short ten-minute stroll from the arena. After Enron became inseparable from outrage, Paul Krugman, a New York Times editorialist, made sense of McKinsey's part in the organization's death. "Different organizations recruited business masters as experts," he composed. "Enron, in actuality, put the masters in control... . What they made was an organization so stylish that financial backers were stunned. ALso, that let chiefs pull off monetary homicide."

The Title of Krugman's section: "Passing by Master."

McKinsey wasn't embroiled in anything unlawful, a help to the company's overseeing accomplice, Rajat Gupta, who was so stressed he dispatched McKinsey's legal counselor Jean Molino to evaluate what is going on.

In his own life, Gupta wouldn't be so lucky. In the wake of leaving the firm, he was shipped off jail for insider exchanging.

Before Enron, McKinsey's Houston office had been just a little, unimportant station in the company's world wide realm. Paris on the straight it was not, however it offered the chance for daring people to take advantage of the city's boomtown development.

One McKinsey advisor who jumping all over that chance was Jeffrey Skilling, who, after only a Half year in the Dallas office, moved to Houston as the company's third representative there. It was where a splendid alumni of Harvard Business college could carry out his vision of how American enterprises ought to function.

Enron, initially a flammable gas organization, offered him that chance, first as a specialist and later as a leader, during what McKinsey called "the unfolding time of industry liberation." Skilling set off to reorder the gas business. Accepting that the best returns would come not from moving gas however by exchanging it, Skilling created the idea of a "gas bank," where Enron could purchase gas and exchange it, catching the spread between the two, much as banks take in low-premium stores, then loan that cash out at higher rates.

In a little while, Enron — the previous tedious gas organization — was exchanging all that from power, steel, petrochemicals, plastics, water, and paper. It

## [L'influence cache]

turned into an innovation player in the broadband market. For a long time, a significant monetary magazine called Enron America's most creative organization. McKinsey's Houston office turned into a problem area, pulling in $10 million in expenses a year from Enron alone, as the quantity of experts there immediately developed.

Experts tunneled into the organization like multitudes of craftsman insects, remaining weeks, once in a while months. In an uncirculated history of the firm, McKinsey composed that its Enron group worked "throughout each and every year at both the vital and functional levels of the organization." A McKinsey accomplice even went to Enron executive gatherings.

As Enron's stock continued to rise, so did the quantity of positive articles, frequently composed by McKinsey advisors who didn't uncover to perusers that their firm was pulling in huge number of dollars from the organization they were commending. This undercut the company's elevated professions that it could never examine a client's business or the exhortation it delivered. The McKinsey Quarterly commended Enron's "indicated triumphs and resourcefulness something like multiple times" north of a six-year term.

Skilling injected Enron with thoughts he had learned at McKinsey, including the significance of occasionally separating the group. Either advance in the firm or leave. McKinsey referred to it as "up or out." At Enron it was "rank and yank." McKinsey approved Enron's procedure, including risk taking, securitizing credits to gas buyers, and its "resource light" approach. As the McKinsey Quarterly made sense of, Enron turned into a world forerunner in confidential power age "since it saw that benefit didn't rely upon development and activity abilities, however on bargain organizing and risk distribution."

Skilling had been fascinated of securitization since his earliest days at Enron, so in 1990 he set off on a mission to find a broker who knew how to structure a securitization bargain. He found that individual, a youthful broker named Andrew Fastow, at Chicago's Mainland Bank, a trailblazer in securitization. Fastow was quick to move to Houston, his better Half's old neighborhood.

"To that end I was reached, explicitly to sort out an approach to securitize oil and gas holds," Fastow reviewed thirty years after the fact.

Fastow assisted Skilling's unit with its most memorable securitization, which included the making of a unique reason vehicle called Desert plant, which Eliminated obligation from the organization's monetary record. Enron packaged $900 million in credits that it had vowed to pay Petroleum gas makers, securitizing the part and auctioning it off to financial backers, including General Electric . One more reeling sheet substance, JEDI, was planned by Fastow and collaborated Enron with California's Public Workers' Retirement Framework to track down energy speculations.

Skilling's initial work at Enron drew acclaim from four McKinsey partners, who in a 1999 book, Race for the World: Methodologies to Construct an Extraordinary Worldwide Firm, singled out Skilling's Enron Capital and Exchange Assets, the division that did the securitizations. "ECT had the option to fence itself against

## [L'influence cache]

market vacillations and deficiencies through talented monetary designing utilizing instruments, for example, item trades and over-the-counter choices to balance the gamble accepted for every arrangement," they composed.

JEDI was only one of many unique reason vehicles Fastow made at Enron, which swelled benefits and concealed misfortunes, Particularly after he turned into the organization's CFO in 1998. Fastow says that McKinsey experts were not associated with any of his activities.

Guaranteeing that income rose many quarters meant quite a bit to Enron leaders. It made them gigantically affluent while approving their activities according to financial backers. Be that as it may, meeting Money Road's assumptions turned out to be progressively troublesome, so Enron started compromising, utilizing various plans to report higher benefits and to conceal misfortunes. Their casualties were financial backers or banks as well as shoppers. At the point when power costs dropped, Enron kept electrical power, causing brownouts in California. Full assistance was reestablished when costs rose.

While McKinsey was never ensnared in Enron's criminal behavior, numerous inside the firm and out asked why such shrewd Individuals couldn't get a handle on the risk of turning out to be so profoundly engaged with an organization that experienced issues making sense of precisely the way in which it brought in cash. Keeping Enron as a client likewise brought up issues about the nature of the company's gamble directors, a weakness that would surface again and again before very long.

In time, Enron's noteworthy achievement was uncovered to be minimal in excess of a deception. The organization fell after the public discovered that its funds were based "on a trap of fake organizations and plans, not the benefits it answered to financial backers and the general population." McKinsey's true history set out the good aspects of the embarrassment, referring to it as "a dark parody, where the firm starts as a clear headed consultant, becomes energetic supporter and winds up as one of the numerous accidental casualties." The distinction among Enron and McKinsey, the firm composed, was McKinsey's "values."

Veteran business journalists who have autopsied Enron's corpse were not sold on the casualty part. "McKinsey didn't simply cash the checks," Duff McDonald wrote in his set of experiences of the firm. "It completely trusted in the clique and aided spread the gospel."

Not long after Enron collapsed, a book called Moneyball turned into a blockbuster, introducing what one unmistakable sportswriter called the greatest change to proficient baseball since incorporation 50 years sooner. It recounted to the story, later made into a film with Brad Pitt, of how the economical Oakland Sports almost won the flag in 2002 by settling on game choices in view of information examination — investigation for short — as opposed to on informal convictions went down through ages of baseball players.

For McKinsey, the book's prominence made it simpler for the firm to involve its information abilities in the games world. McKinsey assigned Dan Vocalist, a Harvard Business college graduate and a broadly positioned seasoned veteran of

## [L'influence cache]

tackling crossword puzzles, to lead the way. By and large, regulated two types of diversion — sports and betting — which coincided next to each other, however now and again awkwardly.

Throughout the long term, sports associations had participated in a cautious hit the dance floor with the betting business, unfortunate from one viewpoint of giving and taking the respectability of their games while perceiving that betting strengthens interest, especially as innovation significantly extended diversion decisions accessible to general society. The progress of unlawful web betting, a multibillion-dollar industry, was not lost on business people who looked for a lawful cut of that market. The outcome was dream sports, where players are picked in light of past execution and wagers are put over the web on how they will act in real games. Since players are typically drawn from many groups, fixing games would be troublesome, on the off chance that certainly feasible. ALL things considered, it was all the while betting, simply under an alternate name.

Wagering in individual groups is another matter, and that is a side of McKinsey's business seldom examined. The firm educated one concerning the world's most well known sports books, William Slope, which paid the firm as of late nearly $40 million, as indicated by organization records. In that equivalent period McKinsey likewise took in $14 million for prompting Caesars Diversion, the monster gambling club administrator. Caesars in the long run purchased William Slope, extending its versatile wagering activity to eight states with the possibility of more coming on the web.

McKinsey has bragged helping the "main club gaming organizations" grow their business through faithfulness programs pointed toward actuating speculators to bet more. Under one arrangement, called "bleeding edge strengthening," McKinsey said an orderly could offer players $50 when they are going to leave. Moreover "high-esteem clients can get passes to Celine Dion shows as well as room overhauls, while low-esteem clients get free air terminal rides."

Vocalist, who was instrumental in rearranging dream sports when its practices experienced harsh criticism, had a foot in the two games and betting. As per his authority McKinsey bio, he filled in as "an essential counsel to seven of the ten biggest games associations on the planet as well as various games groups, gatherings, and government bodies." He likewise counseled for gaming organizations, including club, sports books, horse racing, and e-sports.

While Vocalist's name seldom surfaced in news records of games, his experiences were esteemed by information examiners who don't make their living scoring runs or scores.

McKinsey developed its skill in information science by purchasing a little, tip top counseling organization called QuantumBlack, which utilized information to assess competitors in the US and Europe. One of its claims to fame was injury expectation — an undeniable area important to card sharks. Knowing whether certain players were inclined to injury could impact wagering chances, however there is no proof this kind of data was spilled to card sharks.

## [L'influence cache]

As indicated by QuantumBlack's landing page, it assisted a soccer with joining survey the "strength of its players and recognize the actual measurements that could flag looming wounds." QuantumBlack's assessments were so nitty gritty they included taking spit tests. "Utilizing objective clinical markers and data from earlier wounds, we distinguished the elements that correspond to injury beginning in the hamstring, upper leg, and lower leg," the organization said. As though to separate its work from the speculative babble of sports radio and television experts, the organization announced that its visually impaired authentic testing "accurately conjecture 170 out of 184 non-influence muscle wounds."

The organization is more meticulous in examining its work in the US.

In September 2013, players on the New York Knicks were frightened to see unidentified Individuals taking notes at shut rehearsals and in group flights. The group's proprietor, James Dolan, at last recognized that the outsiders were McKinsey experts and that their recommendation drove him to fire the group's head supervisor, Glen Grunwald, after the Knicks had arrived at the second round of the end of the season games, a high-water mark that hasn't been copied since. Dolan believed McKinsey should revamp the group, accentuating innovation, without determining what that implied.

This command perplexed Dave Hopla, a Knicks shooting trainer, who told The Athletic, "I wouldn't have an issue in the event that a counseling firm came in and it was Hubie Brown and John Thompson or something, yet not a counseling firm with a few young lady from MIT and some person from Stanford that don't understand anything about b-ball."

During one stretch mentors were told not to watch game film with players. Their need became finishing up definite reports on players' exhibition and perspectives. Hopla turned out to be so baffled with what he considered a generally useless activity he once kept his reports in the men's restroom, where he thought they had a place, as opposed to on the work area of a McKinsey representative.

That season, the Knicks missed the end of the season games by a solitary game and didn't make the end of the season games until 2021, when they lost in the primary round.

Had the players known all that McKinsey was doing, there could have been more prominent disagreement in the group as well as around the association. Previous QuantumBlack representatives told the writers of this book that they were subtly utilizing clinical data to anticipate lower-body wounds. "It was exceptionally secretive inside at the group, working straightforwardly with the group specialist," one previous expert said. "They didn't believe the players should be aware." Should a player be recognized as prone to be harmed, the expert said, that could influence contract exchanges.

The discoveries eventually demonstrated of negligible worth, yet they highlighted a waiting worry about whom group specialists should serve — proprietors or players. This issue would turn out to be colossally dubious in the Public Football Association when some group specialists made light of genuine proof of extremely durable mind harm from blackouts.

## [L'influence cache]

However, it was Significant Association Baseball, explicitly the Houston Astros, where McKinsey had its greatest effect

Another age of video gear delivered gigantic measures of granular information on each pitch and each batted ball. Therefore, a few long-held presumptions about how to dominate matches were tested. Presently players were told to pull the ball, to change their swing plane to create more homers, as opposed to line drives. Pitchers were told to toss more bends, less sinkers, and more four-crease fastballs high in the strike zone as opposed to at a hitter's knees. The most outrageous experts of baseball investigation accepted that the whole game could be diminished to numbers, uncontaminated by human opinion, feElings, or, incidentally, even morals.

The inquiry hiding underneath this was when does information examination get over from assisting competitors with performing better to dehumanizing their game. That issue took on new importance due to what a man named Jeff Luhnow — a previous McKinsey expert — was doing down in Houston.

A Wharton School graduate with a MBA from Northwestern, Luhnow had a fan's advantage in baseball and measurements yet didn't at first seek to work in sports. During his five years at McKinsey, his obligations remembered working for the association's abundantly defamed Allstate account. As a lesser individual from the Allstate group, Luhnow is probably not going to play had an impact in contriving that plan, however it makes one can't help thinking about what examples, if any, he could have taken from the experience.

Then Moneyball went along, and it aroused his interest and incited the St. Louis Cardinals to reexamine their baseball activity. With the assistance of a previous McKinsey partner — the child in-law of the Cardinals' proprietor — Luhnow found a new line of work as the group's VP for exploring and player improvement, a shockingly significant situation for a rookie with no proper foundation in baseball.

Luhnow immediately flagged his obligation to examination by employing Sig Mejdal, a previous blackjack seller who had likewise filled in as a specialist for lockheed Martin and NASA. He changed vocations subsequent to perusing Moneyball. Mejdal's depiction of present day baseball didn't summon reco1lections of Casey Stenge1 or Yogi Berra. "You will require information base, you will require people with data set abilities, you will require servers, you will require investigators to examine that information, and afterward you will require experts or others with abilities to introduce it to the chiefs."

Luhnow's appearance steamed baseball conservatives. Despite his good faith, Cardinals representatives referred to him as "Harry Potter" or "the bookkeeper." Yet Luhnow tremendously worked on the nature of players drafted by the Cardinals and secured himself as an extraordinary voice in the baseball world .

Luhnow's faith in the otherworld ly powers of numbers in the long run grabbed the eye of the Houston Astros. They, as well, needed more examination, so the Astros employed Luhnow as senior supervisor, the main situation in a baseball association. His work: characterize the group's main goal, pursue the important yet

## [L'influence cache]

questionable choices, and guarantee that everybody acted as one with the group's core values. Which were, basically, to win.

Mejdal, the NASA researcher, accompanied him. Another early recruit was Brandon Taubman, a numbers-sharp speculation financier. He, as well, had no foundation in baseball, however accepted there should be a more legitimate method for pursuing choices on player staff and in-game technique. Taubman would be advanced multiple times in five years, rising to the gig of partner senior supervisor, Luhnow's top assistant. Other tech folks were welcomed on board, with nary a tobacco spitter among them.

Luhnow carried with him the ethos of his old business McKinsey, where accomplishing higher benefits was the norm by which the company's prosperity was estimated. McKinsey had a sweeping perspective on the worth of investigation. "We can utilize it to guarantee that we're enlisting the ideal Individuals," said Dominic Barton, McKinsey's previous overseeing accomplice. "We have a superior feEling of foreseeing who will leave. We have a superior feEling of who makes esteem inside associations. We can be considerably more granular about that. The entire investigation around Individuals has changed."

In the same way as other previous counseling partners, Luhnow embraced the idea of "disturbance," a word progressively used to depict foundational change. He talked about needing to be on the "extreme forefront" of that change. Luhnow accomplished more than channel McKinsey's lessons; he employed the firm to direct the Astros on its new excursion. More Elite level graduates telling baseball Individuals how to play the game.

Similarly as with Enron, the McKinsey Quarterly turned into the congregation ensemble. In a two-section interview with Luhnow, the Quarterly vowed to show "how examination, association, and culture join to make upper hand in a lose industry." In the event that you don't win, you lose. The Quarterly didn't specify that the Astros were likewise a McKinsey client. Luhnow let the questioner know where baseball was going:

>large information joined with man-made reasoning is the Following enormous wave in baseball, and I believe we're simply beginning to start to expose what's underneath. It's a region that I view as exceptionally restrictive, so I don't talk about it before my opposition. Be that as it may, we're making a major interest around here. I think different clubs are too. There's so much being caught. There's radar and video at each office in baseball now, in addition to the significant associations yet the lower levels, universities, beginning to go into secondary schools. We understand what each individual is doing on the field consistently. We understand what the bat and ball are doing on the field consistently.

Baseball is a business, and as the McKinsey Quarterly noticed, "the business is to win." Jeff Luhnow needed to win. "In the event that we're not committing a few errors en route, we're not being sufficiently forceful," he said.

Luhnow's interest with numbers stretched out to the investigation of players' bodies and their penchant for injury, a Specialty of McKinsey's QuantumBlack,

## [L'influence cache]

which likewise worked for the Astros. "We frequently measure imbalances in players' bodies, since those are regions probably going to separate," Luhnow told 200 Individuals at the Singh Place for Nanotechnology at the College of Pennsylvania. "We want to expect wounds, instead of hang tight for them to occur prior to responding." The reason behind combining sports medication and innovation, he said, was "to amplify players' exhibition."

Before long, one more strategy for further developing player execution would be uncovered not by the Astros but rather by the media. Furthermore, that technique would cost the positions of three significant association field chiefs and a senior supervisor — Luhnow.

On a hot Houston evening in September 2017, the White Sox pitcher Danny Farquhar took the hill, endeavoring to safeguard a 3-1 lead over the Astros. The groups were moving this way and that. The Sox were modifying; the Astros were charging ahead to a possible 101-win season.

The retractable rooftop over Minute Servant Park, né Enron Field, was shut, and with the arena just somewhat the greater part full sound voyaged well, a reality that became significant for what was going to occur.

In the eighth inning, Evan Gattis of the Astros stepped in the hitter's container. "There was a banging from the burrow, practically like a bat raising a ruckus around town rack each time a changeup signal got put down," Farquhar said. "After the third one, I ventured off. I was tossing some great changeups and they were getting fouled off. After the third bang, I ventured off."

Farquhar trusted that somebody, some way or another, was involving the banging as a method for motioning toward the player what pitch to anticipate. Groups for the most part attempt to take signs — legitimately — by searching in from a respectable Halfway point to see what pitch the catcher is motioning for and afterward imparting that to the player. Yet, for this situation no sprinter was on a respectable Halfway point.

Pitching from the stretch, Farquhar unexpectedly halted and strolled toward the catcher. They presented and consented to utilize more intricate signs. Another changeup was called, yet this time there was no banging. Farquhar's record was subsequently affirmed by video posted on the web by Jomboy Media Corp.

It was by and large present for anybody to check out or examine. In any case, nobody did. Farquhar was irate that no journalists covering the game asked him what had occurred. The Astros proceeded to win the World wide championship, the primary in Establishment history, in what The Washington Post called "the second the examination development vanquished the game for good."

In 2018, additional troubling episodes happened including Houston. One of the most serious occurred in what might be the third season finisher game between the Cleveland Indians and Houston.

No group had gone longer without winning the World wide championship than Cleveland. Two years sooner, the Chicago Whelps beat the Indians in additional

## [L'influence cache]

innings of the seventh and last round of the World wide championship. Nineteen years before that, Cleveland turned into the primary group to bring a lead into the 10th inning of game 7 and lose — again in additional innings.

In any case, Cleveland — the hard-karma city with evaporating position, awful schools, and government debasement — trusted that 2018 would be the year to break the revile, reestablishing pride in the city. The Indians were an incredible group, having set an American Association record the earlier year of 22 straight wins. The Indians likewise had the association's best pitcher, the Cy Youthful Honor victor Corey Kluber.

Furthermore, that is where matters remained in 2018 when Cleveland met Houston in the best-of-five end of the season games. The initial two games were in Houston, and Cleveland lost them both. However, the third would be in their home ballpark. Win or be killed.

Then something bizarre occurred. A man with Houston certifications acquired unapproved admittance to the media-just camera pit quickly close to Cleveland's hole. When inside, he involved his PDA to keep action in the hole clandestinely. That baldfaced act surprised Andre Knott, a veteran live field correspondent who covers Indians games. "I was taking a gander at his certifications and considering what is somebody from the Houston Astros doing here?" Knott said. Was it to take signs from the seat mentor, Brad Plants, or to see data that the director, Terry Francona, taped to the burrow wall, showing pitcher-hitter matchups?

Knott said he isn't a nark however regardless thought the man's direct so strange he snapped an image of him in the demonstration and communicated it to Indians authorities, who informed MLB security. The covert agent, recognized as Kyle Mclaughlin, was accompanied from the field and his accreditations seized. Then, at that point, Houston attempted it once more during the game, an Indians leader said.

As news spread the Indians burrow that Knott got an Astros agent seeing, the players were enraged. The occurrence validated their intuitions — and those of different groups — that the Astros would successfully win. While playing the Astros, players said they some of the time heard whistles, applauds, and banging before pitches, conceivably flagging what pitch was coming. After Cleveland's most memorable game in Houston, Corey Kluber and his catcher, Yan Gomes, both told partners they were stunned that nobody had swung at Kluber's best pitch, a shooting slider. Not one to rationalize or gripe, Kluber said secretly that he never had hitters lay off each slider he tossed.

Cleveland lost the last game and was dispensed with. After the game, the Indians' beginning pitcher, Mike Clevinger, was inquired as to why Houston won.

"I will keep it truly short," he said. "We... sort of had our options somewhat limited before this series began when it came to the insightful side." His obscure comments turned into the subject of much hypothesis throughout the next weeks. What he implied, Knott said, was that the Astros cheated, something many significant leaguers previously thought. As a matter of fact, during the game,

## [L'influence cache]

Clevinger must be limited while shouting at a Houston player, "We realize you are cheating."

The Indians documented a conventional dissent with MlB and cautioned the Astros' next rival, the Boston Red Sox. For good explanation. In their most memorable game, Boston got a similar Astros official, Kyle Mclaughlin, endeavoring what he had done in Cleveland.

Significant Association Baseball explored the two episodes and gave a short explanation that excused Houston. "An intensive examination presumed that an Astros representative was checking the field to guarantee that the restricting Club was not disregarding any standards." It gave no subtleties.

Scarcely any Individuals trusted the clarification. Knott referred to it as "b.s." Paul Hoynes, a call-it-like-he-sees-it correspondent who takes care of the Indians for quite a long time, concurred. "No, I don't buy that," he said. "I can't completely accept that nothing was at any point finished about it." And that was a disgrace, he added, in light of the fact that the episodes were a harbinger of what might be on the horizon.

The Astros kept up with their account. "We were playing safeguard," Luhnow said. "We were not playing offense. We need to ensure it's an in any event, battleground."

On the off chance that MlB's examination was pretty much as exhaustive as it claims, specialists conversed with some unacceptable Individuals or posed some unacceptable inquiries. The principles preclude utilizing electronic gear during games to take signs, yet The Athletic's Ken Rosenthal and Evan Drellich later found that an Astros chief sent an email to scouts in August 2017, empowering them to take signs — with cameras if essential:

One thing in unambiguous we are searching for is choosing up signs coming from the hole. What we are searching for is the amount we can see, how we would log things, on the off chance that we really want cameras/optics, and so on. So go to game, see what you can (or can't) do and report back your discoveries.

After a year, Houston's Kyle Mclaughlin pointed his camera — without punishment — inside the burrows of Cleveland and Boston during the game's holiest of times, the end of the season games. Houston didn't go to the World wide championship this time, losing to Boston in the end of the season games.

The Astros rehashed win the flag in 2019. In any case, during the boisterous postgame festivity, Houston's painstakingly arranged picture as the savviest, hardest association in the majors started to crumble quicker than anybody might have envisioned. It started when Brandon Taubman, the previous investor turned colleague head supervisor, communicated his scorn for anybody sufficiently silly to scrutinize the insight of Luhnow exchanging for Roberto Osuna, a world class nearer, while serving a 75 game suspension for aggressive behavior at home.

"Express gratitude toward God we got Osuna. I'm so freaking happy we got Osuna," Taubman shouted in the storage space, coordinating his remarks toward

## [L'influence cache]

three female journalists, one of whom wore an abusive behavior at home mindfulness wristband. Taubman said it multiple times. "Express gratitude toward God we got Osuna. I'm so incredibly happy we got Osuna."

The majority of the Astros' front office protested the exchange, as per Ben lindbergh and Travis Sawchik, creators of The MVP Machine, yet "Luhnow... slammed it through notwithstanding," with the help from the Astros' proprietor, Jim Crane. While different groups passed on Osuna, Luhnow's way of life of winning regardless of the profound quality of his activities — a disposition showed some of the time by McKinsey specialists — put the Astros aside. In the event that the numbers shouted "sign him," sign him they did. Luhnow prior must be convinced not to draft an indicted kid molester.

After an overflow of analysis, the Astros terminated Taubman, and the group proceeded to lose the World wide championship to the Washington Nationals. Then, at that point, the genuinely terrible news hit. Ken Rosenthal and Evan Drellich of The Athletic broke the story that Houston cheated to dominate matches. Disregarding association runs, the group utilized live video to take signs from the catcher, which they decoded and imparted to hitters by beating on a garbage bin in the passage prompting the burrow.

Significant Association Baseball examined and found that the sign taking happened all through 2017 — including the World wide championship when the Astros beat the Dodgers — and in 2018. Significant Association Baseball's official, Ransack Manfred, suspended Luhnow and the group director, A. J. Hinch. Despite the fact that Luhnow denied being familiar with the cheating, "there is both narrative and tribute proof that Luhnow had some information on those endeavors," Manfred composed. Hinch opposed the plan however didn't stop it. Soon after the suspensions were reported, both were terminated, as were two other field supervisors who knew about the plan when they were with the Astros.

The report's most accursing end was not the cheating fundamentally however what happens when an investigation driven distraction with winning goes excessively far:

> It is exceptionally obvious to me that the way of life of the baseball tasks division, showing itself in how its representatives are dealt with, its relations with different Clubs, and its relations with the media and outer partners, has been extremely dangerous. To some degree in my view, the baseball tasks division's separate culture — one that esteemed and compensated results over different contemplations, joined with a staff of people who frequently needed heading or adequate oversight, drove, to some degree to a limited extent, to the Brandon Taubman occurrence... lastly, to a climate that permitted the lead depicted in this report to have happened.

McKinsey's name didn't show up in Manfred's report, and no proof arose connecting it to the outrage. Yet, the company's job in forming the way of life of the Astros was evident. "The Astros didn't recruit McKinsey to audit ticket deals, concessions or product," one veteran baseball author from The Athletic finished up. "This was about baseball tasks and baseball tasks just, an eagerness to open up the most fundamental and isolated region of the group to finish pariahs."

## [L'influence cache]

Mejdal, the previous Astros official, said in a meeting that McKinsey's work was not quite so significant as certain Individuals accepted. "My general sense was they were investigating our cycles, how would we foster players, what's our framework for our information frameworks, and the reinforcements we had for them, how is our front office coordinated. That's what things like." Mejdal was not engaged with the bamboozling embarrassment and presently works for the Baltimore Orioles.

One baseball insider said McKinsey for the most part utilized its connections to the Astros to intrigue clients and expected clients, as opposed to score enormous expenses.

There's no questioning that Luhnow's stewardship of the Astros thought about inadequately McKinsey as well as on the illustrations he would have taken from his time at the firm. Had he not been terminated, the magistrate would have requested Luhnow to partake in "a proper program of the executives/authority preparing to guarantee no episodes of the kind portrayed in this report happen from now on."

Instead of finishing the discussion, the magistrate's report made another one. Players who contended and lost to Houston, including probably the calmest, greatest names in the game, whined furiously that no Astros players were focused. The group kept its World wide championship Title, and the Astros' short however strong second baseman, José ALtuve, kept his American Association Most Significant Player grant.

"Scorn for the Astros runs profound — and has a long time before this episode," ESPN's Jeff Passan composed. "Desire breeds some of it. The association's self-importance represents the rest. The Astros painted themselves as a disrupter and delighted in the uproar."

The outrage went far past gloating privileges. It impacted players' livElihoods. "It's miserable for baseball," said Mike Trout, baseball's ideal and least questionable player. "Folks ' vocations have been impacted. A many Individuals lost positions."

The deceiving hurt youthful pitchers battling to remain in the majors after unfortunate excursions. Furthermore, it could have kept the Yankees star, Aaron Judge, from winning the Most Significant Player grant, and the profit that accompany it. "Baseball has lost its spirit under a developing technocracy," the veteran baseball essayist Tom Verducci finished up. "The Astros are the admonition shot of what happens when it goes excessively far."

Houston's examination insurgency subverted two customary mainstays of the game — scouts and Small time Baseball. The Astros destroyed their exploring division by putting a higher worth on numbers to the prohibition of human perception. What's more, it facilitated the way for the Houston-drove intend to dispense with many small time groups, frequently the monetary and Social focus of unassuming community America, as well as the door through which ages of youngsters have fostered a supporting interest in the game.

## [L'influence cache]

The amount McKinsey could have added to these choices isn't known, yet it was no mysterious that McKinsey met with Astros scouts — some of whom scarcely understood what the firm did. Furthermore, at the command of Chief Manfred, McKinsey likewise embraced a "full-scale" survey of Significant Association Baseball that created changes to the association design and faculty.

Examination drove pitchers to increment turn rates to create greater development, players to hit more homers, and defenders to reposition themselves to interfere with fair hits. One thing it hasn't done is to figure out how to carry more Individuals to the ballpark. Participation at major-association games had fallen in six of the last seven pre-Coronavirus years. Baseball essayists who once celebrated examination are presently addressing whether it made the game less invigorating. Presently baseball stresses homers and strikeouts, instead of pitchers tossing total games or sprinters progressing from first to third on singles.

One McKinsey expert wailed over Luhnow's methodology of "destroying" ineffectively paid work in the minors to help a multibillion-dollar industry.

In the mean time, McKinsey, perceiving that it had outfitted some unacceptable pony, withdrew the article lauding Luhnow's "examination, association, and culture." As opposed to take ownership of its misguided thinking, the McKinsey Quarterly offered this faltering and to a great extent reality free clarification: " 'How the Houston Astros are winning through cutting edge examination's was Eliminated considering resulting improvements proposing that elements past information examination were critical supporters of the Astros' prosperity."

ALL in all, they cheated.

## *[L'influence cachée]*

### Section 12

**"Clubbing Seals"**

**The South Africa Catastrophe**

Molded by a first class life experience school in the forested lower regions of the Himalayas, Vikas Sagar was taught from the get-go in the qualities that McKinsey apparently upheld: civil rights, uniformity, and administration. His coed school, one of the most seasoned and most lofty in Asia, anticipated that understudies should live by the witticism engraved in the school peak: "Never yield." As though to demonstrate fealty to those words, a few understudies really scaled Mount Everest.

Years after the fact, Sagar carried that outlook to his occupation as an expert in McKinsey's Johannesburg office. He ran. He swam. He cycled. McKinsey values competitors for their capacity to persevere through extended periods of time of work, travel, and absence of rest. Sagar's physicality made him fit in.

In alternate ways, however, he was unique in relation to the rest. His extravagance — fast to embrace nearly anybody — hung out in an organization characterized by numbers, calculation sheets, and PowerPoint slides. Bianca Goodson, a chief in a little counseling organization, recalls Sagar well. One night after a long conference inside McKinsey's Johannesburg office, Goodson said Sagar unexpectedly moved on the meeting room table and moved. Nobody who realized him found that story astonishing.

Since he was famous and amusing to be near, Sagar's character helped him create and sustain client connections. His capacity to get business dazzled senior McKinsey chiefs, energizing his ascent in the association, first as an accomplice, then, at that point, as a senior collaborate with a base compensation of no less than $1 million every year, excluding rewards.

He joined the Johannesburg office at an advantageous time. South Africa was opening its wallet to McKinsey, and the firm anxiously spent that cash. It moved into new twin glass towers, associated by raised walkways. Free beverages on Fridays streamed to those not currently welcome to private, wine-drenched evening gatherings. One accomplice drove a yellow Ferrari, others Porsches or BMWs.

This didn't be ignored among government authorities whom McKinsey rElied upon for contracts. "When am I going to get my Porsche?" asked one.

At the point when politically-sanctioned racial segregation ruled as the rule that everyone must follow, an UN exchange ban looked to pressure South African pioneers into changing their racial strategies. The impulse to break that ban was perfect. The nation had a high level economy and an abundance of regular assets, including precious stones, gold, Coal, and platinum. McKinsey nearly surrendered to the allurement. Three years before the stain of politically-sanctioned racial segregation was taken out, Standard Bank of South Africa attempted to employ McKinsey. Interested, yet mindful of the reputational harm that would result,

## [L'influence cache]

McKinsey sent a group to Johannesburg to examine. Independently, the firm asked a fresh recruit, Susan Rice, the future public safety consultant to Obama, for her viewpoint. The firm eventually declined the bank's proposition.

Years after the fact, the senior accomplice David Fine, a white local South African, talked proudly of his company's refusal to take clients there until free multiracial races were held. At the point when that at long last occurred in 1994, experts at the firm clamored to be a piece of South Africa's resurrection.

However working in South Africa was not generally so basic as assisting Allstate with selling more protection or Philip Morris sell more cigarettes.

Nelson Mandela's ideological group, the African Public Congress, concluded that a solid focal government ought to lead the way in changing society, a methodology that put a significant weight on a country with no just practices and an untested general set of laws. It didn't help that McKinsey fabricated its standing exhorting organizations, not states.

For quite a long time McKinsey had moved toward government work warily after a humiliating episode in 1970 when a paper revealed that the firm had benefitted from New York City contracts while a McKinsey accomplice worked free in the city financial plan office. New York answered by ending $1 million in installments to McKinsey. No charges were recorded and the city ultimately continued installments, yet the episode showed the firm that administration work conveyed uplifted investigation and reputational risk.

McKinsey's demeanor, in any case, relaxed over the course of the years as the firm perceived that to hold its roost on the counseling industry, a bigger client pool was required. By the early long periods of the twenty-first hundred years, the firm had reappeared the open arena in a significant manner — in America, yet entirely all over the planet.

In South Africa, McKinsey felt it had no real option except to take on government work and the gamble that accompanied it. "To be significant in a nation like South Africa, you need to engage in the public area," a previous chief of the Johannesburg office noticed.

In any case, the early positive sentiments that came from aiding Dark South Africans started to blur as Mandela's vision of a kinder, more impartial country gave way to defilement and savagery in the ANC. Party agents were siphoning tremendous amounts of public assets intended to lift up Dark South Africans. At first this wilderness stayed behind the scenes, however that changed as ANC legislators started killing each other to conceal their burglary. After it was uncovered that the ANC's public representative, Mucks Ngonyama, remained to make up to $10 million through a public agreement, he answered, "I didn't join the battle to be poor."

Western organizations were not blameless onlookers.

Chime Pottinger, perhaps of London's most persuasive public connection firms, fanned racial divisions in South Africa in a ploy to redirect consideration from a

## [L'influence cache]

client's bad open agreements. The marketing specialists did this through counterfeit Twitter accounts and by mixing outrage about "white syndication capital" in South Africa.

The goliath German programming firm SAP paid a go between $9 million bucks regarding getting contracts with state-possessed offices. KPMG, the evaluating firm, assisted President Jacob Zuma with eviscerating the state charge organization, preparing for him to fire the money serve, a pundit of a strong Zuma partner.

McKinsey entered the fight in 2005 when it started exhorting Transnet, the state-claimed rail and port organization. To counsel for a state-claimed undertaking, McKinsey needed to follow an administration order expecting workers for hire to impart a part of their business to a Dark possessed subcontractor, a type of financial reallocation. Assuming the relationship was appropriately taken care of, these subcontractors would ultimately foster the abilities expected to go out all alone. It worked like an organized marriage with every one of the orderly issues of two outsiders figuring out how to live respectively.

It was significant for McKinsey to observe the guidelines and do it rapidly in light of the fact that Transnet direly required redesigning. A fundamental piece of the country's economy, Transnet utilized 60,000 specialists and upheld another 200,000 to 300,000 positions. The mining business required cargo trains to move minerals around a country almost two times the size of Texas. Power plants rElied upon ordinary shipments of warm Coal to create power. Furthermore, the port city of Durban required Transnet to convey freight for send out.

McKinsey's most memorable Transnet subcontractor was a little counseling organization called letsema. Generally that marriage was a blissful one, however clashes emerged over how much work letsema contributed and how some McKinsey experts treated letsema representatives. In 2013, McKinsey headed out in different directions from letsema in the wake of discovering that it was prompting General Electric — a possible bidder for a train supply contract that McKinsey was supervising for Transnet.

McKinsey currently needed to find one more accomplice when these Dark financial strengthening organizations were progressively utilized as fronts for degenerate exercises. The nation was set out toward inconvenience, and most everybody knew it, compromising South Africa's dElicate majority rule government and McKinsey's developing business.

To try not to become trapped in these bad plans, McKinsey expected to completely vet its new Dark strengthening accomplice and clients too. That didn't occur. ALL things being equal, the firm erroneously regarded Transnet like it were a privately owned business, not government possessed, which would have set off a more elevated level of a reasonable level of investment. So when Transnet suggested that McKinsey employ Regiments Capital as its accomplice, the firm did a generally superficial survey and tracked down no critical issues.

To work on Transnet's administrations, McKinsey gathered a group that in the end expanded to 100 specialists, helped by 94 global specialists and many Transnet

## [L'influence cache]

representatives. The company's advisors tunneled so profound into the organization that one Transnet official considered how the office might at any point work without them.

For such a significant, remote, McKinsey had needed areas of strength for a the pioneer country. That individual ended up being David Fine, the South African-conceived expert. Savvy, noble, yet not Particularly famous, Fine didn't act like Sagar, his more wicked partner. Nobody could envision him rashly embracing outsiders or moving on a meeting table. A couple of partners called him socially abnormal.

Transnet ended up being a rowdy client.

The rail office had rehired its previous cargo rail boss, Siyabonga Gama, who had been terminated before for contracting abnormalities. Furthermore, Jürgen Schrempp, a previous DaimlerChrysler CEO, unexpectedly left the Transnet board on the grounds that the organization neglected to counsel him prior to naming another CEO, Brian Molefe. The choice to sidestep him, Schrempp said, was "absolutely unseemly" and an impression of "poor corporate administration" — words that ought to have resounded with McKinsey, Particularly since Schrempp was notable to the company's German accomplices.

While Schrempp stayed in obscurity, the arrangement did not shock Ajay, Atul, and Rajesh Gupta — three émigré Siblings from India who were quick turning into the nexus of supposed plans to attack the public depository through front organizations. A Gupta-claimed paper revealed the arrangement months before it was openly declared.

Since showing up in South Africa during the 1990s, the Guptas had utilized Individuals near President Zuma to assist with building a business domain that included mining, transportation, PCs, and the media. The family even recruited two of Zuma's kids.

Their most bold presentation of riches and impact came in 2013 when the Guptas organized "the wedding of the hundred years" for a family member, a multiday issue for which the lady of the hour's folks booked each room in one of South Africa's most lavish hotels in Sun City. South Africans were infuriated by how a Gupta-sanctioned fly with 200 visitors from India had been allowed to sidestep Johannesburg's business air terminal so it could land at a profoundly safe army installation nearer to Sun City. As revealed by The New York Times, the visitors were carried to the wedding site at the Royal residence of the lost City "in extravagance vehicles joined by a rambling security escort, alarms blasting."

The Guptas welcomed conspicuous South Africans to the wedding, including McKinsey's David Fine, who said he didn't join in, adding that he had never met the Guptas and had no clue about why he was welcomed. McKinsey leaders demanded they knew nothing about the Guptas' political impact.

Others were more attentive.

## *[L'influence cache]*

In late February 2011, a South African paper cited Sdumo Dlamini, a strong worker's organization president, communicating worry about the Guptas. "We are concerned that we are progressively seeing serious deals occurring in a dubious way," Dlamini said. A long time later, South Africa's Mail and Gatekeeper detailed comparable stresses over conceivable Gupta impact in state-claimed offices.

Indifferent, McKinsey assumed on the liability of directing a dangerous new framework plan inside Transnet's cargo rail division run by, as a matter of fact, Siyabonga Gama, a similar leader who had been terminated for contracting inconsistencies and afterward mysteriously rehired.

Transnet's arrangement was an immense bet.

As opposed to put resources into framework in light of current orders, Transnet wanted to contribute without affirmed orders, basically wagering a huge number of dollars on business that didn't yet exist. To succeed, the program required McKinsey to foresee future financial movement precisely. The association's hopeful figure drove Transnet to arrange the greatest capital acquirement in its set of experiences — the acquisition of 1,064 trains.

For a thought of what could lie ahead, Transnet expected to look no farther than its sister organization, the Traveler Rail Organization of South Africa. In Walk 2013, PRASA paid generally $200 million for trains in an arrangement that, as per court reports, "was saturated with debasement and bid-fixing." The end result demonstrated diverting. The overrated trains were excessively tall for the South African rail framework or were rarely conveyed. One wrecked during a test, and those excess were set available to be purchased.

Transnet's train buy was greater and more noteworthy for the country's economy. McKinsey fixed the worth of Transnet's buy at around $2.6 billion. After a progression of deferrals, Transnet unexpectedly concluded in mid 2014 that the obtainment must be made right away. Awkward with the short cutoff time, McKinsey quit exhorting on that acquirement similarly as the triumphant bidders were going to be chosen.

Practically short-term, the price tag hopped almost $1 billion. Fine said the higher installments included "superfluous variables which generally speaking are difficult to make sense of." as a matter of fact, he added, "they are not reasonable." Another McKinsey senior accomplice was distrustful. "I've never heard that the cost goes up after exchanges," he said. "You have a proposal on the table and the chief arranges the cost upwards?"

McKinsey was not chaste in this disaster. The firm had misjudged customer interest for the trains, making Transnet purchase overrated trains that it didn't require. In contrast to Transnet, be that as it may, McKinsey really benefitted off its defective gauge by getting the occupation of fixing the issue it assisted with making. Its new task: cut expenses and lift incomes.

Matthew Chaskalson, a protected regulation master and an individual from a legal commission examining what it called "state catch" — basically a quiet overthrow — said McKinsey started packing enormous Transnet contracts in the wake of

## [L'influence cachée]

employing a subcontracting accomplice, Regiments, which ended up having connects to the politically strong Gupta family. "There is an unprecedented progression of sole-source contracts," Chaskalson expressed, highlighting the company's seven sole-source contracts in under eighteen months. During that period, he noticed, McKinsey's charges developed "dramatically."

Questions were raised, unobtrusively from the start, inside McKinsey's Johannesburg office about those agreements.

Colin Douglas was at his home in Cape Town when he discovered that McKinsey had been making a few inquiries on the off chance that anybody knew about dubious way of behaving at the firm including Transnet. An early recruit in McKinsey's Johannesburg office, Douglas had filled in as the occupant essayist and specialized expert for a long time prior to passing on to independent in 2004. While at the firm, he got to know Sagar, so when he learned of McKinsey's request about Transnet, Douglas recalled something surprising and he reached the firm.

The outcome was full-scale alarm in the Johannesburg office and across McKinsey's world wide realm.

Douglas recounted an unusual solicitation two or three years sooner from Vikas Sagar to assist with composing somebody's MBA proposal. That somebody ended up being Siyabonga Gama, the famous head of the cargo rail bunch when McKinsey chipped away at the train acquirement. In spite of the fact that Douglas communicated reservations, he felt free to compose somewhere around two parts with help from McKinsey staff.

For his work, Douglas got around $7,000 charged to two distinct Transnet accounts, excluding the worth of commitments from other McKinsey representatives. McKinsey quickly perceived the ghost of a potential infringement of the U.S. Unfamiliar Degenerate Practices Act — for giving what could be seen as a pay off, inciting an excited interior examination.

The firm reasoned that the worth of its administrations to Gama must be accounted for as a potential FCPA infringement. Yet, the U.S. government made no move after McKinsey said it found no connection between aiding Gama and contract grants.

On the off chance that McKinsey's seniors had required some investment to truly get to know Sagar, they could have seen this coming.

Sagar had developed associations with pioneers at Regiments and Transnet, and his progress in dealing with those connections — and the cash that moved from them — dazzled his McKinsey accomplices such a lot of that they chose him a senior accomplice.

He had prepared for his position at McKinsey in the US, getting a college degree at the College of Michigan and a MBA from the Wharton School. After a concise spell in McKinsey's Chicago office, Sagar began a little data the board organization

## [L'influence cache]

in Kuwait, then rejoined McKinsey in Africa in 2001. Sagar arrived in the company's Johannesburg office quite a while after Fine.

A female business chief who went to gatherings with Sagar depicted him as presumptuous however Bollywood attractive, decorated with a Hermès belt, Montblanc sleeve buttons, and a Louis Vuitton folder case. "The main time Vikas at any point addressed me," the chief said, "was the point at which I took my pristine Prada pack to a gathering and he murmured 'dazzling sack' — prior to adding that I ought to have purchased a Celine."

Fine and Sagar moved toward work in an unexpected way. Fine followed organization methodology, counseling accomplices on significant choices. He rose rapidly from accomplice to senior accomplice to chief of the Johannesburg office and later to a territorial director. Sagar, by dint of his character, liked to manage clients, barring even his partners. Office seniors cautioned Sagar that acting alone was flippant, however they for the most part taken no notice. In the event that Sagar's strategies added to higher year-end rewards for accomplices, they were ready to Acknowledge his irregular practices.

McKinsey's problematic however beneficial work for Transnet filled in as a get ready for the company's next huge score: fixing the state-possessed power organization, Eskom. In the event that all worked out in a good way, McKinsey remained to gather more cash from Eskom than from practically some other organization on the planet, with a likely worth of $700 million. The optics were sufficiently terrible — an overwhelmingly white firm looking for that measure of cash without cutthroat offering from a ruined government. In the US or England, this charge could draw in little consideration, however not in that frame of mind, with a pay hole more extensive than generally anyplace on the planet and youth joblessness besting 50%. To separate that sort of cash from a state-possessed organization soaking under water with a background marked by blunder was unreasonable.

Eskom's concerns reduced to this: the mainland's most progressive economy could never again depend on the power organization to keep the lights on. In the main portion of 2015, South Africa experienced power outages or power decreases on the greater part of the days. Every week appeared to bring new issues. Eskom terminated 1,000 specialists at one power plant. 21 thousand provisional laborers picketed fighting unfortunate everyday environments and low compensation. Four chiefs were suspended, inciting Standard and Poor's to slice Eskom's credit score to garbage. The earlier year a significant kettle exploded.

Frantic to right the boat, Eskom employed another CEO, Brian Molefe, who had directed the train disaster at Transnet.

Sagar knew Molefe from Transnet. Another senior accomplice, Alexander Weiss, had exhorted Eskom beginning around 2005. Weiss' accreditations included two doctorates, one in structural designing and one more in business organization. Despite the fact that he resided in Berlin, Weiss barely cared about making 26 hour full circle flights, some of the time week after week, to Johannesburg, where he counseled close by in excess of twelve CEOs and CFOs at Eskom.

## [L'influence cache]

To agree on what should have been finished — and the amount it would cost — Eskom and McKinsey haggled for over twenty days spread over almost a Half year. The discussions created a ruckus inside McKinsey's glass tower in Sandton, Johannesburg's monetary focus, said to be the most extravagant square mile in all of Africa.

Interviews with in excess of sixteen current and previous McKinsey representatives, including accomplices and senior accomplices, recounted a sharp split in the workplace between the people who needed to put everything on the line shot, accepting they could change Eskom, and the Individuals who saw the power organization as nitwit's gold and a significant reputational risk. The remote chance group won, the gamble legitimized by the possibility of a mammoth payout.

Formally, McKinsey described the exchanges as exhausting with a ton of to and fro. Yet, in private, somewhere around one previous accomplice proposed McKinsey effortlessly got what it needed. "These discussions resembled Clubbing Seals," the accomplice said. A partner added, "Ravenousness had overwhelmed good judgment."

Different worries focused on the shortfall of cutthroat offering and a questionable outcome based expense structure, known as an in danger contract. Not at all like standard fixed-charge arrangements, the last bill for an in danger contract is obscure until the gig is finished. McKinsey could work for a really long time and get no compensation on the off chance that settle d upon objectives were not accomplished. Then again, the payout could be gigantic. "You are risking everything and the kitchen sink," one accomplice cautioned partners. If the last payout becomes public, the accomplice added, "you will be butchered only for the size."

An outcome based agreement conveyed different dangers. In the last part of the 1980s, Jeffrey Skilling of Enron notoriety sat on a board of trustees thinking about whether McKinsey ought to get compensated in view of the effect, like a level of accomplished cost decreases. The board called that imprudent, in light of the fact that it could boost the firm to advise clients to diminish costs when that was not to the client's advantage. "Doing that," Skilling said, "could obliterate" the firm. McKinsey at last dismissed that view since clients requested it and contenders were utilizing it.

"Attempting to do a 100% in danger contract at Eskom is attempting to play God," a previous South African expert said. "You are ensuring that I can pivot everything, no issue." That's what to do, McKinsey could require more political clout and skill than it had. "It is most certainly far past what McKinsey can create."

In any case, the possibility of a significant bonus made the Eskom project famous in Johannesburg and in other McKinsey workplaces. Allies remembered two senior accomplices with oversight for energy and power — Moscow's Yermolai Solzhenitsyn, the author Aleksandr Solzhenitsyn's oldest child, and Thomas Vahlenkamp in Düsseldorf, Germany.

## [L'influence cache]

The enormous Eskom project started in January 2016 however immediately ran into inconvenience. The McKinsey group neglected to affirm Eskom's confirmations that the Public Depository had endorsed the unconventional charge game plan as legally necessary. It was only after numerous months after the fact that McKinsey learned it had been working unlawfully.

McKinsey likewise needed to track down a dependable Dark strengthening subcontractor subsequent to unloading Regiments in February 2016 over the nature of its work. In view of Sagar's suggestion, the firm picked Trillian, another organization that had been veered off from Regiments. Once more, McKinsey failed — this time by beginning work without an agreement and without affirming that Trillian was Dark possessed and liberated from unwanted people.

Trillian's own conduct exacerbated things. While prompting Eskom on purchasing another evaporator, it was likewise exhorting the dealer, a Chinese organization. "What was especially disturbing about this was that Trillian had not unveiled the possible struggle," Weiss said, taking note of that McKinsey just scholarly of the contention during a gathering at Eskom.

Trillian had its own explanations behind being angry at McKinsey. Bianca Goodson, who ran Trillian's administration counseling unit, said McKinsey regarded her and her organization as undesirable stuff. At an initiative gathering one night at McKinsey central command — the one where Goodson saw Sagar dance on the meeting room table — Goodson held up a few hours to talk, yet when her opportunity arrived, Weiss left the room. A McKinsey accomplice, lorenz Jüngling, told her not to stress on the grounds that Trillian "will in any case get their 30%." Goodson said that the next day Jüngling implied that Trillian simply needed cash "as a trade-off for not much work."

These trades helped Goodson to remember guidance she got from an impressive man impact inside Trillian.

"These McKinsey dicks — in the event that they give you any difficulty, call me," he told her. That man was Salim Essa, a Trillian proprietor and a shadowy figure who might arise as a critical course through which the Gupta family purportedly looked to "catch" South Africa's administration.

The Following day Sagar called to apologize for the lead of his associates.

In the mean time, Fine had developed progressively worried about Sagar's confidential gatherings with authorities at Trillian and Eskom. "This was an issue I raised with him, and my other partner Norbert Doerr raised with him also. We even had a supper to examine this matter."

Sagar didn't take the analysis well. "You are not confiding adequately in," he said.

Facing Sagar conveyed a gamble, given his prevalence and his prosperity as an income generator at Eskom and Transnet. As per one gauge, those two records addressed almost 50% of the Johannesburg office's pay.

## [L'influence cache]

ALbeit Fine didn't deal with the Eskom account, as a director he needed to realize who claimed Trillian. "I had asked on various occasions, all things considered, who is Trillian?" he said. "There was no response impending." The main individual Fine knew at the organization was Eric Wood, Trillian's CEO, whom he depicted as "a white South African beginning a dark warning firm."

To press the issue, Fine organized two gatherings with Sagar and Wood at Tashas, an eatery in Mellrose Curve, an Island of high-design retail locations, in the open air feasting, an inn, an exercise center, and business workplaces. "Who are the financial backers?" Fine requested. Wood answered with a couple of names. After finding out about those names later, Fine turned out to be considerably more concerned. They were politically associated, he finished up.

The possibility that McKinsey's reasonable level of effort on one of its greatest undertakings comprised of an accomplice researching names showed how poorly pre-arranged the firm was to take on this task. In the end, McKinsey recruited agents to analyze Trillian's experience, and the proof they saw as highlighted the contribution of Salim Essa, the Gupta family partner.

Sagar had guaranteed his partners that he had never met or addressed Essa. That was false.

As a matter of fact, McKinsey found that Sagar had been discussing routinely with Essa and that Sagar had attempted to conceal it. He introduced a program to clean off his PC memory and utilized a confidential email to speak with Essa's own covert record. He likewise sent Eskom a letter bearing McKinsey's logo that approved the power organization to pay Trillian straightforwardly for subcontracting work, refering to an "understanding" that McKinsey had with the organization.

McKinsey informed Eskom in Walk 2016 that following three months of cooperating with Trillian, it had cut attaches with the organization. The firm had at long last stood firm, yet immediately undercut that choice by proceeding to work close by Trillian.

McKinsey had up to this point figured out how to pack down fresh insight about its contribution in spoiled agreements by saying scarcely anything. However, in June, only a Half year into its three-year contract, Eskom ended McKinsey, refering to serious contracting anomalies.

McKinsey accomplices, who thought they had to a great extent contained reputational harm, were in for a major shock.

McKinsey had long benefitted from government contracts without tolerating the obligation to represent how it spent the public's cash. In the US, its eminence and political associations, as well as the country's positive administrative regulations, frequently protected the firm from inquiries concerning those agreements. It is astonishing, then, that it took South Africa, a dElicate vote based system scarcely twenty years old, to show McKinsey examples responsibility that it hadn't learned in the US.

## [L'influence cache]

That training started in October 2016 after specialists sent off a progression of examinations concerning "state catch," characterized as when confidential people and organizations assume control over state offices to divert public assets into their own hands, while debilitating the Establishments liable for ferreting out that debasement.

The principal examination was by the public defender, Thuli Madonsela, who delivered her discoveries three months after McKinsey quit prompting Eskom. She referred to contract inconsistencies including McKinsey's work at Transnet and Eskom, however gave not many granular subtleties on the grounds that, as she composed, the exchanges "stay a secret as all gatherings won't deliver subtleties of the arrangements." The report scratched yet didn't wound McKinsey.

The next month, another examination started, this one by Supporter Geoff Budlender, a generally regarded basic freedoms dissident. With additional time, he dug further into the agreements. Budlender requested to talk with McKinsey, however the firm declined, saying it would just response composed questions. One sentence in McKinsey's responses grabbed Budlender's eye: "McKinsey worked on no tasks on which Trillian filled in as SDP [supply improvement partner] or a subcontractor to McKinsey."

Budlender realized more than he was letting on and had laid a snare for McKinsey. After accepting McKinsey's refusal, he delivered the letter from Sagar to Eskom expressing the specific inverse. "As you probably are aware," Sagar stated, "McKinsey has subcontracted a piece of the administrations to be performed under the consent to Trillian." Sagar likewise approved Eskom to straightforwardly pay Trillian.

Budlender requested a clarification. Benedict Phiri, a McKinsey legal counselor, said he would examine the matter with his partners and hit him up. A large number of weeks went by with no answer, regardless of continuous updates from Budlender. At long last, over two months after the fact, McKinsey said it would be "unseemly" to answer Budlender's "casual" request.

"Why that would be 'improper' has not been made sense of," Budlender composed. "I need to say that I view this as strange, especially having respect to the way that McKinsey introduces itself as a global forerunner in administration counseling and given the far and wide open interest in this." Budlender's last judgment: McKinsey had submitted misleading data.

By suggesting that McKinsey was deceptive, Budlender's report incurred in excess of a surface injury. It cut profound, and that's what the firm understood. With additional examinations arranging, McKinsey's quietness was becoming indefensible. Holding up in trap were specialists from the Public Depository, the Parliament, the media, and the greatest of all, the Commission of Investigation into State Catch, led by Raymond Zondo, vice president equity of South Africa.

McKinsey's hesitance to connect about open agreements persisted to the media. In an article about McKinsey's association with Regiments, Amabhungane, the nation's head insightful news unit, expressed, "More than two months, amaBhungane has sent six solicitations to McKinsey finding out if it knew about

## [L'influence cache]

the luxurious expenses Regiments paid to different 'business improvement accomplices.' McKinsey evaded the inquiry each time."

The Public Indicting Authority turned up the intensity by freely denouncing McKinsey for empowering defilement. The NPA reasoned that the firm had been instrumental "in making a cover of authenticity to what was generally a nonexistent unlawful game plan." The NPA, alluding to McKinsey's Eskom work, conveyed this judgment when Parliament was profound into its hearings on government defilement.

McKinsey concluded the opportunity had arrived to persevere, and to do so not through an unremarkable corporate explanation but rather through a thoughtful McKinsey accomplice, David Fine, faithful South African expert had ascended to lead the company's world wide public-and Social-area practice. Presently living in Europe, Fine flew down to tell Parliament of McKinsey's profound lament for not conversing with Promoter Budlender and to recognize a plenty of different mix-ups.

"I comprehend it caused extreme horror inside about how we would or ought to help out an examination without our client's assent," Fine said. "We ought to have had a discussion with him to make sense of these issues and I'm humiliated that we didn't do that." Probably, Budlender was less keen on McKinsey's thinking for not talking and more intrigued by how it did or didn't empower state catch.

The public's all in all correct to know how the public authority spends its cash is crucial in a flourishing vote based system. That right, as a rule, not move to McKinsey's confidential clients, and the firm certainly realize that administration counseling conveyed extra liabilities. McKinsey's involvement with South Africa brought that distinction into sharp concentration: Should the firm talk about government clients when there is an assumption for secrecy?

There are just two valid reactions: don't take government business, or answer the inquiries. McKinsey offered a third, saying specialists are urged to bring up troublesome issues inside, however that missed the mark regarding public responsibility.

In South Africa in any event, McKinsey adjusted its perspective. Confronting the deficiency of clients and probably the end of its South African office, the firm gone with a monetary choice. It consented to respond to inquiries in a public gathering — not once, yet multiple times — a circumstance not yet experienced in the US.

Fine was first, responding to inquiries for four hours before a parliamentary board of trustees. He conceded botches yet no violations. He was sorry in the interest of the firm and reported that it would discount the aggregate of its Eskom charges. "We ought to have totally had an expense structure that was covered," Fine said.

McKinsey authorities presented Sagar — not the firm — as a penance, saying he caused the company's inconveniences and reporting that he had left the firm while under suspension. The firm didn't make reference to that he left with full advantages. The firm likewise authorized his co-chief in the Eskom group, Alex

## [L'influence cache]

Weiss, without uncovering the idea of that approval. Weiss kept his work. Sagar presently runs a product organization in London.

With a quickly contracting client base, McKinsey moved many workers to posts outside South Africa. The overseeing accomplice, Dominic Barton, situated in New York City, made six tiring excursions to South Africa to stop the draining.

However, one more examination concerning debasement and "state catch" — the greatest yet — started in June 2018 and before it finished would take declaration from multiple hundred people. Driven by Vice president Equity Raymond Zondo, the commission proceeded with its function admirably into 2021.

While witnesses were being called, Barton's replacement, Kevin Sneader, thought it was critical to visit Johannesburg, where he expected to quench any leftover Coals of outrage. Addressing a business bunch from the get-go a Monday morning in July 2018 — fourteen days after The New York Times distributed a basic article about the company's work in South Africa — Sneader utilized "sorry" multiple times. "The accounts expounded on us in South Africa hurt profoundly as they strike at what we esteem more than anything more — the trust we have worked with our clients through the judgment, character, and notoriety of our kin."

Sneader conceded that McKinsey was excessively far off to get a handle on the rising resentment in South Africa. "Our administration processes fizzled. Our business approach prompted an expense that was excessively enormous. We didn't concede we were off-base. What's more, more awful, we didn't say sorry rapidly enough and obviously enough." Sneader additionally recognized that McKinsey shouldn't have proceeded to "communicate" with Trillian at Eskom after the organization had bombed its expected level of effort audit.

South Africa, however, wasn't finished with McKinsey.

After Sneader's discourse, all the more terrible news arose in the Zondo Commission hearings. Around the finish of 2020, the commission astounded the firm by finding two more corrupted McKinsey contracts with state-claimed endeavors.

One was with South African Aviation routes, where McKinsey and Regiments were recruited to "open" the carrier's functioning capital. This time, no sole-source contract was important on the grounds that Regiments paid off the carrier's financier to get the work. As per the legal commission, Regiments got the agreement particulars ahead of time, then, at that point, changed the assessment Models before the solicitation for proposition was given. Regiments additionally got "secret data" on the assessment interaction, including offers from its rivals. The carrier guaranteed that the agreement sum didn't surpass a worth that would have set off a board survey.

A little less than Half of Regiments' portion of the carrier contract — 6.2 million rand, or generally $420,000 — went to a Shell organization that washed installments to the Gupta family. McKinsey said it didn't realize that the agreement was gotten through a pay off.

## [L'influence cache]

The second spoiled McKinsey contract was with Transnet, where Regiments redirected great many dollars to front organizations constrained by the Guptas.

McKinsey again took the place that it didn't know anything about these installments. Its specialists had said they investigated more than 1,000,000 messages, monetary records, and different reports and directed 115 meetings. The firm needed summon power, however McKinsey's refusals brought to mind Claude Downpours in the film Casablanca: "I'm stunned, stunned to observe that betting is happening in here."

The commission raised another humiliating issue: Weiss affirmed that he had demanded that Trillian give reported confirmation of its proprietorship. "I requested this in an exceptionally difficult, profoundly successive way," he said. In the event that narrative confirmation was so significant, the commission needed to be aware, for what reason did he antedate his particular by just about nine months on McKinsey's Eskom contract. Weiss recommended that misdirection was inconsequential.

The commission deviated, saying an appropriately dated signature "would have hailed something that would have emerged as an inconsistency that might have set off more noteworthy examination of the agreement." Weiss apologized for any disarray he could have caused. Not to be neglected, he said, was that in a brief time frame McKinsey "had a genuine, apparent effect on Eskom's functional execution," including further developed accessibility of power.

McKinsey looked to stop the revelation of the two extra corrupted agreements by consenting to a commission solicitation to discount more than $40 million from those agreements — despite the fact that the firm and the commission declared it was not complicit. That evoked commendation from the commission for being a "dependable corporate resident." Along with the Eskom discount, McKinsey was currently on the snare for more than $100 million.

The commission's commendation irritated David lewis, chief head of Debasement Watch, a South African support bunch. "To repay your expense just on the grounds that you were gotten with your ridiculous hands in the till is, honestly, not compensation," lewis said. "They are associated with such dodgy movement across the world that I think there are grounds to Eliminate their permit to work, unquestionably in this country. That would be the fitting degree of repayment."

McKinsey's inconveniences in South Africa provoked a lot of soul-looking through in the firm. Might the company's directors at any point have figured out how to stop the emergency sooner? What did they foul up? Probably the most extreme analysis came from previous associates in the Johannesburg office. "It was a fender bender in sluggish movement," one representative said.

Everybody appeared to concur that the firm took excessively lengthy to perceive the profundity of South Africa's resentment. Dominic Barton, overseeing accomplice while the emergency unfurled, said senior accomplices had "somewhat of an inability to listen" in their initial reaction. His ancestor, Ian Davis, censured the firm for saying 'sorry' comparing it to a confirmation of culpability, as per a source with direct information on information disclosed. (Davis declined to talk

## [L'influence cache]

on the record about whether this record is precise.) Others thought Kevin Sneader, who succeeded Barton, went excessively far in his statement of regret.

In South Africa, the legal commission legal counselor, Matthew Chaskalson, asked the company's new boss gamble official, Jean-Christophe Mieszala, why no one at McKinsey scrutinized the association's "cosmic expansion in the charges."

"As far as anyone is concerned it was not something gotten," Mieszala replied.

The commission found no proof recommending that McKinsey as a firm had taken part in degenerate direct, however Mieszala conceded that it is "ethically off-base" to seem eager when your client is battling.

The image was less clear for Sagar, a reality featured by the commission. "A connection among Sagar and Essa went far past inappropriate relationship," Chaskalson told Mieszala. "It really elaborate indecency toward Eskom." He finished up the proof "ensnares Sagar in state catch." Sagar was no low-level analyst, however a believed senior accomplice working for the benefit of McKinsey.

McKinsey attests that it has resolved issues in South Africa by reinforcing its inner administration, including more examination of public-area work. Chaskalson pushed back, saying the slip-ups mirrored McKinsey's way of life more than powerless administration.

The Financial expert appeared to concur. Under the Title "The Smuggest Folks in the Room," the distribution believed,

For very nearly 95 years, McKinsey has tried to depict itself as a cultured proficient administrations organization, not a dirty business. Dissimilar to, say, a benefit hungry Goldman Sachs financier, who strolls into a room mindful she might be murmured at, a McKinsey expert anticipates that his radiance should be taken note. Whatever amount of its senior accomplices demand that they are not persuaded by outsized benefits, they can procure as much every year as that Goldman broker.

For sure, the company's incomes nearly multiplied in 10 years to more than $10 billion, provoking The Financial specialist to finish up, "The association's representatives revel in the emanation of the old McKinsey — of independence, carefulness and scholarly distinction — while embracing the development, benefits and power that have come in later years. Seldom do they question whether they can have everything."

McKinsey's Mieszala appeared to recognize that reality.

"At the point when you have Individuals who are overachievers, it can produce terrible way of behaving and to this end we must be cautious," he said. "It is certain that the South Africa circumstance has shown us a thing or two and we are exceptionally lowered by that illustration."

Eskom probably scholarly an illustration too. In January 2020, the organization had to cut such an excess of force that mines and processing plants shut down

## [L'influence cache]

and families went dim. Weeks sooner, South Africa's leader had sliced short a conciliatory visit to the Center East to manage the emergency. After one year, business as usual.

The media revealed that 2021 could be the most terrible year for power reductions in almost a long period.

# [L'influence cache]

## Section 13

### Serving the Saudi State

During the 1970s, Saudi Arabia was blasting. Unrefined Petroleum costs multiplied, then, at that point, quadrupled, right after the Middle Easterner oil ban. The realm, flooded with cash, had enormous plans — new urban communities, new enterprises, new air terminals, new treatment facilities — yet required unfamiliar skill to pull it off. A huge number of expats overflowed the nation, frequently bringing their families.[*]

Among the numerous Americans who came was a star McKinsey expert and previous armed force insight official, Sandy Apgar. The downturn that the oil ban assisted with starting had destroyed the work he'd been doing in London on land, so he made a beeline for Saudi Arabia and "thumped on entryways and tents."

Apgar tracked down a lot of work. He exhorted the state-possessed oil organization, Aramco, as it went through a monstrous extension and furthermore won business to assist the realm with arranging its progress from a country of Bedouin wanderers to a cutting edge, metropolitan economy. Over forty years after the fact, McKinsey's work in Saudi Arabia actually spins around those two support points, the nearest thing in counseling to an ideal fence: exhorting Aramco and the Energy Service and assisting the public authority with creating some distance from an economy absolutely reliant upon Aramco's oil.

Apgar, who proceeded to be an associate secretary of the military under President Bill Clinton, immediately found that monetary power in the nation was, as he put it, "somewhat concentrated in the possession of government pastors, senior authorities, and an enterprising tip top, the greater part of whom are either Individuals from or near the regal family." His replacements found a way phenomenal ways to construct connections to that world class, recruiting their children and little girls.

Opportunity coaxed for American advisors. To draw nearer to the activity, in 1996 McKinsey set up an office in Dubai, the Persian Bay exchanging center point. Saudi rulers needed to imitate the outcome of Dubai, then arising as a multicultural worldwide vehicle and monetary focus. The Saudi counseling flood was on.

Winning the greatest agreements in Saudi Arabia was reliant upon the public authority, the main thrust behind all of the Persian Bay economies. That wasn't lost on Kito de Boer, the Dutch McKinsey accomplice and ardent workmanship authority who directed the district and later proceeded to act as head of mission for the Group of four, the gathering comprised of the Unified Countries, the European Association, the US, and Russia, that intervenes among Israelis and Palestinians. De Boer kept an exceptional sort of association diagram on the workplace walls of McKinsey's Dubai office: banners spreading out who was who in the district's imperial families.

In 2009, McKinsey opened an office in Riyadh, the Saudi capital, and business inside the realm truly took off. The firm landed one of the greatest development

## [L'influence cache]

organizations in the Center East — one with a name in a split second conspicuous all over the planet in view of its scandalous relative — the Saudi Binladin Gathering. It additionally moved forward work with Aramco, instructing on its rebuilding ahead concerning its possible Initial public offering.

From just 2 positions in 2010 in Saudi Arabia, the firm took on 47 ventures the next year, as per interior McKinsey figures on "Know," the company's intranet, where experts can draw on the aggregate work of their partners, for example, instant slide decks. By 2016, McKinsey had 137 activities in Saudi Arabia.

So instilled was McKinsey into the realm's undertakings that the Arranging Service became known as the Service of McKinsey. A portion of the company's specialists who worked for a Saudi auxiliary procured in 2017 even utilized government email addresses, one previous expert said. McKinsey said it didn't know about any advisors who were given Saudi government email addresses.

One power that drove McKinsey's hazardous development in Saudi Arabia was a political peculiarity the imperial family needed frantically to avert: the Bedouin Spring. The rush of transformations and rebellions that moved throughout Egypt, libya, Bahrain, Yemen, Syria, and Tunisia in 2011 and 2012 was possibly an Elimination level occasion for the imperial family. "The counseling blast happened on the grounds that despots would have rather not turned into the Following Mubarak," one previous Dubai-based McKinsey advisor expressed, alluding to the late Egyptian pioneer who was expelled in the distress Following quite a while of pallid development and far and wide defilement.

The possible arrangement, wherein McKinsey and its rivals assumed a focal part, was to loosen up a portion of the realm's notorious Social limitations, for example, the restriction on ladies driving and cinemas, while simultaneously expanding constraint of protester voices.

Some McKinsey specialists, Particularly more youthful ones, were irritated that the firm would so energetically help the Place of Saud, a family from Riyadh whose patriarch vanquished a large part of the Bedouin landmass during the 1920s and whose children have supervised a merciless religious totalitarianism from that point onward. They contended that the firm ought to lessen, or potentially even end, its work there. Said one, "Saudi Arabia is a country that shouldn't exist."

They were overruled by the accomplices, who contended that it wasn't McKinsey's responsibility to condemn the upsides of its clients. left inferred was the effect on yearly rewards on the off chance that the Saudi work evaporated. In guarding McKinsey's choice to remain in Saudi Arabia, its senior accomplices definitely depend on political contentions, saying its work helps hold Saudi Arabia back from going the method of Syria or other bombed states, in spite of the company's frequently rehashed guarantee that it doesn't include itself in legislative issues.

"Assuming you take a nation like Saudi, and you project it forward assuming that nothing changes, the ramifications for that locale are simply critical," said one senior accomplice who directs work in the district. The issue is that after 2015, McKinsey's work in Saudi Arabia was obliged to a man who was working, as Ben

## [L'influence cache]

Hubbard of The New York Times expressed, "a lab for another sort of electronic dictatorship."

McKinsey was assisting him with getting it done.

The five-part assignment from the Saudi Illustrious Court was getting out and about in Washington, visiting think tanks like the Brookings Foundation and guard workers for hire like lockheed Martin and Raytheon, the provider of the bombs the Saudis were utilizing to kill great many regular folks during the conflict in adjoining Yemen.

It was February 2016, and the Saudis were there to discuss the new political reality in Saudi Arabia Following the passing of Ruler Abdullah a year sooner. It came as the chunky young fellow Mohammed canister Salman, who was the most loved child of the octogenarian lord.

As of now, enough was had some significant awareness of MBS to have made McKinsey or any Western organization question the insight of carrying on with work in the realm. MBS was savage. One story makes them send a solitary projectile in an envelope to a land-library official who wouldn't give up a package of land to him, procuring him the epithet Abu Rasasa, or "father of the slug." He even kept his own mom, because of reasons that aren't clear. Anybody checked out Saudi legislative issues knew the tales. Before long, the whole world would know exactly the way in which far he would go to quiet his apparent foes.

Yet, that wasn't the message his messengers were bringing to the American capital. They informed their hosts concerning MBS's excellent objectives to change Saudi life. Their local area experts — McKinsey and its main adversary, Boston Counseling Gathering — dwarfed the Saudis. The advisors sat discreetly, taking notes.

After four years, McKinsey documented an exceptionally late exposure with the Equity Division under the Unfamiliar Specialists Enlistment Represent that work. It is the main documenting by McKinsey on the office's site. The documenting laid out McKinsey as something other than experts to the realm. They were currently addressing that nation's advantages in the US. The firm had before let columnists know that it saw no great explanation to make a FARA documenting.

McKinsey was working with the Saudi government to reinforce its discretionary effort, helping set up what turned into the Saudi Community for Global Vital Associations, which, McKinsey said, was "a substance whose reason is assist oversee and work on Saudi Arabia's associations with various nations all over the planet." A portion of McKinsey's greatest stars were involved, including Gary Pinkus, then the overseeing accomplice for North America. McKinsey got $4.8 million for its work, paid by its client of close to 50 years, Aramco.

These were occupied days for American advisors in Saudi Arabia. The youthful sovereign was enchanted of them. Also, he assumed he wanted their skill to transform his large dreams into the real world, like the city representing things to come. On the off chance that there was any inquiry concerning that, the city's name, NEOM, is an abbreviation for "new future," got from the Greek word neo

## [L'influence cachée]

and the Arabic word for future, mustaqbal. Such an endeavor was aggressive to the point that "uber project" just wouldn't do. This was a giga-project. Plans call for flying robot taxis, a fake moon, and automated Jurassic Park-style dinosaurs for this space-age city on the Red Ocean. McKinsey charged large number of dollars to exhort on the venture, inside organization records show.

The entryway of the Riyadh Ritz-Carlton was brimming with McKinsey men. Dominic Barton, then McKinsey's overseeing accomplice, showed up in Riyadh, astounding McKinsey's nearby specialists with the recurrence of his visits. Indeed, even cab drivers could recognize individual advisors and their organizations.

In years past, specialists developed connections in the heap services, constrained by different fiefdoms of the rambling regal family. Presently MBS was solidifying power, and he carried the experts into the Imperial Court, an uncommon honor under past rulers, one long-lasting specialist in the district said. "There was no doubt about working with MBS," one previous McKinsey advisor told Ben Hubbard. "They were holding nothing back."

From the get-go in MBS's ascent to control, McKinsey found a difficult task — a public change project, pointed toward weaning the realm off its reliance on oil. In December 2015, McKinsey's research organization, the McKinsey Worldwide Foundation, carried out the result of a portion of that work, "Saudi Arabia Past Oil." The report cautioned that by 2030, Saudi Arabia confronted mass joblessness that could be deflected by a $4 trillion venture go overboard in regions like mining, the travel industry, and money. The prize: a multiplying of Gross domestic product and 6,000,000 new positions. Oversight of this aggressive task would by configuration rest with the Service of Economy and Arranging.

However McKinsey was not almighty in Saudi Arabia. An opponent, Boston Counseling Gathering, had developed the youthful ruler years sooner, prompting his Establishment, MiSK, which says it is "committed to develop and support learning and initiative in youth for a superior future in Saudi Arabia." It was BCG that got probably the greatest positions, for example, working with the country's sovereign abundance reserve as well as the Service of Safeguard. Furthermore, it was BCG's "Vision 2030" that won the day, not McKinsey's arrangement.

Yet, McKinsey wouldn't surrender to its adversary with such ease. One way McKinsey could solidify its impact was through politically associated employs. This it did with energy.

Back in 2003 the firm recruited Mazen AL-Jubeir, the more youthful Sibling of Adel AL-Jubeir, the future Saudi minister to the US and the cajoling public face of the realm in Washington right after the September 11, 2001, assaults. Mazen AL-Jubeir was, as so many McKinsey experts, an alum of Harvard Business college and was named a Bread cook researcher. As rivalry warmed up with BCG, McKinsey returned to this playbook, however this time a portion of its recruits didn't have such sparkling scholarly list of references.

In 2017, The Money Road Diary revealed that over the past two years McKinsey utilized two offspring of the previous Aramco boss as well as the child of a money serve, two offspring of a previous national bank boss, and the top of a state-claimed mining organization. Featuring the closeness of McKinsey to the system, somewhere around five previous McKinsey representatives have proceeded to work at MiSK, MBS's Establishment, as indicated by their linkedIn profiles. One of those was Sarah ALkhedheiri, the girl of a previous data and culture serve. She and her Sibling worked at McKinsey after they completed their undergrad learns at Northeastern College in Boston.

By 2017, two years into the time of MBS, McKinsey took an extremely strong move to solidify its place in Saudi Arabia and strike back at BCG's strength: it purchased a very much associated Saudi counseling organization.

In 2005, Hani Khoja, a previous Procter and Bet chief, established his own counseling organization, Remedy, at the encouraging of a McKinsey accomplice. Khoja had close connections to the arranging priest, and Solution's workers, situated in Jeddah and Riyadh, had tunneled profound into the service, winning significant agreements.

On April 1, 2017, McKinsey declared that it had purchased Remedy. It was an exceptionally interesting procurement by McKinsey, which for the initial ninety years of its presence had basically depended on "natural" development, shunning consolidations and acquisitions, despite the fact that it frequently exhorted and upheld for them for its clients.

Purchases "purchases nothing like this anyplace on the planet," said one previous McKinsey accomplice who worked in the locale, talking about Remedy. "The word was that it was only for the connections." In a moment, McKinsey's staff in Saudi Arabia expanded by 140 Individuals, adding just about 50% to its staff in the locale.

"Four or five months in, you sort of acknowledge it for what it is, which is a hiring organization for the public authority," a previous Saudi Solution representative said.

Remedy's experts are so near the Saudi services that they're frequently undefined from government workers, said a previous Mixture representative, a Saudi employed after the McKinsey takeover. "At the point when you come at them with an administration email, they will converse with you," the individual expressed, alluding to government officials.

That put McKinsey experts extremely near their client. One more previous McKinsey advisor in Saudi Arabia portrayed the relationship as one of business worker: gone was the customary relationship that — from a certain point of view — permitted McKinsey experts to talk hard bits of insight to their clients. The expert reviews Ian Davis, then McKinsey's overseeing accomplice, let youthful recruits know that they ought to see themselves as present day "squires and viziers."

ALL things considered, it was, this individual said, "Don't suspect the same thing; simply do as I tell you."

## [L'influence cache]

McKinsey workers acting basically as government authorities would be dangerous enough in a majority rules system. To do it in a flat out government where its true chief correctional facilities or kills his political foes made McKinsey surprisingly helpless against the impulses of a tyrant.

Promptly after the securing, that sounds plainly self-evident, truly.

In the primary seven day stretch of November 2017 a greater number of than 350 sovereigns, priests, and finance managers met on the Saudi capital. They were welcomed there, under different guises, for the sake of the ruler or his child MBS.

At the point when they showed up in Riyadh, security authorities seized their phones, pens, and wallets. They were bound to the Ritz-Carlton. The rooms were sumptuous, however sharp items — whatever they might use to hurt themselves — were mysteriously absent. Individually, they were given proof of their wrongdoing — defilement — and many were offered bargains that elaborate giving immense bits of their resources up to the Saudi state. Some were beaten, and no less than one was clubbed to death.

Among those kept was Hani Khoja, the fellow benefactor of Remedy and shiny new McKinsey accomplice. He was held for over thirteen months, and as per a report in The Money Road Diary he was likewise beaten.

One more loss from the Ritz cleanse: the arranging clergyman responsible for "the Service of McKinsey." He was accused of defilement.

Starting a new business with go betweens in a profoundly bad nation can jeopardize the standing of American organizations. McKinsey knows this as a matter of fact. In South Africa, it confronted a comparative quandary and decided to bounce in any case, no matter what the dangers. In any case, in contrast to South Africa, where the impurity of debasement crushed its business, that didn't occur in Saudi Arabia, clearly on the grounds that McKinsey's work was seen by MBS and his administration as critical to the actual endurance of the Place of Saud.

Falling unrefined Petroleum costs were destroying the Saudi financial plan, and authorities there were thinking about whether to cut oil endowments, conceivably raising the cost of fuel in the realm. Since they would have rather not started fights that could bring the Bedouin Spring into the country, Saudi pioneers needed to check the disposition of the majority toward cutting sponsorships. That's what to do, they went to McKinsey, Boston Counseling, and a third firm, the London-based SC1 Gathering, better known through its auxiliary, Cambridge Analytica, famous for impacting decisions across the globe for any up-and-comer able to pay its expenses. Cambridge Analytica's President, Alexander Nix, bragged to secret columnists from England's Channel 4 News that the organization would be able "send a few young ladies around to the competitor's home" to entangle them, saying he jumped at the chance to utilize Ukrainian "young ladies" for the gig. The organization likewise inappropriately got to Facebook information to assist the Trump with battling make mental profiles of millions of electors who were then besieged with designated content.

## [L'influence cache]

In Saudi Arabia, SC1 and Cambridge Analytica were basically exchangeable: the work there was directed by the individual who succeeded Nix as Cambridge Analytica's President. The point was to lead center gatherings across the realm, inquiring as to whether the cost of fuel expanded. McKinsey and BCG would then deal with that data and present it to senior authorities at the service. This profoundly political work went a long ways past the customary McKinsey dispatch of giving exhortation to privately owned businesses on the most proficient method to set aside cash by being more productive. One previous Cambridge Analytica leader engaged with the Saudi work with McKinsey said the reason behind it was "to decrease the gamble of turmoil."

McKinsey was guaranteeing the reasonability of a ruthless, tyrant system. "Putting the pieces and pieces together, looking back I don't feel far better about it," said one more previous Cambridge Analytica specialist whose work converged with Mckinsey's. "It is a kind of support, or adding to their combination of force."

McKinsey said it didn't work with Cambridge Analytica or the SC1 Gathering for the Saudi Service of Economy and Arranging.

McKinsey's work with the Saudis went a long ways past center gatherings. Saudi Arabia's populace is one of the most youthful on the planet and quite possibly of the most connected on stage like Twitter and Facebook. Another procedure — "opinion examination" — dug online entertainment posts for watchwords, permitting organizations to gauge mentalities about their items. McKinsey became amped up for the procedure, referencing it in numerous reports. So did the Saudis; a gathering of Saudi researchers referred to it as "assessment mining."

The Saudis locked onto the way that feeling examination had possible far past deciding how Individuals had an outlook on their pizza conveyance experience. In a nation like Saudi Arabia, where it appeared everybody was visiting on Facebook, Instagram, or Twitter, it very well may be utilized by the public authority to take the public's temperature and smoke out compelling grumblers.

Around a similar time McKinsey was working close by SC1, one of its Dubai-based senior accomplices, Enrico Benni, was searching out Individuals across the firm for another expected Saudi task: to perform feeling examination in Arabic, one previous representative said. McKinsey's Saudi-put together representatives featured this work with respect to their public profiles. One Saudi-based Remedy worker, Ahmad Alattas, recorded "virtual entertainment observing to direct and concentrate on open feeling examination" among his positions. Before long, this new profession yielded results, however maybe not the caring McKinsey had as a main priority.

In mid 2018 an individual from Saudi Arabia called Omar Abdulaziz to determine the status of him. He hadn't seen much from him as of late via virtual entertainment; Abdulaziz had countless supporters on Twitter and YouTube. Is it safe to say that he was alright?

Abdulaziz, a Saudi public who had been living in Montreal for very nearly 10 years, answered that he was fine. Be that as it may, the individual had valid justification to be stressed. He let Abdulaziz know that he had been working with

## [L'influence cache]

McKinsey on an undertaking for MBS. McKinsey had arranged a report about how the realm's subjects were responding to government strategies. The report distinguished Abdulaziz, alongside a few different Saudis, as being exceptionally persuasive in forming the general's perspective, and not in a positive way.

"I thought, 'Goodness, that is perfect,' " Abdulaziz reviewed over two years after the fact. "To start with I didn't realize that it would be a Particularly significant thing. I was unable to envision how MBS would be keen on my work. So I figured nothing would occur."

The dull Title of the nine-page report, "Somberness Estimates in Saudi Arabia," misrepresents its hazardous substance. It was opinion investigation: weaponized. "Omar has a huge number of negative tweets on subjects like gravity and the regal declarations," read one McKinsey list item.

That May, Saudi messengers headed out to Montreal to encourage Abdulaziz to get back to his country. As a youthful, hip YouTube star, he'd be a big name, they told him. As an additional motivator, they carried along his Sibling to assist with persuading him.

Abdulaziz disputed. The next month, his telephone was hacked, however he knew nothing about it for quite a long time, as indicated by a report by the Resident lab, an association at the College of Toronto that examines computerized reconnaissance against common society. In August, Abdulaziz's two Siblings were tossed behind bars. One more powerful web-based pundit featured in the McKinsey report was likewise captured, and a third record considered negative by McKinsey vanished from Twitter.

The telephone hack likewise undermined Abdulaziz's interchanges with an unmistakable Saudi writer. The two had been devising a game plan to counter MBS's arising techno-dictator state, which utilized multitudes of web savages, called flies, to distinguish and overpower any disagreeing on the web voices.

In September, the writer had wired Abdulaziz $5,000 to kick the undertaking off. The arrangement was to counter the flies with a multitude of "honey bees" — Individuals zeroed in on countering the Saudi savages.

The writer's name was Jamal Khashoggi.

On October 2, 2018, Khashoggi, a journalist for The Washington Post, entered the Saudi department in Istanbul to get some desk work for his marriage. His Turkish life partner hung tight outside for him.

A Saudi death crew, cautioned that he was set to visit the legation, was set up. After entering, Khashoggi was informed he was returning to Saudi Arabia. A specialist advised him to compose a message to his child, telling him not to stress "in the event that you don't hear from me in some time." He rejected. "We will anesthetize you," he was told. There were hints of a battle, Khashoggi saying, "I can't inhale, I can't inhale," then quietness after Khashoggi was infused with a medication. Then came the humming sound of a saw as his carcass was dissected. American insight organizations reasoned that MBS was behind the homicide.

## [L'influence cache]

The presence of the McKinsey report focusing on his partner Omar Abdulaziz became public in the weeks after Khashoggi's homicide, remembered for a New York Times tale about the Saudi multitude of online savages. The story incited shock the world over: in the US, Representative Elizabeth Warren of Massachusetts sent a letter to McKinsey's overseeing accomplice, Kevin Sneader, requesting that he give her office data about who could have seen the report.

"I'm worried that McKinsey's report on open discernment might have been weaponized by the Saudi government to pound analysis of the Realm's strategies, no matter what McKinsey's expected reason for the data," Warren composed.

At that point, McKinsey said it was "frightened by the chance, but remote, that it might have been abused in any capacity." The firm said the report's "expected essential crowd was inside" and that it was assembled by a scientist in Riyadh. "In the same way as other large companies including our rivals, we try to explore a changing international climate," the organization said, "yet we don't uphold or take part in political exercises."

One previous McKinsey expert gave a totally different reaction. "The company's reaction to the web-based entertainment mining stuff in Saudi is complete horseshit," the previous specialist said. "I was associated with the discussions that hinted at that work with Saudi, and it was a lot bigger and more had some significant awareness of by the forerunners in the district than that 1udicrous 'it was just a single examiner' story they delivered."

McKinsey says that the report was "made completely out of freely accessible data" and that it has "seen no proof that the record being referred to was abused."

Truth be told, McKinsey's "interior" report was a lot of outside. Abdulaziz's source, who was working with McKinsey on the undertaking, let him know it had been introduced in 2017 to MBS's partners, and he sent Abdulaziz an electronic form, which was disclosed in a claim. The Times got a duplicate from another source.

McKinsey had been working with the Saudi government starting around 2015 on precisely what was in the report — an examination of how general society would respond to cuts in appropriations. It was a strongly political action, pointed toward protecting the Saudi government, dealing with center political assignments for one of the world's most oppressive systems.

Kevin Sneader, McKinsey's overseeing accomplice at that point, protected the work in Saudi Arabia on CNBC, outlining it with regards to international affairs, not business. "The world doesn't maintain that Saudi Arabia should p1unge into where there aren't occupations, and where it gets truly extreme in an exceptionally terrible manner," he told CNBC in Walk 2019, adding that he trusts the firm makes "a positive commitment" there.

The disclosure prompted scaffold humor among McKinsey's staff members all over the planet, a large portion of whom, in light of the deliberately stovepiped nature of McKinsey's work, were surprised by the Times story. In one office, an instructional meeting took an exceptionally dim turn:

# [L'influence cache]

Your client is the Saudi Middle Eastern Government. They have recruited McKinsey to investigate ways that they can smother writers and nonconformists who censured the Realm's imperious approaches.

You've been approached to decide the number of protesters you that can place into a tank of corrosive to break up and conceal their bodies. Expecting that you have a 10' x 10' x 10' tank of hydrochloric corrosive, what number of nonconformists could fit? Make sense of your methodology.

Abdulaziz in the long run sued McKinsey, with his legal counselors writing in the objection that "McKinsey really set an objective on Offended party's back." McKinsey convinced the appointed authority to excuse the case, documented in California, on jurisdictional grounds. McKinsey said in court papers that Abdulaziz was a notable pundit of the system for a really long time who had been conceded political refuge in Canada and that the report was referring to freely accessible tweets.

Abdulaziz sued McKinsey again in 2021, this time in bureaucratic court in New York, claiming that the slide deck that recognized him as a system pundit was seen by delegates of MBS and that after its distribution he "was constrained into stowing away and needed to move from one inn to another for a really long time to try not to be grabbed or hurt." McKinsey again asked the appointed authority for the situation to excuse it, and in September 2021 she did, referring to, among a few reasons, a passed legal time limit and a disappointment on Abdulaziz's part to show McKinsey had any command over how the Saudi government would involve the data in the slide deck.

After Khashoggi's homicide, Saudi Arabia was radioactive. Huge names like Blackstone's Chief, Stephen Schwarzman, Jamie Dimon of JPMorgan Pursue, and Christine lagarde, then top of the IMF, pulled out of a Riyadh meeting supported by MBS — named Davos in the Desert — that happened only weeks after the homicide.

McKinsey and a portion of the other counseling organizations decided to remain. The firm driven boards on cash and energy, as indicated by the program.

In 2019, the year after Khashoggi's killing, McKinsey's income in Saudi Arabia seems to have expanded from the earlier year, as per one inside measure. The rundown of clients, and the hours charged, are overwhelmed by government organizations.

Inward records from 2018 and 2019 show McKinsey's work in Saudi Arabia fixated on tasks for the nation's Money, Monetary, Wellbeing, and Schooling Services, including many positions connected with NEOM, the arranged city representing things to come on the Red Ocean. There were no records of any work with the Inside, Equity, or Guard Services that are integral to the public authority's concealment of protesters and its capacity to keep up with power. However, as per one previous McKinsey representative acquainted with the company's work in Saudi Arabia, it wasn't so much for absence of endeavoring. McKinsey had pitched for such work however missed out. "It went to BCG," the individual said.

## [L'influence cache]

In 2019 inner records show that McKinsey took on work for an administration possessed organization, the AL-E1m Data Security Organization, which contracts with the Inside and Equity Services. McKinsey said it doesn't take care of business for these services and doesn't prompt privately owned businesses "regarding how to draw in with these services."

"I fee1 so gu1lible now thinking back," a previous McKinsey expert engaged with the Saudi work on opinion examination said by means of a protected informing framework. "looking back it's SO clear what this work could be utilized for, yet at the time it didn't actually occurred to me. I thought we were doing something worth being thankful for, assisting the public authority with getting criticism from their kin, perhaps a minuscule step towards a majority rules government."

When asked on CNBC in Walk 2019 what McKinsey would do on the off chance that it figured out its client was a killer, Sneader, the company's overseeing accomplice, had a two-word reaction: "You Walk."

In Saudi Arabia, McKinsey most certainly didn't Walk.

The Saudi and China-related work is important for a bigger example at McKinsey that is grabbed hold as of late. The firm is progressively working with dictator legislatures the world over or for the state-possessed organizations that undergird their power. Furthermore, as in Saudi Arabia, the Elites of those countries can be tracked down working inside McKinsey's workplaces.

In Russia, the state-possessed VTB Bank, which has worked under U.S. what's more, EU sanctions beginning around 2014, positioned among McKinsey's top clients by income as of late, as did Gazprom, the state-controlled energy monster, McKinsey records show. The top of Russia's sovereign abundance reserve, Kirill Dmitriev, is a McKinsey alum.

In Ukraine, the country's most extravagant oligarch employed McKinsey to exhort the supportive of Russian president, Viktor Yanukovych, assisting in the work with reworking this significantly bad man as a financial reformer. Simultaneously, Paul Manafort, Trump's previous mission director, was polishing Yanukovych's political picture. McKinsey has additionally worked straightforwardly with other tyrant systems, including the legislatures of Azerbaijan and Kazakhstan, records show.

In 2019, Following reports in The New York Times about the association's work in South Africa, China, Ukraine, and Saudi Arabia, McKinsey presented new principles adding layers of oversight in the client-choice cycle.

## *[L'influence cache]*

Section 14

**Chumocracy**

**50 years at England's NHS**

The news snapped through radio sets across England. Triumph over the Nazis in Egypt. In the wake of persevering through routs on combat zones in Europe and Asia, after the Barrage decreased English urban areas to rubble, the news that day in November 1942 was downright sublime. Church ringers — quiet the nation over for over two years — rang in festival.

With the Americans now in the conflict and Field Marshal Erwin Rommel's Afrika Korps in full retreat, there was trust. Winston Churchill, the wartime top state leader, communicated it as no one but he could: "Presently this isn't the end. It isn't even the start of the end, however it is, maybe, the finish of the start."

Days after the fact, Britons realized what could look for them when triumph at last came: an all the more society. An administration report spread out an arrangement for a government assistance state, with help for poor people and, as its focal point, free medical care for all. In the expressions of Aneurin "Nye" Bevan, the Welsh Coal digger turned Work Party legislator who imagined what might turn into the Public Wellbeing Administration: "No general public can truly call itself enlightened on the off chance that a wiped out individual is denied clinical guide as a result of absence of means."

Before the NHS appeared in July 1948, England's medical services framework mirrored the inconsistent class-befuddled society based on the backs of assembly line laborers where having cash was the method for getting "anything simple clinical benefits were accessible." By September of that year, 93% of the English populace had pursued the help. The deficiencies of the past framework were borne out by the thing Individuals were arranging for. Before the NHS, a large number of Britons couldn't stand to see the dental specialist. In the initial nine months of the assistance's presence, a few 33 million arrangements of false teeth — or two for each three Britons at that point — were requested. Eyeglasses — up to that point seen as an extravagance by poor people — were another famous thing.

The NHS was certainly not a public medical coverage framework. Clinical consideration was free at the mark of conveyance; citizens subsidized it, and the public authority nationalized the majority of the clinics also. It was flawed, however it worked. Nye Bevan, then, at that point, the wellbeing pastor, said that the NHS "should constantly be changing, developing and improving; it should continuously seem, by all accounts, to be deficient."

Starting around 1948 the NHS has served England well. For a more modest level of Gross domestic product than the US spends, the NHS obtains far superior outcomes. Maternal death rates are about 33% of what they are in the US. England's future, in lockstep with a large portion of the world, has been consistently rising. In America — alone among created countries — Individuals are kicking the bucket more youthful.

## [L'influence cache]

Surveys have demonstrated the NHS to be the most dearest foundation in England: more well known than the military or the sovereign. It's respected to such an extent that it was exhibited at the initial functions for the 2012 London Olympics. Like Government managed retirement in the US, the NHS is the third rail of English governmental issues, or, as two antiquarians of after war England put it, the "heavenly of holies."

But, as of late, England's chiefs have sanctioned significant changes to the NHS, directing a little however expanding portion of the country's medical care spending to the confidential area and opening the entryway for American organizations to enter the market.

McKinsey assumed an outsized part in molding and carrying out these changes. Two of its greatest American clients profited from them. The narrative of how the firm became the dominant focal point in redesiging the NHS says exactly that about the U.K. as it does about the firm.

For in England, McKinsey had tracked down an ideal host.

Over sixty years prior, McKinsey entered the English circulatory system with dazzling pace and grabbed hold of the country's mind such that never occurred in the US.

By the last part of the 1950s, European organizations were rising up out of the desolates of The Second Great War and were quick to become familiar with the insider facts of huge American enterprises like General Engines and GE, at the time the unchallenged heads of the business world . For McKinsey, the time had come to go worldwide, and, exactly as expected, it outlined its choice in the most decent terms.

In a reminder that opened with citations from the French political mastermind Alexis de Tocqueville, Charles H. lee, a McKinsey senior accomplice, composed that the world had entered "a period where America has been given a world job of initiative."

"Our exercises currently rise above public outskirts and they are equipped to a worldwide stage," lee composed. "Our community obligations have been developed, and our new job calls for us to practice these obligations in this more extensive setting."

In 1957, McKinsey had taken on a task with Illustrious Dutch Shell — the Dutch and English oil organization — to assist it with fostering a multidivisional business structure spearheaded by GM, which gave divisions inside enterprises more independence. Estimated in expenses, it was a major achievement, achieving in $720,000, an enormous sum in that period. That prodded the firm to set up a London office in order to land all the more large clients.

McKinsey opened an office on Ruler Road, a location at the core of the power construction of the quickly b1urring English Domain. It was ventures from the grip of Social c1ubs where matters of state were much of the time chose and a short stro11 from the public authority workplaces and the Places of Parliament.

## [L'influence cache]

More significant was the man McKinsey decided to lead the workplace: Hugh Parker, an American, who had moved on from Cambridge College, which alongside Oxford has for quite a long time taught England's first class. While at Cambridge, Parker paddled group. He went to the positions of the leander Club, one of the world's most seasoned paddling clubs, for a portion of McKinsey's most memorable English experts. Parker looked and sounded the part, wearing quintessentially English pinstripes, his American pronunciation imbued with an English accuracy.

"Obviously the primary thing I needed to do was to attempt to become known in Britain. What's more, I committed the Following decade of my life seriously to doing exactly that," Parker, who passed on in 2008, reviewed in a meeting for Bosses of the Universe, a narrative about specialists that broadcasted on England's Divert 4 out of 1999. "I made it my business to be seen and heard, I made discourses, I composed articles, my entire time was spent becoming known and perceived. Also, Following quite a long while this started to work."

McKinsey's blend of new American administration thinking conveyed by "clubbable" youthful experts was a hit. The grandees of English industry came hurrying to McKinsey for counsel. After its prosperity at Shell, a procession of other enormous organizations needed to get familiar with the insider facts of American administrative ability. The synthetics bunch ICI, one of the country's biggest makers, endorsed on in 1961, trailed by different heavyweights like Rolls-Royce, Cadbury Schweppes, Unilever, Rio Tinto, and Tate and lyle.

Then came the state area: the BBC, the Nuclear Energy Authority, and, fundamentally, the Bank of Britain. McKinsey even assisted with the nationalization of English Steel (and with its ensuing privatization years after the fact).

McKinsey was all over the place and Individuals took note. "If God somehow happened to redo the world, he would call upon McKinsey for help," composed the London reporter for the diary Science. The columnist Stephen Aris, who in 1968 profiled Hugh Parker for The Sunday Times, said that the name McKinsey was "becoming as inseparable from administrative change as Hoover is with vacuum cleaning." He even offered a definition: "McKinsey: n and v.t. 1. To stir up, revamp, announce repetitive, nullify council rule. Basically applied to enormous modern organizations yet in addition relevant to any association with the executives issues."

With surprising pace, McKinsey had vanquished England. By the mid 1970s, it had rebuilt 25 of England's main 100 organizations. "When we truly got moving in Britain — this would be the mid-to late 1960s, a decade after we opened an office there — we were truly on a roll," Parker said.

McKinsey hadn't Recently joined the club; it became, it might be said, the club. Parker and another McKinsey accomplice, Roger Morrison, initiated what they called "Executive's Meals" in the penthouse set-up of the Dorchester lodging, the craftsmanship deco milestone in London's princely Mayfair region. The thought was for England's skippers of industry to chat with McKinsey Individuals and "not be introduced to," as per McKinsey's in-house history book. It developed

## [L'influence cache]

into a little Model of the World Monetary Discussion, where business pioneers could accumulate to talk among themselves.

Yet, one organization — the greatest business in England — evaded McKinsey. The NHS. That was going to change.

By 1970, after over twenty years of activity, the NHS required an update. Since Britain's wellbeing framework had three branches — essential consideration, NHS-run medical clinics, and nearby administrations, for example, nursing home and emotional well-being care — organizing therapy demonstrated troublesome and inefficient. This "three sided beast" prompted silly choices, for example, lodging the old in stuffed clinics as opposed to in nursing homes.

Both fundamental English gatherings — Work and Moderate — perceived the issue, however they disagreed on the most proficient method to fix it. The public authority went to McKinsey. As one authority put it many years after the fact, "You were the administration masters. You had some awareness of the board and the Division had barely any insight into the executives."

McKinsey helped produce what was known as the "Dim Book," distributed in 1972, spreading out an arrangement to coordinate the three sections of the medical services framework along geographic lines. Directing everything were groups of specialists, medical attendants, and clinic administrators who might pursue choices by agreement. Yet, as one member noted, "when everybody is capable, nobody is mindful."

The upgrade, carried out in 1974, demonstrated generally ineffectual. McKinsey regretted a "expansion of paper" and the confounding, covering organizations. Yet, it likewise denoted a significant achievement in McKinsey's world wide development — a task at the NHS, one of the world 's biggest associations. The firm would remain for a considerable length of time, exhibiting its capacity to adjust to the nation's changing political perspectives.

One major change would come soon. The U.K., broadly viewed as the "wiped out man of Europe," fell behind most other European nations monetarily. A regarded editorialist conjectured that England could turn into the primary country in present day history to progress from a created country to an immature one. In 1979, citizens picked an extreme break, guiding into office an intense pupil of unregulated economy financial matters: Margaret Thatcher.

For McKinsey, the Thatcher years were generally excellent. Her way of thinking fit flawlessly with the company's own arising perspective — that public issues can frequently be addressed by the confidential area.

Thatcher pushed to privatize the indispensable state-claimed enterprises — steel, shipbuilding, flying, and broadcast communications, which, over going before many years, had been nationalized by Work legislatures. What's more, McKinsey was there to help. "It was a free for all for them," said Andrew Strong, a teacher at the College of Bristol who concentrates on McKinsey and other administration counseling organizations.

## [L'influence cache]

England's ideal and most splendid free advertisers clamored to work at McKinsey. There was William Hague, future head of the Moderate Party and unfamiliar secretary, and Adair Turner, top of England's monetary controller, generally likened to America's Protections and Trade Commission.

However dubious, privatization earned well known help as the media supported the public authority's mission to grow divide proprietorship between the majority. A large number of Britons purchased shares in recently privatized syndications like English Telecom, English Gas, and English Aviation routes, while other state-claimed organizations were auctions off to private proprietors.

In any case, for certain ventures, particularly those that were basically open utilities, privatization blew up, prompting costs far in abundance of what they had been under public control. One eminent fiasco was English Rail, the nation's railroad framework privatized under Thatcher's replacement, John Major.

Changing a framework with in excess of 10,000 miles of track in a country that brought forth the railroad almost two centuries sooner was not easy at all. McKinsey improperly referred to this task as "Venture Predetermination." In 1994, with guidance from McKinsey, the nation's rail foundation was put heavily influence d by another organization, Railtrack, which sold shares in 1996.

McKinsey's methodology included counsel to diminish upkeep spending and supplant framework like rails and signals just when broken or going to break. The fundamental assignments would at this point not be finished in-house however be reevaluated. "They are attempting to work more use out of existing asset[s]," one project worker said.

Then, at that point, in August 1999, Railtrack's high ranking representative directing track upkeep went for a stro11 along a stretch of the bustling East Coast rail line that ran from London in the south to Edinburgh in the north. He found it was inadequately kept up with. That November he cautioned his bosses, in exemplary English misrepresentation of reality, that the track's condition was "going towards the limit of agreeableness," adding that the "balance between business drivers and security are as of now predominantly towards the business."

His bosses ought to have tuned in. On October 17, 2000, a traveler train wrecked on that line close to the town of Hatfield, killing four Individuals and harming more than seventy. An administration examination found the track loaded with breaks, subverting its underlying honesty. The report faulted Railtrack for neglecting to appropriately keep up with it, with a few contemporaneous reports refering to McKinsey's Task Fate. Railtrack was soon renationalized.

Planes, trains, and corner stores were sufficiently provoking to privatize, however England's cherished NHS remained as a far greater and all the more politically loaded focus for any ideological group.

Dissimilar to Thatcher, who had held on until her eighth year of office prior to rolling out little improvements at the NHS, for example, privatizing janitorial and catering work, Significant pigeon right in. His administration presented contest,

## [L'influence cache]

permitting patients to pick their clinical suppliers. Inadequately performing medical clinics would, in principle, miss out.

Truly, rivalry didn't function admirably in an emergency clinic setting. That was certainly not confidential: one of the most commended business analysts of the 20th hundred years, Kenneth Bolt, had finished up many years sooner that the wizardry of business sectors didn't work for medical services in the manner it would for selling bread, vehicles, or boarding passes. Patients simply didn't have the data to wisely cost medical services administrations, and generally their need was getting the best consideration straightaway, not tracking down the least expensive oncologist.

Significant's changes, in any case, made new layers of organization supervising this new interior market. Subsequently, organization costs for the NHS took off. During the 1970s they absorbed around 5% of the organization's financial plan. By 2003 that number had ascended to 13 percent, as indicated by one review.

Major likewise presented a strategy, known as the Confidential Money Drive, which permitted the NHS to contract with privately owned businesses to construct clinics. It prompted gigantic expense overwhelms, burdening the NHS with £80 billion in the red for projects that were initially expected to cost £11.4 billion.

At the point when the Work Party finished Moderate rule, there was the assumption that the NHS would to a great extent be let be — if just because Work brought forth the NHS in 1948. Yet, the Work chief, Tony Blair, similar to his contemporary Bill Clinton in the US, fit no unbending philosophical shape. Under Blair, top NHS clinics were further reconfigured, with McKinsey's assistance, to work like organizations. To make preparations for exploitative, another guard dog office called Screen was set up to direct NHS clinics.

On occasion, McKinsey experts and government authorities seemed like tradable parts. A youthful specialist, Penny Run, assisted Blair with molding NHS strategy prior to joining McKinsey two years after the fact in 2002. Heading the other way was David Bennett, a McKinsey senior accomplice, who in 2005 turned into Blair's head strategy consultant. Blair's replacement, Gordon Brown, likewise inclined intensely on McKinsey for wellbeing strategy exhortation.

Then the monetary emergency hit. Following quite a while of more cash being siphoned into the NHS, which had forcefully helped staffing levels and diminished patient holding up times, the cash stream stopped. Confronted with a colossal spending plan shortage, the public authority went to McKinsey to manage the NHS spending plan. In Walk 2009, McKinsey conveyed its arrangement in a 123-slide PowerPoint show.

The proposition illustrated a pathway to save the NHS as much as £20 billion ($32 billion at that point) by cutting around 10% of its labor force, or very nearly 140,000 positions, amidst the most keen monetary slump in many years.

Individuals who remained would need to work harder. McKinsey determined that 1.7 percent of a specialist's time was lost to lunch breaks and said £400 million in

## [L'influence cache]

reserve funds could be understood if frail clinical suppliers "accomplish standard execution."

In any case, it wasn't sufficient to slice occupations. McKinsey likewise required the finish of "low worth added medical services mediations." Interpretation: scaling back what McKinsey considered superfluous operations. For instance, lessening specific hysterectomies by 70% could yield £80.6 million in reserve funds; one more £118 million could be saved by cutting knee joint medical procedures by 30%.

One McKinsey slide commended Kaiser Permanente, the American wellbeing support association, as a Model of somberness. However, the extremely next slide showed that the typical emergency clinic stay in the U.K. cost a little more than 33% of what it did in the US.

A portion of England's driving specialists joined lawmakers in reprimanding McKinsey's proposed cuts. "A significant number of these techniques might be of evidently little or even peripheral direct advantage at the time they are performed, however will forestall possibly serious medium and long haul issues," John Dark, leader of the Regal School of Specialists, said at that point.

The Moderate Party's wellbeing representative, Andrew Lansley, happily seized the opportunity to stick Work, which for quite a long time had reprimanded endeavors to cut the NHS financial plan.

The Work government repudiated the McKinsey slide deck. However, the thoughts in the slides were nowhere near dead.

On Monday, May 10, 2010, London was a city on the move. The Work Party — in power for the past thirteen years, had been completely squashed in the public political race four days sooner. Inside 48 hours David Cameron would be state head.

At 1:18 p.m., McKinsey's London office sent an email to two government authorities, offering them free passes to a presentation the next seven day stretch of Verdi's la traviata at the Illustrious Show House. The two authorities were no paper-pushing administrators. They held senior posts at Screen, the guard dog association that directed the presentation of NHS medical clinics — the very medical clinics that were likely to McKinsey's approach proposals. One of those authorities, Adrian Experts, had worked at McKinsey prior to turning into Screen's head of technique.

Before long another greeting came, this time tickets for their families to go to a presentation of Cirque du Soleil, the Canadian gymnastic group, joined by the McKinsey senior accomplice Nicolaus Henke. McKinsey had valid justification to lay on the appeal. The new wellbeing secretary, Andrew Lansley, would before long discuss making changes to the NHS "Sufficiently large to be seen from space." The Conservative's enormous novel thought: bring significantly more rivalry into the NHS through a demonstration of Parliament.

## [L'influence cache]

McKinsey, by righteousness of its associations, was in an excellent situation to assist with molding that regulation, giving the public authority its phalanxes of Oxford-and Harvard-taught medical care specialists.

Only days after the new government shaped, McKinsey handled a £330,000 agreement to prompt Screen, the public authority administrative office. It later won a far greater, £6 million agreement, for "administrations to the NHS initiative group." By May 31, a McKinsey specialist sent an email to two Screen authorities, telling them that the firm has "been gathering our reasoning on the ramifications of the new Taxpayer supported initiative for the NHS [and] have begun to impart this to clients" (italics added) and inquiring as to whether the two authorities would "like to meet to examine it."

The authorities on the less than desirable finish of that email were Adrian Experts and his chief, David Bennett, the previous McKinsey senior accomplice, who was currently Screen's leader administrator.

It addressed the comfort in England between government authorities and corporate chiefs. "You can't get a cigarette paper between the convictions of numerous administration priests and global Chiefs," the English writer Tamasin Cavern, who uncovered the McKinsey messages, wrote in a 2014 book.

McKinsey besieged the in-boxes of Screen authorities with talking solicitations. Aces Acknowledged a deal that June to talk at McKinsey's Central Specialist Roundtable Supper at St. Stephen's Club, when an Individuals just club for Moderate Party Individuals. Messages show that he Acknowledged undoubtedly two different solicitations to talk at McKinsey occasions in the approach the entry of the NHS regulation.

The firm was so near Screen that it helped pick speakers for the public authority guard dog's own occasions. In October 2010, a McKinsey expert welcomed Ian Dalton, a senior authority in the division of wellbeing and future head of Screen, to talk at one such occasion. The next year, Dalton Acknowledged a talking gig at a McKinsey medical care occasion in Paris. Members were reserved at the extravagant Westin Paris and at Eatery le Meurice Alain Ducasse, including two MichElin stars. McKinsey said it would take care of the check for the lodging and feasts.

This consideration came amidst gatherings with similar authorities — at government services and even now and again at McKinsey's own office — as the Moderate government's arrangements for the NHS started to come to fruition.

Acquiring a second rent on life was the McKinsey study from 2009, made under the Work government and broadly panned. Presently the Moderates were promoting its expense saving potential.

Scratch Seddon, a high ranking representative in the conservative research organization Change, who might before long join Cameron's administration as a consultant, suggested that the NHS lessen staffing by 150,000, kill up to 32,000 emergency clinic beds, and decrease optional strategies "like coronary detour or mastectomy."

## [L'influence cache]

Writing in The Watchman, Seddon said McKinsey had tracked down that these actions, among others, could prompt yearly reserve funds of over £20 billion out of 2014-2015.

Seddon fought that the answer for the post-monetary emergency financial crush was more confidential medical care spending. "A guarantee to public wellbeing isn't equivalent to a pledge to the NHS, or each nation would have a NHS, which they don't," he composed. "It's time we found the remainder of the world ."

The McKinsey study was then heated into another administration report that framed ways of managing £20 billion from the NHS spending plan.

Two months in the wake of taking power, the new government provided a 57 page white paper spreading out its recommendations. The paper imagined specialists assuming responsibility for the vast majority of the $100 billion or more yearly NHS spending plan and choosing where the cash ought to be spent or, in NHS-talk, "authorized." Already, one more arrangement of government bodies had gone with those choices.

Specialists choosing where medical care cash is best spent may appear to be sensible, yet they are additionally famously occupied, with neither the time nor the tendency to adjust spending plans. Somebody — or some firm like McKinsey — would need to help them. Yet again more privatization appeared to offer an answer, as per Screen's President, Bennett, who joined McKinsey during Thatcher's privatization binge.

"We, in the UK, have done this in different areas previously. We did it in gas, we did it in power, we did it in telecoms," he said as the regulation was coming to fruition. "We've done it in rail, we've done it in water. In this way, there is 20 years of taking on monopolistic solid business sectors and suppliers and presenting them to monetary guideline."

One method for presenting market influence s was for privately owned businesses to purchase NHS clinics, especially failing to meet expectations ones. Dalton, the English wellbeing official who was the focal point of extraordinary McKinsey politicking, met with McKinsey experts on December 17, 2010, to figure out their choices. They had an imminent purchaser as a top priority — Helios — a confidential German clinic chain. Inner records showed that the parent organization of Helios had been a McKinsey client as of late.

Be that as it may, privatizing NHS emergency clinics, which would have a free hand in overseeing workers, could mix resistance. So the choice was made to gradually begin. The objective: privatize ten to twenty clinics yet begin "at the mentality of 1 all at once with different political imperatives," a McKinsey specialist kept in touch with Dalton.

When officials and civil servants started to consider the new NHS regulation, advisors were profoundly implanted in England's administration. In 2010 the NHS alone burned through £313 million on administration advisors. Many years sooner, the English government carried out a public medical services program

## [L'influence cache]

without the assistance of experts. In any case, similar as their American partners, that changed over the long haul and their impact developed.

On February 14, 2011, McKinsey circulated a 47 page slide deck, bearing the NHS logo, that depicted the public authority's arrangement to redo the office.

One slide seemed to recommend that the motivation for the new NHS Model came from the US, noticing similitudes to the HMO Kaiser Permanente, for a long time a McKinsey client. Kaiser looks to contain costs by covering installments for clinical benefits and paying specialists pay rates, rather than the charge for-administration Model. The Kaiser framework has its intense allies in the US, yet in addition naysayers say it needs straightforwardness and spends unreasonably on organization.

Six illustrations filled slides were dedicated to spreading out the Kaiser Model. Two different choices got less consideration.

As the regulation came to fruition, McKinsey worked with a natural crowd — Paul Bate, a previous McKinsey specialist and the top of the top state leader's wellbeing strategy bunch, and Nicolaus Henke, the McKinsey senior accomplice and a noticeable individual from what was called Cameron's kitchen cupboard on medical care.

Presently the public authority — and McKinsey — needed to offer the arrangement to legislators who might decide in favor of it and the authorities who might execute it.

Welcome on the conflict games.

A portion of London's most senior wellbeing authorities were welcome to join McKinsey experts on Walk 4, 2011, at a gathering place close to the Pinnacle of London to partake in a reenactment practice on how the new framework would function. As indicated by a slide deck McKinsey arranged for the occasion — this time with the McKinsey logo — members were given "job cards" addressing the organization they would play as they reproduced "the fate of the London wellbeing economy."

The slide deck commended the proposed regulation, taking note of that the NHS update would "put patients first" and further develop wellbeing results. McKinsey imagined a framework where enormous gatherings of private specialists covered a huge number of patients.

McKinsey likewise intensified the arrogance that England, with one of the world's most practical medical care frameworks, actually expected to cut its wellbeing financial plan. "The ongoing framework will at this point not be reasonable soon — genuine groundbreaking change is required quickly," it said.

The truth was that the Moderate government had picked a way of monetary somberness in the midst of a financial slump, a choice that opposed the compositions of England's own John Maynard Keynes. Furthermore, with the NHS in its sights, one gathering reproachful of the Moderate plan said, "The

# [L'influence cache]

people who keep up with that we can't manage the cost of the NHS should be made to respond to the main question — on the off chance that we can't bear the cost of the most practical wellbeing support on the planet what could we at any point bear?"

McKinsey put its support behind the Traditionalists, who, similar to David Bennett, the previous McKinsey senior accomplice, needed to bring the sorcery of the unrestricted economy to medical care. As though to commute home that point, on June 8, 2011, McKinsey was the corporate supporter for a gathering at the Illustrious School of Nursing, which had transformed its dazzling Georgian manor on Cavendish Square into a setting accessible for corporate occasions.

The meeting, put on by the traditional research organization Change, was named "Significantly Something else for much less: Troublesome Development in Medical care." "Problematic" implied a more extensive compartment for privately owned businesses. That's what the gathering contended "for-benefit organizations and not-revenue driven associations are conveying medical care effectively all over the planet and doing as such at more prominent worth and with equivalent, while possibly worse, quality."

The McKinsey senior accomplice Nicolaus Henke, the company's agent on the state leader's kitchen cupboard on wellbeing, partook in the one-day meeting, joined by two other McKinsey experts. They again promoted the advantages of the Kaiser Permanente Model and proposed the NHS "enable patients to embrace their very own greater amount care themselves." "Whether in web-based registration for carriers or self-administration works at general stores, clients in different areas are taking on more prominent jobs prompting both more productive organizations and higher fulfillment," Henke and a partner composed.

The McKinsey pair referred to the therapy of ongoing sicknesses like diabetes, which could be overseen by patients "in organization with experts" through calls as opposed to through visits.

As the medical care bill moved nearer, the numerous McKinsey veterans tucked away in England's wellbeing organization kept on getting a constant flow of messages to go to occasions for McKinsey "graduated class." On September 14, 2011, it was a solicitation to the London office's yearly party, held at the Public Exhibition on Trafalgar Square. The respectable visitor: the overseeing accomplice, Dominic Barton, who might be talking about his new article in the Harvard Business Survey, "Private enterprise as long as possible."

Written directly Following the world wide monetary emergency, Barton's exposition encouraged business pioneers to look past momentary objectives and ponder the higher reason for free enterprise, citing the eighteenth-century Scottish financial expert Adam Smith: "The insightful and prudent man is consistently willing that his own confidential interest ought to be forfeited to the public interest."

The new bill — the Wellbeing and Social Consideration Act — became regulation in mid 2012. By far most of England's medical services spending would now be steered through new specialist drove gatherings. Segment 75 of the bill

## [L'influence cache]

commanded that those specialists' gatherings put out their agreements for delicate: meaning privately owned businesses would get a turn the greatest spending plan thing in the country.

As anticipated, the specialists' gatherings required help dealing with their new job as financial plan aces. It shocked no one that McKinsey was essential for a gathering of specialists that won a £7.1 million agreement to prompt the specialists.

McKinsey assisted the public authority with trim the regulation and, at the same time, was paid by the gatherings generally impacted by it. "So they were picking pockets on the two sides of the separation," said Jacky Davis, a specialist who battled against privatization of the NHS.

Other American organizations were additionally prompting the specialists' gatherings, including UnitedHealth Gathering, the monster American guarantor, which works in the U.K. as Optum. As of late, UnitedHealth was among the best 10% of McKinsey clients with regards to income. It straightforwardly profited from McKinsey's work in assisting with molding the 2012 regulation.

By 2014, Simon Stevens, a previous chief VP of UnitedHealth, was running the NHS in Britain. In Washington, he had presented a defense against greater government contribution in Obamacare, contending that the US didn't require a framework like the NHS.

As the 2012 regulation grabbed hold, the portion of NHS cash going to privately owned businesses expanded, incompletely because of the necessity that crafted by the specialists' gatherings be put out for offers, a strategy choice that McKinsey assisted with molding. At the point when John Major filled in as top state leader during the 1990s, the public authority spent about £96 million on medical care administrations from privately owned businesses every year. Under Work, that figure rose to £8.4 billion. Following 10 years of Conservative rule, it remained at £14.4 billion, as per figures distributed in 2021 by the Work Party.

ALL things considered, privatization has its cutoff points. Such a great deal what the NHS gives, for example, trauma center administrations, isn't appealing to the confidential area. Scores of organizations with NHS contracts deserted them subsequent to neglecting to turn a meaningful benefit. One organization even took over administration of a NHS medical clinic, just to leave the undertaking in 2015 in the midst of falling apart consideration and cost overwhelms.

"This multitude of privately owned businesses, they need to realize they can get a surefire return," said John lister, a specialist on the NHS who screens endeavors to siphon general wellbeing assets into private hands. "The last spot you can get a surefire benefit is running a full scope of NHS administrations."

McKinsey said its work with the NHS was to help the organization's "essential goals." "McKinsey didn't promoter or campaign to impact the public authority's position, and completely doesn't have a plan for the privatization of the NHS," McKinsey said because of inquiries regarding its work.

## [L'influence cache]

At the NHS, the utilization of specialists had its cutoff points. As per one definitive review, advisors made the NHS less productive, and the typical measure of cash every emergency clinic spent on experts might have paid the pay rates for 35 medical attendants or ten specialists.

Fair and square, with his experience at UnitedHealth, saw the constraints of privatization and proposed rejecting area 75. In 2015, as head of NHS Britain, he attempted an alternate methodology, welcoming McKinsey to help set up the "supportability and change organization" framework. The point was to set up a medical services organization that united the NHS, nearby specialists, psychological well-being offices, and the neighborhood government — in each geographic region of the NHS in Britain. At the end of the day, McKinsey was being approached to assist with figuring out generally similar issue the NHS confronted when it previously got the firm almost 50 years sooner and to switch large numbers of the arrangements of the 2012 regulation that it had assisted with making.

London was a significant proving ground for this coordinated framework, and McKinsey's Penny Run was at its focal point. In 2020 she was designated nonexecutive director of the organization in northwest London, where McKinsey had been working for quite a long time assisting with setting up a pilot project for the new framework close by a major specialists' gathering called AT Surgeons. Under the new regulation a portion of these specialists' gatherings had quickly extended. AT Surgeons managed care for in excess of 300,000 Londoners. McKinsey said Run took the post just as she was getting ready to leave the firm and that during the cross-over period she didn't chip away at NHS projects for McKinsey and wasn't engaged with any choices that granted agreements to counseling firms.

In February 2021, the news broke that AT Surgeons had been purchased by Operose Wellbeing, an English auxiliary of Centene, the enormous American health care coverage organization that has been one of McKinsey's top worldwide clients. Nearby specialists, dreading the takeover of such an enormous piece of the English clinical framework by a confidential American organization, mixed to go against it. Be that as it may, the takeover was a done deal.

The Coronavirus pestilence gave a significant trial of the nation's retooled medical care framework. State leader Boris Johnson shared the extremely significant test-and-follow exertion with the previous McKinsey specialist Dido Harding, presently Noble Harding. She and the nation's top wellbeing authorities went to privately owned businesses, not the NHS, to run the program. McKinsey alone charged £563,400 to give a "dream, reason and story" of the Harding-drove program.

Test and follow was a debacle. In excess of a fourth of Individuals presented to Coronavirus didn't know that they expected to self-quarantine, a serious weakness that added to the country's inability to control the spread of the Covid. The country's passing rate surpassed even that of the US for a significant part of the pandemic.

## [L'influence cache]

The Gatekeeper reporter George Monbiot suddenly erupted against U.K. wellbeing authorities. "The public authority has circumvent the lean and effective NHS to make a re-appropriated, privatized framework portrayed by ineptitude and disappointment," Monbiot composed. "The framework's waste is estimated in pounds, however in living souls."

The public authority's "Anticorruption Champion," whose transmit would incorporate investigating the large number of no-offered agreements granted to private firms, was John Penrose, a Moderate individual from Parliament who is likewise Noble Harding's significant other. They met while both were working at McKinsey. Harding had gone to Oxford, very much like Johnson, David Cameron, and 26 other English state heads. The English old young men's organization, which currently included ladies, had another name: the chumocracy.

By the spring of 2021, Johnson's prominence had risen. One explanation: England's unchallenged accomplishment at getting its populace inoculated. The U.K. was a world forerunner in carrying out its Coronavirus immunization program, and it was to a great extent because of the hierarchical capacities of the public authority's NHS, whose specialists and medical caretakers gave the infusions, for nothing.

## [L'influence cache]

### Epilog

Among the many difficulties to composing a book about McKinsey, none is greater than its way of life of mystery, the Establishment whereupon its business is constructed. Specialists in their most memorable days at the firm are modified to not say anything freely about clients or their recommendation. Most view that commitment in a serious way. A long time after representatives leave, whether enjoying a positive outlook or terrible, they are as yet hesitant to disregard that vow.

Unhampered by government oversight, McKinsey is responsible just to its clients, who anticipate that their weaknesses, errors, and business techniques — all in all, their mysteries — will stay simply that, confidential. Furthermore, envisioning any foundation that knows a greater amount of those mysteries than McKinsey is hard. Under these conditions, writing about the consultancy is likened to pursuing shadows, in the US and all over the planet. Yet, nothing entices analytical columnists more than strong organizations that accept they are excluded from public investigation.

One previous McKinsey specialist composed namelessly, "To those persuaded that a cryptic secrecy controls the world, the typical suspects are Illuminati, Reptile Individuals, or 'globalists.' They are off-base, normally. There is no mysterious society forming each significant choice and deciding the course of mankind's set of experiences. There is, be that as it may, McKinsey and Company."

The specialist utilized humor to come to a meaningful conclusion, a serious point: McKinsey has an inconspicuous presence at the table inside the world 's most important organizations and states.

In spite of the association's data lockdown, buttressed by nondisclosure arrangements, we had the option to talk with almost 100 current and previous McKinsey workers. They decided to talk not on the grounds that they were unfaithful but since they were the very kinds of advisors McKinsey looks for: savvy Individuals of rule, attracted to the organization due to its expressed qualities.

McKinsey takes extraordinary measures to underline its great deeds, and there are quite a large number. In a 2018 report named "Making Change That Is important," the company's world wide overseeing accomplice stated, "Safeguarding our planet, empowering significant work in our networks, and making comprehensive Social orders that honor our variety are key."

However, as the firm found, employing Individuals with a reason more prominent than bringing in heaps of cash can have a drawback. At the point when these optimists see a lot of sunlight between McKinsey's words and activities, they become disenthralled; they get clarification on pressing issues. Some even consented to converse with us.

This book depends on significantly more than the verbally expressed word. We turned into the principal outcasts to look inside McKinsey's mystery vault of

## [L'influence cache]

clients and billings — data forbidden to legislatures, clients, contenders, and, surprisingly, its own representatives. With this data, we had the option to reveal a large number of layers of possible irreconcilable circumstances, including its "well established strategy" to serve contending clients with clashing interests, "as well as counter-parties in consolidation, procurement and union open doors."

Bain and Company, a contender, accepts that is some unacceptable methodology, and says it acknowledges just a single client at a time in a similar area. McKinsey guards its choice, saying that an inward wall forestalls the death of classified data.

McKinsey's free enterprise style of the board has permitted its specialists to harvest enormous paydays advancing habit-forming items, suggesting approaches that extend pay imbalance, and serving agitators on the global stage, including significant polluters. There is no scrutinizing McKinsey's longing to accomplish something beneficial, to offer in return. However, as one previous expert said, McKinsey ought to likewise figure out how to cause less damage.

# [L'influence cache]

### A Note on Sources

Our giving an account of McKinsey started vigorously in mid 2018, in the midst of the commotion over the association's work in South Africa. Our work was helped immensely by the forceful South African press, especially the analytical columnists at Amabhungane. McKinsey specialists were experiencing the intensity, and they started to talk. McKinsey itself, for this underlying story, made a few senior accomplices accessible to us too, including its soon-to-leave overseeing accomplice, Dominic Barton. They had a story to tell: what occurred in South Africa was sui generis, for the most part because of a couple of troublemakers yet with more extensive examples for the firm. McKinsey said measures were taken to ensure it at no point ever occurs in the future.

After that underlying article, distributed in late June 2018, McKinsey as an association moved in. While their representative kept on being responsive, getting interviews with top McKinsey experts wouldn't occur. The South Africa story likewise referenced McKinsey's work with ICE, generating shock inside the firm when the misfortune on America's southern line was overwhelming Titles. More Individuals approached. Different articles followed. They included reports about McKinsey's work with Saudi Arabia and with bad and tyrant pioneers in pre-Zelensky Ukraine and China. Even more Individuals opened up. With a considerable lot of these sources, we conveyed through scrambled voice and informing applications.

While we called the South African Failure the greatest contention in the company's almost very long term history, it took under a year for that emergency to be supplanted. In mid 2019 subtleties arose about McKinsey's broad work with Purdue Pharma and its mission to "turbocharge" deals of the profoundly habit-forming pain rEliever OxyContin.

That report was not driven by sources, yet rather by the summon force of the Massachusetts head legal officer, Maura Healey. Abruptly hundreds, soon thousands, of pages of messages, bookkeeping sheets, and slides became public, chronicling McKinsey's work with Purdue and other narcotic creators.

In many stories, McKinsey's own words assumed a focal part, frequently as slide decks never planned for public utilization. A nine-page show made in Riyadh, the Saudi capital, clarified how for recognize powerful voices via web-based entertainment who may be reproachful of the public authority. Many reports, returning sixty years, showed its cozy relationship with Enormous Tobacco. Others showed its work with Juul, the predominant vaping organization. Great many pages of records itemized McKinsey's cozy relationship with government authorities in England who directed the Public Wellbeing Administration.

While investigating the book, we ran over a startling wellspring of data: carefully hidden inner records that recorded McKinsey's clients as well as billings that assisted us with figuring out the degree of McKinsey's counseling domain. What stuck out: the conspicuousness of the large American medical organizations and the public authority offices that manage them.

## [L'influence cache]

We moved toward McKinsey various times throughout the years to demand interviews. Most were denied. We likewise gave the firm a complete rundown of questions.

The book mirrors McKinsey's reactions, particularly where the firm disagrees with explicit discoveries from our detailing. A portion of the responses were brilliant: McKinsey, for instance, said it as of late quit counseling for tobacco organizations, however the firm didn't respond to the subject of precisely when it halted or why it had kept on serving Enormous Tobacco a very long time after cigarettes were well known to dangerous be.

Answering our part on security issues, U.S. Steel said it works distinctively today than previously. "Our general change endeavors have worked on our organization's exhibition, made an economical support program, and further developed worker security over the long haul," the organization said. With respect to McKinsey, the steelmaker said the firm had no dynamic power. Disney declined to remark.

McKinsey likewise resolved inquiries concerning expected irreconcilable situations, remembering serving different organizations for similar industry and their administration controllers. "We illuminate our clients about our classification and struggle strategies," McKinsey said. "Clients work with us since they believe that we will guard their private data."

McKinsey recognized that it has a "well established strategy to serve contending clients and clients with possibly clashing interests as well as counter-parties in consolidation, obtaining and union open doors, and to do as such without undermining McKinsey's expert obligation to keep up with the secrecy of client data." "In the event that a worker disregards our arrangements, we can and do make a fitting disciplinary move including end where justified," McKinsey said. Asked how frequently this had occurred, the firm didn't reply.

Concerning questions encompassing its work for drug makers and the Food and Medication Organization, McKinsey expressed that since it didn't exhort the office on unambiguous drug or tobacco items, then, at that point, its work with these confidential clients represented no contention. In any case, McKinsey said its agreement proposition "regularly" referenced its work with the drug business.

## *[L'influence cache]*

### Affirmations

Quite a long while prior, the leader proofreader of The New York Times, Senior member Baquet, came by a gathering of our insightful unit to figure out what was ready to go. Prior to leaving, Dignitary said in such countless words that he'd be keen on a profound, granular glance at a large company as a method for assisting perusers with understanding how power is used in our general public. We accepted Senior member's recommendation and decided to look at McKinsey, the clandestine advocate to not one yet huge number of organizations around the world .

We owe Senior member our gratitude for sowing the seed that turned into this book and for his immovable help of analytical revealing in all sides of the newsroom.

There are many strides among thought and book. With the assistance of two of the country's best news editors, Paul Fishleder and Matt Purdy, we started our McKinsey announcing for the Times. Backing us up was David McCraw, the Times' legal counselor, a legend to each insightful columnist in our organization. Also, for good explanation. He has a spine of steel, wonderful judgment, and a dedication to First Correction standards top notch. At the point when our examination moved abroad, we profited from the insight of Michael Slackman and Greg Winter, editors on our worldwide work area.

Among the a great many Individuals who read and remarked on our McKinsey stories were two scholarly specialists at ICM Accomplices, Alexandra Mechanical engineer and Amelia Chart book, who accepted there was a bigger story to tell. Maybe a book? We were not prepared for that, but rather we continued to talk due to their excitement — and they were downright enjoyable to be near. At the point when M&A, as we tenderly consider them, let us know that one of the distributing scene's most recognized editors, William Thomas, supervisor and distributer of Doubleday, needed a McKinsey book, we perceived this as a remarkable open door, Particularly since he had altered a few of our #1 journalists. Bill's commitment to this venture won't ever falter. He kept us centered, offering support and direction when we really wanted it. It shocked no one that his altering made our book limitlessly better. Daniel Novack, our brave Doubleday legal advisor, raised our lawful survey with very much coordinated humor, a quality not generally present in both of our callings. A unique holler to Nicole Pedersen, who put forth a valiant effort to persuade perusers that we got passing grades in English. Others at Doubleday to whom we owe thanks incorporate Michael Goldsmith, Todd Bold, Kathy Hourigan, and Khari Dawkins, alongside every one of the people who assumed imperative parts in distributing this book.

Many Individuals contributed somehow to our detailing. Is Kate Bakhtiyarova, our main scientist and an alum of the Columbia News coverage, most importantly, School. We could never have envisioned anybody whom we'd prefer have close by. Another Columbia understudy, Bridget Hickey, co-thought of one of our articles for the Times. We additionally need to thank the previous Columbia

## [L'influence cache]

understudies Champe Barton, Sachi McClendon, Caterina Elly Barbera, Natasha Rodriguez, Eileen Marie Grench, and Effortlessness Ashford.

Duff McDonald, the first writer of McKinsey's mysterious history, was unfailingly useful. His work enlivened us. Different essayists who got through McKinsey's cleaned adaptation of occasions included Bethany Mclean, Anita Raghavan, Anand Giridharadas, Post Exquisite, Erik Edstrom, and Ian MacDougall of ProPublica.

There's a well-known adage in the paper business: don't cover the lead. On this, we confess, for this book would never have been composed without the assistance of bold McKinsey experts who ended their promises of quiet since they figured the firm should improve. Three hang out specifically, yet one individual, whose help blew away the call, gave us a pen name for this event. Much obliged to you, Cooper G. Duncan.

Individuals with a heart and a limit with regards to shock are indispensable to truth searchers all over the place. Without them, a majority rules system doesn't have a potential for success. We are profoundly thankful that we saw as so many of them at McKinsey.

www.ingramcontent.com/pod-product-compliance
Lightning Source LLC
Chambersburg PA
CBHW052349220526
45465CB00003BA/1024